MODERN LEGAL STUDIES

THE GOVERNANCE
OF POLICE

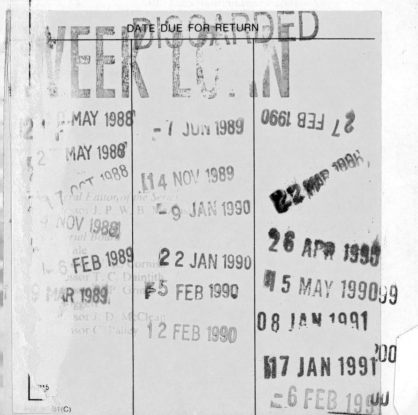

AUSTRALIA AND NEW ZEALAND
The Law Book Company Ltd.
Sydney : Melbourne : Perth

CANADA AND U.S.A.
The Carswell Company Ltd.
Agincourt, Ontario

INDIA
N. M. Tripathi Private Ltd.
Bombay
and
Eastern Law House Private Ltd.
Calcutta and Delhi
M.P.P. House
Bangalore

ISRAEL
Steimatzky's Agency Ltd.
Jerusalem : Tel Aviv : Haifa

MALAYSIA : SINGAPORE : BRUNEI
Malayan Law Journal (Pte.) Ltd.
Singapore and Kuala Lumpur

PAKISTAN
Pakistan Law House
Karachi

MODERN LEGAL STUDIES

THE GOVERNANCE
OF POLICE

by

LAURENCE LUSTGARTEN

LONDON
SWEET & MAXWELL
1986

Published in 1986 by
Sweet & Maxwell Limited of
11 New Fetter Lane, London.
Computerset by Promenade Graphics Limited, Cheltenham.
Printed in Scotland

British Library Cataloguing in Publication Data

Lustgarten, Laurence
The governance of police.—(Modern
legal studies)
1. Police power—England
I. Title   II. Series
344.205'52   KD4839

ISBN 0–421–31900–3
ISBN 0–421–31910–0 Pbk

PREFACE

For a surprisingly long period, the police were the most taken for granted of all major institutions of government. Virtually no research was conducted and, panegyrics apart, little was written about them. As often happens, sustained research only really got underway after policing became the focus of fierce political controversy. There is now a substantial body of sociological and historical writing, much of it of very good quality. There is also a large literature on what is termed, too narrowly, "police accountability." The Police and Criminal Evidence Act 1984 and the debate surrounding its enactment produced a great deal of legal and political commentary on police powers. What has been missing, however, is any systematic treatment of police within the broad framework of public law. This study attempts to fill that void. Such an approach requires drawing upon work done in all those areas, and integrating it with writing on administrative law, local government, and constitutional and political theory. Writing the book has not been easy but was certainly stimulating and mostly enjoyable.

I have had the advantage of gaining information and ideas from interviews and conversations with a wide range of people concerned with the subject: police officers, politicians, civil servants and scholars. Many people have given generously of their time and intellectual energy; I have tried to acknowledge them all in footnotes in appropriate places. More generally, I am much in debt to the secretarial staff of the University of Warwick Law School, nearly all of whom typed or word processed bits of the manuscript as they coped with the chaos of personnel changes and adjustment to new technology. The work as a whole has benefited greatly from the critical scrutiny of Marian FitzGerald, who commented in detail on several draft chapters and whose emphasis upon structure was indispensable to making the argument more coherent.

I could only take account of material available to me before November 1, 1985.

Laurence Lustgarten
University of Warwick

April 1986

CONTENTS

OTHER BOOKS IN THE SERIES

Anatomy of International Law (Second Edition), by J. G. Merrills
Compensation and Government Torts, by C. Harlow
Confessions, by Peter Mirfield
Constructive Trusts, by A. J. Oakley
Council Housing (Second Edition), by D. C. Hoath
Court of Justice of the European Communities (Second Edition), by L. N. Brown and F. G. Jacobs
Development Control, by J. Alder
Emergency Powers in Peacetime, by David Bonner
Exclusion Clauses in Contracts (Second Edition), by David Yates
The Family Home, by W. T. Murphy and H. Clark
Grievances, Remedies and the State, by Patrick Birkinshaw
Homelessness, by David Hoath
Human Rights and Europe (Second Edition), by Ralph Beddard
Immigration Law (Second Edition), by John Evans
International Dispute Settlement, by J. G. Merrills
Law, Legitimacy and the Constitution, by McAuslan and McEldowney (eds.)
Law of the Common Agricultural Policy, by Francis G. Snyder
Local Government in the Modern State, by Martin Loughlin
Natural Justice (Second Edition), by Paul Jackson
Registered Land (Third Edition), by David J. Hayton
Remedies for Breach of Contract, by Hugh Beale
Security of Tenure under the Rent Act, by Jill E. Martin
Small Businesses (Second Edition), by Michael Chesterman
Strict and Vicarious Liability, by L. H. Leigh
Taxation and Trusts, by G. W. Thomas

TABLE OF CASES

TABLE OF STATUTES

TABLE OF STATUTORY INSTRUMENTS

PROLOGUE

I

The level on which debate over the role of the police in the British[1] constitution is most often conducted is that of constitutional and political theory—conceptions of liberty, democracy, social order and the rule of law. Clearly these considerations and their institutional corollaries are vital, indeed fundamental, but to restrict the debate within their boundaries ensures that it will remain unsatisfactorily inward-looking, and lead us to treat matters that are historically contingent, even accidental, as though they were essential elements of a democratic polity. This produces a wholly unwarranted exaltation of the status quo.

A glance across the North Sea or the Channel makes one point very clear: there is no necessary connection between democracy and any particular mode of organisation and control of the police. Unless one is to assert that democracy speaks only the Queen's English, a view over the water produces the unsettling conclusion that England is very much in the minority among democratic nations in the extreme degree of self-governance it permits its police, and—a separate but connected point which increases the importance of the first—in the breadth of discretion they exercise within the structure of criminal justice. Some of the difference may be due to divergent concepts of democracy, or divergent histories of the growth of the state in England and on the Continent.[2] But a good deal of it must also be attributable to differences in the sphere of criminal justice, more particularly in structure and institutions. As this aspect has been ignored entirely in the debate over what has come to be called "police accountability,"[3] this study

[1] Apologies to those north of the Border: despite the use of the word "British," although a few references are made to Scottish experience, no real attempt is made here to analyse Scottish legislation or case law.

[2] See especially Dyson (1980), pp.36–47, emphasising Britain's uniqueness in this respect. A thoughtful attempt to relate features of criminal process to political tradition and ideology, which draws a sharp distinction between Anglo-American and Continental traditions is found in Damaska (1975).

[3] "Accountability" is often used as a weasel word. What is really at issue is the degree of control various political institutions are to have over the police. Accountability in the sense of after-the-fact explanation means acceptance of a sharply limited degree of control, a point recognised by its more candid exponents, notably Marshall (1984); see below, pp.165–167.

1

begins by examining its importance, perhaps even overstating it in order to shift the perspective from which the problem is normally viewed. The exaggeration stems in part from the fact that I am talking in terms of ideal types, not empirically precise descriptions. In Chapter 10 I shall rejoin the mainstream and discuss the issues in more traditional constitutional terms.

II

The English police operate in the context of an adversarial, not inquisitorial, system. (The difference is neatly symbolised in the style of criminal prosecutions: *R.* v. *Smith* becomes Az JS VII/ 103–85 or BGHSt 26, 263 in Germany.) In practical terms, this means a system in which the trial is of much greater importance. It is true that most accused persons plead guilty even when facing serious charges,[4] but the police must do their work in preparation for the possibility of a proceeding which Professor Damaska describes as a "party contest" rather than the Continental "official inquiry."[5] This trial is governed by rules erecting relatively high evidentiary barriers to conviction; in the adversary system "there is a greater divergence between what the police actually know and what can be introduced as evidence at trial."[6] Moreover the verdict at that trial is reached by persons without legal training who, unlike mixed Continental tribunals, need not give reasons for their decision. Thus the English police take an avowedly partisan stance in a system in which partisan contest is supposed to produce truth. And the evidentiary barriers reinforce bureaucratic and resource imperatives of avoiding trials in the vast majority of cases by producing guilty pleas. This is impossible in Continental systems, where the accused is not permitted to plead guilty.[7] This gives the English police substantially greater incentive to seek to obtain a confession from the suspect; more generally and ominously, it would seem to be a constant pressure leading them to overstep their powers against those they "know" are guilty.[8]

---

[4] For statistics, see Bottoms and McClean (1976), pp.105-108.
[5] Damaska (1975), p.481 n.1.
[6] *Ibid*. p.523, n.109. In this quotation and that in the previous footnote, Professor Damaska draws upon his earlier article, Damaska (1973).
[7] Sheehan (1975), pp.26–27. See Langbein (1977), pp.96–97, for a description of the West German procedure (*Strafbefehl*) analogous to a guilty plea but which is only operative in relation to payment of "penance money for petty infractions."
[8] McConville and Baldwin (1982), in an important article, emphasise the overwhelming importance of obtaining statements from a suspect, which makes police interrogation rather than the trial the central focus of criminal justice.

The role of the police in conducting investigations is also very different. "French police are expected to prepare an investigative record that is complete and formally correct, available to the defence as well as the prosecution and able to withstand a searching examination [by a judge at trial]."[9] The investigative police are called *police judiciaire,* and in this capacity are subject to the supervision and control of the *procureur,* a member of the magistracy who sees his role as that of a judicial officer; in some difficult cases they are directed by a judicial figure, the examining magistrate. Even though in the great majority of criminal incidents, which inevitably involve minor matters, the police will conduct their investigations entirely on their own,[10] this structure creates a radically different ethos among the police, and in practical terms—notably their career ladder and the supervision and investigation of their conduct by both judicial and non-police administrative superiors[11]—places them in a much more subordinate position to judicial and ministerial hierarchies. The activities of the German police, for example, are subject to review in the administrative law courts under the legal principle of "proportionality," which permits judges to determine whether they could have used methods less restrictive of personal liberty in pursuit of legitimate ends.

Further, there is nothing in England corresponding to the principle of compulsory prosecution. Although this is subject to countervailing principles and practices, it serves as the point of departure for the decisions to be made in individual cases. In particular, on the Continent the discretion not to prosecute is not exercised by the police, who are required to report all offences that have come to their notice to the public prosecutor.[12] It is the latter, a much more formidable figure than his quasi-counterpart in most English speaking countries (a point taken up below), who exercises the discretion.

Finally, and here one begins to move away from consideration of criminal procedure strictly speaking to wider political institutions, Continental police are so much a part of a centralised, nationally uniform structure that, to quote a distinguished comparative lawyer, "It may be said with only a modicum of exaggeration that both in England and America a police system in a continental sense hardly exists."[13] Professor Damaska bases this rather star-

---

[9] Langbein and Weinreb (1978), p.1554.
[10] Goldstein and Marcus (1978), pp.247–250.
[11] A point emphasised by Langbein and Weinreb, above n.9, in relation to both France and Germany (1978), pp.1555 and 1560, respectively.
[12] Damaska (1975), pp.502–503: Sheehan (1975), p.20.
[13] Damaska (1975), p.511.

tling conclusion on the absence of "the dominant structural principle of all continental systems," namely, centralisation of police and prosecution corps, within which "central authorities issue binding general directives to local officials and can give specific instructions on the handling of a particular case."[14] This fundamental difference is doubtless in some ways connected to equally significant differences in political culture and institutions, which in turn may reflect a basic difference in political philosophy concerning the relationship between the individual and state authority.[15] What is of critical relevance, however, is that none of these features, so alien to the English experience, makes Continental countries any less democratic or libertarian, nor makes their police into greater instruments of political oppression.

Thus the police in England work in what, in comparative terms, is a very unusual context. Their task is to play an avowedly one-sided part in an adversary contest in which the accused may present a contrary version of the facts, and in which a verdict will be delivered by lay persons whose reasons remain inscrutable and from whose judgment of acquittal there is no appeal.[16] They are entirely independent of judicial supervision, and the notion of a judicial or even quasi-judicial role is no part of their occupational ethos. They are unrestricted by ministerial control in relation to particular cases and adoption of general practices. They cannot be required to act in particular ways in order to achieve uniformity in enforcement practices throughout the country. They alone decide whether to investigate, how to conduct the investigation and, save for minor exceptions where the Director of Public Prosecutions must be consulted, whether to charge a suspect and what charges to lay. Viewed from the east, the scope of their authority, and the lack of control over its exercise, is awesome.

III

The adversarial, as opposed to inquisitorial, nature of English criminal justice thus has profound implications for the constitutional position of the police. Yet even with the genus of adver-

[14] *Ibid.* pp.487–488. A caveat should be entered here, however. Centralisation does not necessarily entail direct control; it can coexist with constabulary independence, as in the case of the Royal Canadian Mounted Police.
[15] *Ibid.* Part IV, for one attempt to relate these ideological influences to the structure of criminal justice in the Anglo-American and Continental traditions.
[16] In West Germany both prosecution and defence enjoy liberal rights of appeal, which is one reason why, as also in France, the verdict must be fully reasoned. See Langbein (1977), pp.63, 84–85.

sarial systems, the *species Anglica* contains some virtually unique features, whose effect is to extend the range of unchecked police power still further.

Perhaps the most obvious is the absence of a separate institution responsible for prosecution of offenders. Put another way, the police in England and Wales combine the functions of investigation and prosecution, thus possessing a degree of control over the processing of suspected lawbreakers that has few equals even in adversarial systems. The police not only decide whether to arrest and charge a suspect; they also decide whether to proceed with prosecution and on the specific charge to be brought; this often determines which court will hear the case. In relation to minor offences, they may physically present the case to the bench. More important, in their use of solicitors, whether specifically engaged or employed by the local council, they retain the dominant role as client, a relationship noted and criticised by the Royal Commission on Criminal Procedure.[17] It is the police, rather than a lawyer, who retain control over the proceedings, and if they choose to drop the case, there is no equivalent of the French *action civile* which might enable the victim to force the authorities to undertake further investigations on proceedings.[18] By contrast the private prosecutor in England must assemble his own case, without the benefit of police powers of questioning and search for evidence, let alone the resources to conduct an investigation.

This combination of functions has a clear historical origin. In theory the police prosecute as private individuals who happen to have information about lawbreaking by the accused. This now patent fiction exists because only surprisingly recently have they come to stand in the shoes of victims of crime: not until around 1870 did they replace private associations as the most frequent initiators of criminal prosecutions.[19]

It may be thought that the creation of an independent prosecution service under the Prosecution of Offences Act 1985 will radically limit their role, but evidence from other jurisdictions suggests that the real change may be less than one might expect. The Scottish procurator fiscal occupies in strict law a supervisory position over the police; indeed under Scottish law a chief constable may be required to initiate a particular investigation at the direction of a

[17] Cmnd. 8092 (1981), para. 6.5.
[18] Sheehan, *op. cit.* pp.20–22, explains the role of the *partie civile*.
[19] On these associations, see Phillips (1977), Chap. 4 and his subsequent paper "Good Men to Associate and Bad Men to Conspire," in Snyder and Hay (forthcoming). The date of 1870 is an approximation offered by Douglas Hay in conversation.

fiscal.[20] Recent research into the way fiscals in various offices
actually conduct their work, however, suggests that they are
largely dependent upon the police as "reporters" of crime. In only
six per cent. of cases did the prosecutor request further information from the police; in all the rest he proceeded entirely upon
the material in the file they had prepared. In only eight per cent. of
cases did the lawyer, purportedly an independent professional
serving the public interest, drop the charges laid by the police.[21]
Similarly, an earlier study of the crown attorney's office in Toronto
concluded that "In effect great confidence is placed by the prosecuting authorities in the competency of the police officer on the
beat, for his decision to arrest is adopted as their decision to prosecute."[22] The emotional sense of being "on the same side" and the
personal relationships that grew up as individual prosecutors and
police repeatedly worked and socialised together reinforced the
tendency for the prosecutor to serve as a sort of police advocate,
rather than an independent check. Only in the higher courts,
where more experienced lawyers dealt with a small number of the
most serious cases were "police pressures" effectively resisted.[23]
As the new legislation establishes a system similar to that of
Ontario, in which full-time lawyers function primarily as a courtroom processing and pleading service which only comes into operation after the police have laid the initial charge, it is unlikely that
the effective police dominance of the prosecution process will be
much diminished.

A very different type of prosecutor would be required to dimin-
ish the pre-eminence of the police in the prosecution process. The
only example in countries with adversarial systems is the American
District Attorney or his federal counterpart, the United States
Attorney, whose office was significantly based on the French
model, which commanded admiration during the early years of the
new republic.[24] As well as handling cases brought to him by the
police, the district attorney can initiate his own investigations.
Within his office under his command are a large number of investigators who enjoy law enforcement powers identical to the police;
and there is a tendency in large urban areas for some of them to be
deployed on difficult and complex cases which the police are

[20] Police (Scotland) Act 1967, s. 17.
[21] Moody and Tombs (1982). The figures quoted in the text are found at pp.47 and
57, respectively.
[22] Grosman (1969), p.27.
[23] *Ibid.* pp.44–50.
[24] Grosman provides a good brief description: *ibid.* pp.13–14.

believed to be less capable of managing.[25] The district attorney thus generates an important part of his own case-load, and may receive reports of crimes directly from the public. A very important consequence of his investigatory capability is that the district attorney may pursue police corruption or other misconduct with adequate legal powers to compel information employed by an expert staff who are not fellow police officers. The obstruction that so effectively made a fiasco of Operation Countryman[26] could have been more readily overcome by a determined district attorney. The proposals for independent investigation of complaints against the police in England have always been bedevilled by the absence of any pre-existing body of skilled and experienced investigators whose friendships and careers lie outside the police organisation, a deficiency the Crown Prosecution Service will do nothing to remedy.

IV

Thus in the edifice of English criminal justice the police are the keystone. Institutions with which elsewhere they would have to share or to which they would have to subordinate their powers are either non-existent or have left them undisturbed on their patch. And comparative analysis at a quite different level further emphasises the extraordinary freedom from restraint they enjoy. This is the level of constitutional structure, and can be seen in sharpest relief by comparison with certain salient features of the American system.

The first point is that the absence of the American brand of federalism, with parallel systems of criminal law, means that there can be no equivalent of federal law enforcement officials who can prosecute venal or brutal local police on charges of federal crime. This machinery has sometimes been of value in instances of maltreatment of racial minorities or widespread corruption. More important, the existence of federal constitutional rights has given rise to what has been called a "constitutional tort"—a civil action for damages in a federal court for denial of any of those numerous rights by public officials, including the police. In England victims of police misconduct can avail themselves only of the protections afforded by the common law, which comprise a much narrower range of rights and interests, embodied in actions for false

---

[25] The Royal Commission visited and described one such D.A.'s office in San Diego, California: above n.17, para. 6.33.
[26] For a good description see Doig (1984), pp.245–252.

imprisonment, assault and trespass[27]. Though the so-called "sec. 1983 action" is flawed in many respects, thousands of Americans invoke its provisions annually.[28] It can provide a means of redress and, at least potentially, a deterrent to police misconduct, that has no parallel here.

Two further controls on the American police derive from constitutional provisions. The Fourth Amendment requires that arrests and searches be based upon "probable cause," a more stringent standard than the "reasonable suspicion" sufficient for the so-called "stop and frisk"—or on the street "pat down" for weapons justified by the potential danger to the officer.[29] It is the lower, more permissive standard of reasonable suspicion which has always governed major police power of arrest in England[30] and now, under the Police and Criminal Evidence Act (P.C.E.A.) 1984, a general power of search as well.[31] Thus the English constable may quite lawfully exert far greater control over the ordinary citizen, in the sense of arresting and searching him and his home in circumstances indicating a lesser degree of likelihood that he has committed a crime, than is available to the American policeman. Correspondingly, of course, the citizen cannot lawfully resist or seek redress for intrusions that satisfy this minimal criterion.

Moreover, the English courts have steadfastly refused to adopt the exclusionary rule in cases where the police have obtained evidence unlawfully. This rule, judicially derived from the Fourth Amendment though not found in its text, was from 1961 to 1984 interpreted to require that matters unlawfully obtained be automatically excluded as evidence in court.[32] The approach in England, as in all common law jurisdictions other than the United States, is to admit reliable evidence however obtained,[33] leaving the prob-

---

[27] These are discussed in Chap. 9 below.

[28] For two substantial critiques, including extensive empirical analysis, see Newman (1978) and Project (1979). The latter study, at p.781, n.3, reveals that the number of sec. 1983 actions against the police trebled to over 6,000 annually between 1971 and 1977.

[29] *Terry* v. *Ohio*, 392 U.S. 1 (1968).

[30] Criminal Law Act 1967, s. 2, now replaced by s. 22 of the P.C.E.A. 1984.

[31] s. 1. See also ss. 18 and 19.

[32] *Mapp* v. *Ohio*, 367 U.S. 643 (1961) announced a general exclusionary rule applicable to state as well as federal prosecutions. However, in *U.S.* v. *Leon*, 104 S.Ct. 3405 (1984), the Supreme Court created a novel exception, denying the exclusion where the evidence is seized in the good faith execution of a warrant subsequently ruled invalid. Some fear, and others hope, that this decision portends further relaxation of the exclusionary rule.

[33] See the discussion below, pp.143–146.

lem of punishing and preventing police illegality to civil actions for damages, criminal prosecutions, or internal disciplinary procedures. Since these mechanisms seem to be remarkably ineffective in curbing police abuses, one might advocate adoption of the exclusionary rule if there seemed a credible case that it would have a serious deterrent effect on police misconduct. However, American studies do not support any such conclusion; the only defensible position on this empirical question is agnosticism.[34] These studies, however, by their nature cannot identify instances where the police officer was deterred from making an unlawful search[35] because he was concerned about possible suppression of evidence, or put another way, where he complied with legal standards in order to ensure that the evidence would be admissible. The exclusionary rule may thus exert some undetectable influence towards inhibiting unlawful practices by American police, which would have no counterpart in English law.

From comparative analysis there emerges a striking conclusion. Police in England work within a system whose ethos is that of partisanship and competitiveness, in which the surest way to "victory" is aborting formal combat—the trial—by obtaining the other side's "surrender"—a guilty plea or at least a confession. This system equips them with wide powers of compulsion and intrusion, along with the motivation (they would say the necessity) to use them. They enjoy a unique dominance within the institutional structure of law enforcement. In a liberal society, this degree of coercive authority *prima facie* calls for vigilant external control. Yet the police in England are subject to fewer constitutional, legal and political restraints than in virtually any other Western democracy. This paradox is the signal feature of the problem of police governance.

---

[34] See sources cited in Newman (1978), p.448, n.3. The Royal Commission considered only one or two of these studies, but reached the correct conclusion: above n.17, paras. 4.125–4.126.

[35] Most of the studies concerned illegality in searches, rather than in arrests or obtaining confessions. Exclusionary rules apply to these activities as well. A few studies of the *Miranda* rule have been conducted; extracts may be found in Kamisar *et al.* (1980), pp.631–635.

Part I

Chapter 1

POLICE DISCRETION

One of the concepts central to nearly all literature concerning the police is that of discretion. Joseph Goldstein's classic article[1] introduced two important ideas: that the police are virtually unique among bureaucratic organisations in that the degree of discretion is greatest at the lowest level of the hierarchy, and that decisions by policemen in their dealings with the public are of "low visibility"—inaccessible to their ostensible superiors and effectively unreviewable by any authority, particularly where they have decided *not* to arrest someone. Discretion here is used in the sense familiar to administrative law: in K.C. Davis' words, it exists "where effective limits on a public officer's power leave him free to make a choice among possible courses of action or inaction."[2] This "room for decisional manoeuvre" is a matter of degree, which varies with the precision of the standards governing an official's discretion.[3]

Yet the points Goldstein emphasised may themselves in part be merely a reflection of a more fundamental fact: that in taking the sort of decision that is the quintessence of their work, the police are guided by virtually no legal standards at all. More precisely, whilst the police may not violate general criminal or civil law,— *e.g.* by accepting a bribe or assaulting someone without lawful excuse,—they act within an almost infinite range of lawful possibilities. Consider the choices open to a constable summoned to the scene of a minor fight between two men who in law have been guilty at least of common assault. They include:

1. Breaking it up, with an informal warning to the participants and no other action.
2. Breaking it up, inquiring into the cause and attempting to conciliate or mediate between them.
3. Formally cautioning either or both.
4. Attempting to inquire into the cause of the fight, arresting only the one he believes was responsible.
5. Arresting both participants, on any of a wide range of

---

[1] Goldstein (1960), *passim*.   [2] Davis, (1969), p. 4.   [3] Jowell, (1973), p. 179.

charges relating to public order and/or varying degrees of assault as seem to him appropriate.

Even in this apparently simple situation, the range of permissible choices is extraordinary, and will depend on how the constable, or those who train and supervise him, perceives his task. If it is solely and simply law enforcement, the first two possibilities are excluded: the law has been broken and the offenders must be penalised. If considerations of maintaining the peace and public good will predominate, any of the responses is permissible and may depend upon the character of the people involved, where the fight took place, reactions of others in the neighbourhood, and numerous other highly idiosyncratic factors. Still other factors, notably the dangers of overloading the capacity of the criminal justice system and the cost of processing offenders, will also be relevant, particularly if the legal infraction is seen as minor.

All the suggested options are within the range of the constable's legal powers. To say therefore that he must uphold the law, or is responsible to the law, is in practical terms meaningless. His discretion involves either making value judgments about the worthiness of the people involved, or public feeling, or the seriousness of the incident, or the long-term gains and losses involved in sanctions of varying severity.

Since the constable has acted within the law whichever course he chooses, the question that must be asked is why the choice should be his. He is not making a technical or professional decision beyond the competence of the untrained lay persons, but a sensitive, very specific human judgment. So to describe what is entailed is to emphasise, not to demean, its importance.

The sheer idiosyncrasy, the fact that every decision will require the weighing of different factors means it may be difficult to subject it to preordained rules drawn up by hierarchical superiors.[4] The speed with which the choice must be made is largely responsible for this, for where other highly personal judgments are governed by complex rules—for example, entitlement to supplementary benefit—decisions often take days. However, police discretion at this level differs qualitatively from the exercise of discretion by other public officials only in the specific character of the human relations elements of the decision, not because it is "legal".

Much has been made of the "original authority" and "indepen-

---

[4] For an argument that the police are unique in that everything they do is of such case-by-case specificity that it is impossible to formulate general norms of conduct, see Bittner (1974), p. 18 *et seq.*

dence" of constables (see below, p. 25). This would seem to imply
an unrestricted power of the constable to exercise his discretion
according to his best judgment. One has only to state this to see its
unreality: the very existence of an organised police force precludes
it. Constables are part of a highly disciplined organisation with a
quasi-military structure. They are subject to voluminous standing
orders. More important, their decision to arrest is subject to
review by hierarchical superiors, who may reject a charge or,
indeed, require an arrest where a caution has been proposed.
Despite the rhetoric, the constable's discretion is greatest, paradoxically, when he chooses *not* to invoke the law, for that will seldom come to his superiors' notice. But the restrictions which
membership in the police organisation impose on the constable
appeared most clearly in the well-known case of P.C. Joy. From
this case precisely the wrong conclusion is sometimes drawn.[5] P.C.
Joy had arrested an M.P for a traffic offence and wished to prosecute him. His superiors overruled his judgment and contented
themselves with a caution. The perseverant constable then under-
took a successful private prosecution. Whilst this incident may vindicate the existence of the right to private prosecution in English
law, its primary lesson is how tightly the constable's wings are
clipped by the structure within which he works. P.C. Joy's superiors were able to substitute their discretion for his; so far as the
Kent Constabulary were concerned, the offender was *not* prosecuted.

The courts have come to understand the reality of the hierarchical control of constables. In 1979 the indefatigable Mr Blackburn
(below, pp. 62–66), tried yet again to challenge the enforcement of
the obscenity laws by the Metropolitan Police. He argued that
instructions issued by the commissioner, requiring officers on the
ground to refer all potential prosecutions to a centralised squad,
were an unlawful restriction on the constable's power of arrest.
This claim was rejected: there was in fact no restriction on the
power of arrest, and the lawfulness of an administrative requirement that ensured uniformity of practice throughout the force was
unassailable.[6] The point was addressed even more directly in *Hawkins* v. *Bepey*.[7] Chief Inspector Hawkins of the Kent Police died
after instituting a prosecution of the defendants, who presented

W. Rees-Davies 1974

[5] A brief account of this incident, which received extensive press coverage at the time, is found in Gillance and Khan (1975).
[6] *R.* v. *Metropolitan Police Commissioner, ex p. Blackburn, The Times*, December 1, 1979. (Q.B.D.)
[7] [1980] 1 All E.R. 797.

the ingenious argument that since the proceedings had been taken by a specific individual, his death required that they be terminated. The High Court, *per* Watkins J., would have none of it. Quoting what was almost certainly the precise instruction that had led to the countermanding of P.C. Joy, he noted that there were standing instructions in the force that all informations should be laid by chief inspectors or inspectors. The chief constable issued such instructions pursuant to his power of direction and control of the force (s.5(1) of the Police Act 1964; see below p. 74) and there is "a sound administrative, if not other, reason for it." "The real prosecutor" was therefore the chief constable or the force itself[8]— not the person who instituted proceedings nor, *a fortiori*, the arresting officer.

These decisions simply recognise the reality of the organisational structure within which the constable functions. They do not, however, make incursion upon the legitimate and necessary, indeed inescapable, discretion the constable must exercise. Statutes confer discretionary powers directly upon constables, and establish factual preconditions for their exercise. Thus section 1 of the Police and Criminal Evidence Act 1984 gives a constable power to search any vehicle if he has reasonable grounds to suspect that he will find a stolen or prohibited article, and section 24 grants him power to arrest without warrant anyone whom he has reasonable grounds to suspect is guilty of an arrestable offence, or is about to commit one. The factual condition precedent is his knowledge of certain events and of the behaviour of the person searched or arrested. For the power to be validly exercised, those facts must be known to be, or at least reasonably suspected to be true, by the constable—and by no one else, including a superior officer.[9] This point was emphasised by Lawton L.J. in the *Central Electricity Generating Board* (C.E.G.B.) Case.[10] The Board had sought mandamus against the Chief Constable of Devon and Cornwall, who had refused to order his men to clear a site of demonstrators whose non-violent resistance was obstructing its exploration of the site as a possible nuclear power station. His Lordship's remarks require extended quotation:

---

[8] *Ibid.* p.800.
[9] These limits appear in sharp relief when contrasted with anti-terrorism legislation, in which the requirement of reasonableness does not appear. As construed by the House of Lords in *McKee* v. *A.G. for Northern Ireland* [1985] 1 All E.R. 1, reversing the Northern Ireland Court of Appeal, an instruction by a superior officer to arrest the plaintiff as a suspected terrorist was sufficient to make the arrest valid under the Prevention of Terrorism Acts.
[10] [1980] 1 All E.R. 797, 826.

"[The Board's] application, in my judgment, showed a mis-
conception of the powers of chief constables. They command
their forces but they cannot give an officer under command an
order to do acts which can only lawfully be done if the officer
himself with reasonable cause suspects that a breach of the
peace has occurred or is imminently likely to occur or an
arrestable offence has been committed. [The Chief Constable
could] order some of his constables to watch what was going
on in the field when the Board wanted to exercise their statutory powers; but what he could not do was to give unqualified
orders to his officers to remove those who were obstructing
the Board's work. Any orders he gave would have to have
qualifying words to the effect that those obstructing should be
removed if, but only if, [an offence was imminent]."[11]

The technical legal reason behind the restriction on the chief
constable's power is that, not being *in situ,* he cannot make the
requisite factual evaluation which must form the reasonable belief
necessary to make a valid arrest. The corollary—a matter of vital
importance for police governance—is that no superior officer can
take away the discretion granted to the individual constable by
statute,[12] either by requiring him to arrest, or forbidding him to
arrest, a particular individual or anyone who falls into some prede-
fined category. A chief constable cannot tell his subordinates,
"Arrest those demonstrators" or "Do not search the car of my
friend X, notwithstanding that you reasonably suspect him of
being in possession of stolen goods." It is at this point, and this
point only, that the constable's statutory discretion becomes
"independence," in the precise sense of freedom from interference in the exercise of that discretion. If the balance of power
between chief constables and democratic representatives was to be
altered, and police authorities once again[13] exercised executive
control of their forces, that change would leave the discretionary
power of constables totally unaltered. In other words, democratic
control of the force as an organisation—its priorities, allocation of
resources and methods of operation—could not, as a matter of
constitutional law, detract from the discretion Parliament has conferred on constables. The elected body would in this respect
become, so to speak, successor in title to the chief constable; and

---

[11] *Ibid.* p.835.
[12] In the latest *Blackburn* case, see above, n. 6, the Court also averred that a commanding officer could not take away the constable's power of arrest.
[13] The contention that nineteenth century borough watch committees possessed
and exercised such powers is elaborated in detail in Chap. 3.

all the encumbrances imposed upon him—notably that explained by Lawton L.J. in the C.E.G.B. case—would become theirs.

Political Implications of Discretion

The discretion not to enforce the law—which in terms of the working constable means not to arrest someone who has in a strict sense broken the law—may also arise from the substantive breadth and vagueness of the law itself. J.R. Spencer has noted the characteristic preference of the English judiciary for broadly defined offences, mitigated by "common sense" discretion not to prosecute.[14] This is particularly important in controversial public order matters, where notions of breach of the peace, threatening behaviour, obstruction and the like are so wide that virtually any action can, depending on its context, be plausibly branded criminal so as to justify an arrest.[15] The result is that the police invariably under-enforce the law. This is normally regarded as simple common sense, essential to avoid dragging the law into disrepute, yet the result is to turn conventional thinking about policing on its head. The equation of policing with enforcement of the Law—the august embodiment of state sovereignty—becomes untenable. For most less serious offences under-enforcement is the norm; precisely for that reason, enforcement can be a serious abuse of power.[16] The "common sense"[17] which tempers full enforcement may readily become a cloak for conscious or unconscious discrimination on the basis of political opinion, personal appearance, demeanour, social status or race. Under-enforcement becomes selective enforcement.

In only one reported case has this critical issue been even implicitly raised in the courts. In *Arrowsmith* v. *Jenkins*[18] the defendant, a well-known peace campaigner, challenged the validity of her conviction for a violation of the Highways Act. She had addressed a meeting at a site where others had spoken many times without prosecution. The Divisional Court dismissed the issue in half a sentence: so long as personal guilt was established, non-enforcement against others was legally irrelevant. It is unclear from the

[14] Book Review, 51 *U.Chi.L.Rev.* 1265 (1984).
[15] Other examples offered by Thomas (1982) include obscenity, "reckless" driving, and offences concerning "indecent" matter.
[16] Non-enforcement can also be a serious abuse, as the incident involving P.C. Joy showed. But that problem arises only where enforcement is the norm, which for reasons given in the text is not generally the case.
[17] It is in this sense that Lord Scarman (1981, para. 4.51, 4.58) uses the term "discretion" to which he attributes such importance.
[18] [1962] 2 Q.B. 561.

brief report how forcefully the point was argued, but its curt dismissal evinces an extraordinary indifference to political freedom. The result is to leave the police with vast power which can be abused with no possibility of legal review. The need for the political process to step into the breach is therefore imperative.

Other decisions, whilst not overtly biased, may cumulatively produce collective distortion. Research indicates, for example, that working class and black youths are less likely than middle class and white youths to be cautioned than arrested for the same offence.[19] It is doubtful even in the latter instance that many individual officers say to themselves, "He's black so I'll go harder on him". Yet the resulting structural bias is familiar enough to analysts of race relations, who have documented how, in a wide range of areas like housing and employment, unconscious stereotypes and unthinking habits produce unintentional, but no less effectively unequal, treatment of black people, a phenomenon known as institutional racism. "Institutional class-ism" lacks the same verbal resonance, but is equally illegitimate and socially damaging. The problem cannot realistically be attacked, however, by abolishing discretion and requiring full enforcement[20]; the question is rather what mechanisms, internal or external to the police organisation, can be devised to ensure its fair exercise. That discretion may be exercised in a manner systematically unfair but also lawful is something the courts do not seem to comprehend; since the bias has political implications—its victims are almost invariably people on the Left, those the police define as "troublemakers," and ethnic minorities—control of this sort of discretion must be regarded as a political question.

A Case Study

In April 1985, the following report appeared in the press:

> "Police in London's East End are to institute a much tougher policy against racial harassment or racial attacks on the Bengali minority.
>
> Commander Malcolm Sullivan, of Tower Hamlets police, promised yesterday to lower the threshold of what constitutes an arrestable offence where an attack was racially motivated.

---

[19] Landau (1981); Fisher and Mawby (1982).
[20] Some American states have enacted statutes which require full enforcement of all criminal prohibitions. As K.C. Davis (1975), Chap. 3 notes in his study of police discretion, these are simply dead letters.

He said that where, previously a victim . . . might have had
to pursue the case privately as a common assault, local police
were now more likely to interpret such minor assaults as
actual bodily harm"[21]

This episode illustrates better than any other the breadth and
political character of legitimate police discretion. Racist attacks
have been the subject of concern for many years, but it took years
of victimisation and campaigning before the issue was taken
seriously by the Home Office and years more before the police
were seen to take it seriously.[22] Ethnic minorities, particularly
Asians, and above all Bengalis in the East End, have been the victims of offences ranging from broken windows to murder. Perhaps
the most common and frightening experience is being beaten up by
groups of whites. A frequent and bitter allegation is that those
complaining to the police have been told that they would have to
pursue the matter privately.

As a matter of technical law, assault is a common law offence
committed when a person causes another to apprehend immediate
force, which need amount to little more than unlawful touching.
Assault occasioning actual bodily harm (A.B.H.) is a statutory
offence punishable by up to five years imprisonment and is therefore, unlike common assault, an arrestable offence.[23] The degree
of violence necessary to satisfy the requirement of A.B.H. is relatively low: bruising will suffice.[24] Virtually all racist attacks can
therefore be classified as A.B.H., so that the police will undertake
responsibility for tracking down and prosecuting the perpetrators.
The expense and complexity of proceedings, not to mention the
inability of the ordinary person to conduct an investigation,
ensures that classifying an incident as common assault means
ignoring it.

It cannot be said that previous police practice was unlawful. It is
within their discretion to charge or prosecute for less than the
maximum offence that the facts of an incident might justify, and

---

[21] *The Guardian*, April 10, 1985.
[22] Evidence was first systematically compiled by Stepney Trades Council, whose
1978 Report *Blood on the Streets* was wilfully ignored by government and police.
It took several more years of violence before the Home Office officially acknowledged the problem in its paper on *Racial Attacks* (1981).
[23] "Arrestable offence" is defined in s.24 of the P.C.E.A. 1984 to include *inter alia*
any offence which may attract a sentence of five years of imprisonment. (This
definition does not alter previous law). A.B.H. is an offence created by s.47 of
the Offences Against the Person Act 1861.
[24] *Taylor* v. *Granville* [1978] Crim.L.R. 482, Q.B.D.

there is no suggestion that racially motivated attacks alone have been treated in this way. The revised practice, which followed on from an announcement of the commissioner some weeks previously that racial attacks would be one of the force's priorities in 1985, expresses a judgment that because of the psychological and other effects on ethnic minority communities, and on their relations with the rest of the society, racially motivated assaults will be regarded as more serious than the same physical injury where such motivation was absent. This is also a lawful position to take, but it be distorting words to call it a legal decision. It is a political act— one based on a more sensitive appreciation of the position of a particular group in society, responsive to their organised representations and those of their sympathisers. It is the sort of judgment that advocates of greater democratic control would hope their proposals would produce more generally; indeed greater and earlier police responsiveness of this type would probably have defused the movement for such a programme.

This episode illustrates three important points. First, "the law" does not produce one right answer. Secondly, its administrators can respond to perceived social needs whilst staying within its mandate, a response which can take account of the different social situations of identifiable groups.[25]

Thirdly, the rigid distinction between law and politics is exposed as hollow. In constitutional terms, this is of the highest importance, for the existence of that distinction is the intellectual underpinning of the doctrine of constabulary independence and hence of the current political structure of police governance. Yet in the above example, the substantive law never changed, only the (legally valid) way in which it has been applied. This application, though pursuant to a general policy, occurs at the level of the individual case: a particular assailant will now be treated as having committed a more serious offence if the facts warrant it. The only specifically legal element is the presence of the requisite fact (the degree of physical injury) necessary to bring the assault within the higher category of offence. This alone cannot be treated as a matter of discretion subject to police judgment. All else is political, in the sense of reflecting judgment of social utility and morality that are contro-

---

[25] Jefferson and Grimshaw (1984a), *passim* had previously argued that such a response was not possible, because of the restrictive nature of the "legal mandate" of the police. This argument had always seemed implausible in any number of contexts, and is now explicitly discredited in relation to the problem they had addressed. Their view that something they call a "socialist conception of justice" must be accepted before a response to needs of disadvantaged minorities can be addressed is thereby also rendered suspect.

versial. Just as police discretion is inevitable, so is its ineradicably political character.

Discretion and Capability

Discretion of a very different sort exists at the highest managerial level of policing as well. Indeed this discretion is much the most important, for it concerns the orientation and capability of the particular force as a whole. The concept of capability[26] is crucial here. "You do not have a drug problem until you have a drug squad" runs an adage well known among police officers. The police do not encounter offences "at random." The organisation of the force will structure the occasions on which generalist beat constables or members of specialist squads will receive complaints or information about crime. The particular types of offences and geographic patterns of their commission thus emerging will skew the crime figures and hence the definition of "the crime problem." This prominence will in turn purportedly justify particular emphasis on these offences or areas. In this light, many crimes are seen to be *interchangeable*. Particularly in relation to offences which depend primarily upon self-initiated police work (like drugs or corruption), or which public willingness to report is dependent upon the belief that the police are likely to respond sympathetically (as with rape) or effectively (minor burglary or criminal damage), a change in police attitudes or manpower allocation may produce an apparent increase in one whilst another declines.[27]

Among these critical managerial decisions are:

1. The fundamental style or method of policing—reactive; community-based; "hard" or "soft"; degree of involvement with other agencies.
2. Deployment of manpower, both in terms of the number and quality of constables assigned to a particular area and of the establishment of specialist units, *e.g.* drugs, fraud, Special Patrol Group or equivalent.
3. Emphasis given to a particular offence, *e.g.* the anti-pornography drive launched by the Chief Constable of Greater Manchester, or a response to concern expressed by affected

[26] The term is taken from Grant (1980).
[27] "Decline" is relative. If the "objective" frequency of a particular offence is rising rapidly, a decline in police capability in relation to it may only slow the rate of increase in reported offences, not produce a drop in the absolute number reported. "Interchangeability" of course refers to official statistics of crime, not to its true but unknowable incidence.

sections of the public about, *e.g.* racist attacks, rape, or street robbery.

4. Acquisition, and the rules governing the use of, new technology and weaponry.

Some of these decisions require solely the application of professional experience and expertise. Most, however, are *political* decisions. The word is used, not in the sense of partisanship but to describe the essence of public choice: decisions which entail judgments about moral values, favour certain interests over others, and require weighing competing claims for scarce resources. At this level, policing is politics, just as taxation or education are politics. The choices should be informed by knowledge, and the specialists given the task of carrying out the political decisions should be listened to with care if those decisions are not to be based solely on ideology and hope. But to regard these sorts of decisions as exclusively "legal" is to misunderstand them fundamentally and thereby deliver substantial political power by default to the chief constable to whom they are entrusted.

A False Distinction

In recent contemporary debate about police governance, a distinction has emerged between "policy" and "operations." Those relatively rare police authorities which have sought to exercise their influence have generally found chief constables willing to discuss the former but steadfastly refusing to speak about the latter, and it is a mark of the unique influence and the critical political position occupied by the Consultative Committee established in Lambeth in the wake of Lord Scarman's Report that the local commander has been willing to extend his consultation to detailed operational matters.[28]

The precise pedigree of the distinction is unclear. It appeared by implication in the Police Authorities (Powers) Bill introduced by Jack Straw M.P. in 1980, attracting some bipartisan interest. This would have enabled police authorities to determine "policies." Lawyers will recall its appearance in the speech of Lord Wilberforce in *Anns* v. *London Borough of Merton*.[29] It is possible that this rigid division can coherently be maintained in the relatively uncontentious area of negligence law, but a glance at the above

---

[28] See the papers by Commander Marnoch and Canon Walker, Chairman of the Consultative Committee, in Brown (1985).

[29] [1978] A.C. 728, 754–755.

examples of executive discretionary decisions will show that it breaks down entirely in relation to policing.

More precisely, some of the crucial "policy" decisions are about "operations." The method of policing, for example, will determine whether the force relies on computerised information collected by various forms of pressure on those at the edges of criminal involvement, leading to isolated "swoops" on suspects but otherwise remaining aloof from the public, or an intensive commitment to street patrols leading to personal knowledge of most of the people in the area, involvement in community welfare projects and co-ordination with other "care and control" agencies in crime prevention.[30] The choice could be described as policy, but its concrete manifestations are in the day-to-day contacts with the public—abrasive or supportive—and it is these which may produce dissatisfaction and demands for change. "Swamp '81" in Brixton is only the most spectacularly disastrous example; public strip-searching, excessive force in dealing with youths congregating on the street, or an attempt to gain access to confidential school records of a particular pupil are more typical examples of causes of antagonism.

The distinction becomes even less tenable when one examines the decision to set up a drug squad. This involves allocation of manpower and related resources that would otherwise be used in alternate ways. In other words, it represents a decision that drugs deserve greater or increased attention compared to traffic control, burglary or rape. It may also have serious consequences for relations with various groups within the community—innocent persons who feel harassed by searches; women or householders who feel that the safety of the streets or their property is not receiving sufficient protection. The decision is highly controversial, and a classic example of a political choice. Yet it could equally be well characterised as "operational"—it merely involves reassignment of a limited number of constables to particular duties.

Finally, it is important to recognise that the distinction was developed in a radically different constitutional context, in which the actions of public officials are challenged in the courts on grounds of alleged negligence. These officials serve a Minister (or a local authority) who in traditional constitutional theory is responsible to Parliament and thus ultimately to the electorate for the policy adopted. The exemption of policy from judicial scrutiny reinforces the process of political accountability along the gener-

---

[30] See further Baldwin and Kinsey (1982), Chaps. 2, 3, 8 and 9.

ally accepted lines. Moreover, the choices often involve complex
technical judgments which the courts are not competent to make.
This leaves the secondary and less value-laden area of "operations" subject to judicial evaluation under standards of negligence. However, in the policing debate the distinction is stood on
its head, for "policy" is what is sought to be brought under democratic control and "operations" defines the no-go area; the issue is
not the scope of judicial control but the exclusion of representative
institutions from their normal commanding role. In sum, in the
context of policing it would be a distinct gain if this proposed line
of demarcation vanished from public debate.[31] A more precise
delineation of the sphere from which political control should be
excluded must be formulated, a task taken up in Chapter 10.

Conclusion

Substantive vagueness of the law and limited resources thus
create enormous discretion, at the lowest and highest levels, for
the police. Underpinning both, however, is an even more important consideration. The purposes of policing are much less obvious
than may first appear. Few have been able to share Peel's single-
minded view that the main task of the police is the prevention of
crime. For Sir Richard Mayne, who issued the founding instructions to the New Police in 1829, the tasks were more complex and
diffuse: "the prevention of crime . . . the protection of life and
property, the preservation of public tranquility." Mayne's formulation was quoted with approval by Lord Scarman, who added a
critical rider. The aims, he argued, may conflict; and where this
occurs, preservation of public tranquility must come first.[32] This
view has had great influence on the new regime in charge of the
Metropolitan Police, which embraced it in the principles of Policy
and Guidance for Professional Behaviour issued to the Force in
April 1985. Yet the police officer, at whatever level, taking this
injunction to heart may well ask, but what of my duty to the law?
Am I to turn a blind eye to infractions in the name of public tranquility? If so, does that give any minority, if sufficiently aroused,
the power to nullify Parliament's command? Sir Robert Mark
made this point when criticising Scarman, who had faulted the
police for not exercising the same sensitivity to public feeling in

---

[31] The Canadian Royal Commission of Inquiry into abuses by the R.C.M.P. also
    concluded that the policy/operations division was untenable in the security field;
    see Marshall (1984), pp.125–127.
[32] Scarman (1981), paras. 4.56–4.57.

their manner of law enforcement in Brixton as they show else-where. This, said Mark, meant one law for blacks and another for whites.[33]

Mark's absolutist position has the virtue of simplicity: the law is the law is the law. Law is somehow "above" politics (a dirty word): the courts are its oracles and the police derive their mandate from it. The difficulty with this stance is that it is a recipe for intolerable conflict or, more likely, for its authoritarian resolution. A political and social order which values freedom cannot take law as its foundation: it must rest on voluntary allegiance. If the majority's law is pushed too far or too hard, that consent evaporates and the ensuing coercion will assuredly curb the liberties of the majority as well. The paramountcy of law is not the highest social good.

One critical point, which Lord Scarman explicitly recognised,[34] is that whilst a judge cannot take this view, the constable must. The judge derives his mandate from the law, the constable from the polity. Law enforcement can no more be an absolute than the environment can remain pure in an industrial economy.

Yet Scarman failed to reflect sufficiently upon the implications of his insight. Once it is accepted that strict law enforcement must give way to more important considerations, the idea that the police can somehow stand apart from politics and from the process of public choice becomes untenable. And the problem is much broader. Once it is admitted that discretion in policing is inevitable, and that the choices involved in police managerial discretion are political, there inevitably follows the question, who determines how the discretion shall be exercised? To answer this one needs both a theory of governance—of constitutional allocation of power—and a conception of policing that enables one to identify the ways, if any, in which it occupies a place in constitutional structure different from other public services. These matters are taken up below.

At this point, however, a fundamental axiom must be stated. It is simply that police discretion is not a seamless web. There are different types of discretion, exercised at different levels within the police service. Some are quintessentially political, and should be exercised by elected representatives in the accepted democratic manner. Some involve application of legal standards to specify factual circumstances, for example the degree of suspicion necessary to justify a search of a particular person. To analogise such dis-

---

[33] *Observer*, November 29, 1981.
[34] *Op. cit.* para. 4.57.

cretion to a judicial function merely confuses thought.[35] It is an executive discretion in relation to the administration of criminal law, a function of particular importance to personal freedom and the legitimacy of the state, which should therefore remain free of political control to remove any possibility of its perversion in the service of person or partisan ends. (It is equally important that such perversion is not practised by the police themselves: hence there remains wide scope for political bodies to review police behaviour on both individual and systematic bases). Many, perhaps most, lie somewhere in-between, like the choices available to the constable attending the assault incident. For consistency they require general guidance as to the primary aims to be pursued and the relative weight to be given to various factors which point in different directions, but as a practical matter the decisions will be taken by individual constables in specific circumstances. The essential task is to identify the *degree* of political control appropriate to particular kinds of decision.

---

[35] The 1962 Royal Commission fell into this trap, describing this aspect of the constable's work as "quasi-judicial" (Cmnd. 1728, para. 86). The House of Lords in *Holgate-Mohammed* v. *Duke,* [1984] A.C. 437 has finally scotched this error, and treated constables as exercising executive discretion. See below, pp. 69–71.

Part II

Chapter 2

THE STATUS OF CONSTABLE

The single most important feature of the constitutional position of the police is that they have the status of constable. When organised police forces were established in the nineteenth century, they were grafted onto, and clothed with the powers of, the traditional office. This "ancient and honourable office" is a creation of the common law,[1] a fact that has been made the foundation stone of constitutional doctrine. Judicial decisions concerning the boundaries of policy-making discretion of the head of the police organisation have taken as their fundamental premise his status as constable.[2] It is said that because the constable's powers are inherent in his office and possessed by the office holder alone—"original and not delegated" was the phrase used by the 1962 Royal Commission[3]—he enjoys a freedom from control by elected representatives unique in public law. Commentators like Jefferson and Grimshaw regard this putative corollary of independence as the definitive theme of police governance.[4] Whether as a matter of history the constitutional status of police has generally been understood in this way will be explored fully below. Before considering this point, there remain equally important questions which are generally overlooked. What were the powers and functions of constables before 1829, and how have these changed in the ensuing century and a half? If, as will be suggested, the present day police bear the same relation to the 18th century constable as does the titled president of the National Farmers Union to the followers of Wat Tyler, it follows that continued identification of the police with the status of constable produces confusion and mythology, obstructing clear thought about the nature of the public services they provide in late twentieth century Britain.

The constable was part of the ancient structure of village self-government. Indeed there were elements both of democracy and representativeness in his selection: he was an elected official

---

[1] On the early origins and development of the office of constable, see Simpson (1895); Critchley (1978), pp. 1–18; Marshall (1965), Chap. 2; Allen (1953) *passim*.
[2] These decisions are critically analysed on pp.63–67.
[3] Royal Commission on the Police Cmnd. 1728 (1962) para. 31.
[4] Jefferson and Grimshaw (1984), pp. 14, 24 and *passim*.

(though the franchise was anything but democratic) and a figure of considerable importance whose functions included a number of other matters of local administration. His powers, however, were extremely limited. It was this fact that enabled the 1929 Royal Commission on Police Powers and Procedure to state—more correctly as a matter of history than of contemporary description—that "a policeman possesses few powers not enjoyed by the ordinary citizen" and that "in view of the common law, he is only 'a person paid to perform, as a matter of duty, acts which if he were so minded he might have done voluntarily'."[5] At common law the main difference was that a constable alone could arrest in cases of *suspected* felony or treason. No special immunities protected him. Indeed it was not until 1750 that Parliament granted immunity from civil suit where the constable was executing a magistrate's warrant.[6]

By the early middle ages, however, both the constable's standing and functions began to decline. His broad range of powers were steadily handed over to the justices of the peace, to whom he became increasingly subordinated—so much so that by the eighteenth century, the constable had become little more than a minion of the magistrates.[7] He became one relatively minor cog in the machinery of local government, whose key figure was the justice of the peace.

The latter's responsibility for maintaining the King's peace overlapped with his responsibilities for care and discipline of the poor, maintenance of highways and sewers and the myriad of other functions of local government exercised originally in legal form, through writs issued by Quarter Sessions. The idea that executive and judicial functions are qualitatively different and should be administratively segregated would have been incomprehensible to an eighteenth century Englishman[8] (indeed Britain remains almost unique in the English-speaking world in the absence of either the practice or theory of separation of powers).[9] The justices of the

---

[5] Cmnd. 3297 (1929), paras. 15–16. The source of the quotation is not identified in the Report. It is in fact taken from Sir James Fitzjames Stephen, *History of the Criminal Law* (1889).

[6] Leigh (1975), p. 3. The immunity was granted by the Constables Protection Act 1750.

[7] This was Holdsworth's conclusion in the first edition of his *History of English Law*, Vol. 4, p. 124. (I owe this citation to Gillance and Khan (1975).) See also Marshall, *op. cit.* p. 24.

[8] As is well known, Montesquieu badly misunderstood the English system he extolled as one of separation of powers in his *Spirit of the Laws*.

[9] This point is well made by Professor Hood Phillips in his criticism of Lord Diplock's comments in *Hinds* v. *The Queen*, [1977] A.C. 195, P.C., in (1977) 93 L.Q.R. 11.

peace were responsible for all aspects of the administration of justice and the maintenance of order, and the history of the police as an institution is inseparably entwined with both the reform of the magistracy and the democratisation of local government.

A portrait of the constable at the end of the eighteenth century would emphasise several salient features.[10] First, the constable was part-time, often a shopkeeper or artisan. He was ignorant of substantive law, and may have been the paid substitute of someone who had been appointed to the office by the justices but wished to avoid its burdens.

Secondly, he was unpaid, and therefore took fees for such tasks as executing warrants, searching for witnesses, or even attending court. Fees were essential if a constable was to expend any significant amount of time as this meant loss of earnings or trade.[11] One of the major features of Peel's "New Police" was that they were a full-time paid body of men forbidden to take fees for their services. This was without precedent, though some urban districts had been granted power by a series of Acts of Parliament to employ a paid constabulary.[12]

Thirdly, he took orders from the justices, who exercised "operational" control over specific cases, and who were seised of primary responsibility for keeping the peace.[13] Fourthly, the notion of police work did not exist, or rather was so limited as to be unrecognisable to us. Constables did not engage in detection in any systematic way; they might search for evidence if a victim identified a particular suspect, but there was no notion of specialist skills or indeed special legal powers to track down unidentified offenders. This tradition survived the early years of organised policing; it took years for the Metropolitan Police to establish a Criminal Investigation Division, and many provincial forces functioned without one well into the present century.[14]

Fifthly, the police did not prosecute offenders. Enthusiasts of privatisation would do well to ponder the history in England of criminal prosecutions, which remained a purely private responsi-

---

[10] This characterisation is something of an ideal type, in that local practice varied and in London there were even a small number of full-time paid constables established by an Act of 1792. More important, much of the picture holds good for well into the nineteenth century in most localities.

[11] Phillips (1986), pp. 1, 30.

[12] Maitland (1908), p. 486.

[13] Maitland (1885), pp. 91–92.

[14] Critchley, *op. cit.* pp. 160–162.

bility for most of the last century; perhaps not until 1870 were a majority of prosecutions undertaken by the police.[15] Prosecutions were largely in the hands of private associations, whose moving spirits were often solicitors in search of custom, and whose members paid annual subscriptions entitling them to call upon the organisation if they were victims of crime. Those unable to afford subscriptions—the great majority—might obtain some financial help from public funds specially created for the purpose, but many prosecutions, especially for offences of violence against the person, were stillborn for want of money. Once initiated, prosecutions could be compounded for money, like a civil action for damages. The creation of a state prosecution mechanism—for that is what the police became—available to and used by all social classes[16] and not directly dependent upon the financial interests of the legal profession, was a significant achievement of Victorian government. The abolition of compounding—a corollary of the fact that the police, rather than the complainant, began to assume ultimate responsibility for whether a prosecution would go forward—was a great advance in making justice a public good, rather than a form of negotiable private property. Essential to these developments was a significant alteration in the character of the constable as law enforcement officer.

Sixthly, precisely because in legal theory he was a sort of delegate of the community, the constable exercised common law powers only. Special statutory powers denied to the general public only began to be created after organised police forces had attained some degree of public acceptance. This is seen most clearly in the Metropolitan Police Act 1839, enacted only after a distinctly uneasy decade of sometimes fierce opposition to the new organisation. This legislation, some of which remained in force until the Police and Criminal Evidence Act 1984 took effect, included provisions granting policemen wide powers of search and arrest in particular circumstances.[17] Similar local corporation Acts followed. Indeed, as Maitland noted, Parliament continued to expand the powers of constables throughout the nineteenth century by "heaping other powers and duties upon them," such as

[15] Above, p. 5

[16] Davis (1986) demonstrates that working class people did make use of the police as a law enforcement and prosecution service when it suited their needs, not in the context of public order but when they were victims of theft or assault.

[17] Notably s.66 of the Metropolitan Police Act 1839, which gave constables the power to stop and search persons whom they had reasonable grounds to suspect of possessing stolen property. This power is now enjoyed by constables throughout the land by virtue of s.1 of the P.C.E.A. 1984, which also repeals s.66.

enforcement of the Licensing Acts and various pieces of sanitary legislation.[18] The trend has continued unbroken, as with the creation of special powers for the police to stop and search for illegal substances under the Misuse of Drugs Act 1971 and to detain people suspected of offences under the Immigration Act 1971. The logical culmination has been reached in the 1984 Act, with its wide powers for constables throughout the country to arrest, search, seize property, and conduct intimate body searches.[19] Legally speaking, the constable is indeed now "a man apart" from other citizens.

The contemporary police officer is thus less a descendant of the nineteenth century constable than a distant cousin several times removed. He is part of a large, formally directed body increasingly organised into specialist squads. Consequently large numbers of police devote their energies to uncovering offences of which they themselves are complainants and for which there may be no third party victims: a proactive rather than the traditional reactive approach.[20] Many are engaged in systematic detection, and all are part of a chain of decision which plays the central role in the decision to prosecute, a dominance which, as argued earlier, will not be displaced by the Crown Prosecution Service.[21] They exercise a wide range of legal powers far exceeding those available to the ordinary member of the public whose responsibility for law enforcement is now more theoretical than real. They make regular use of advanced technology, which has profound implications for privacy and other aspects of personal freedom. They carry out, in the context of an organisational structure which channels the exercise of their discretion, a broad range of policies which often involve contentious political choices. At both the level of the police officer on the beat and the chief constable in his office, the

---

[18] Above n. 12, p. 489.

[19] *e.g.* the wide range of powers contained in the P.C.E.A. 1984 which, apart from the "citizens's arrest" power (s.24(4) and (5)), are all restricted to constables; indeed some, such as roadchecks (s.4) and extended detention (s.42) require authorization of high level officers.

[20] This point requires supplementation. Nineteenth century policing contained important pro-active elements, notably in relation to street offences and drunkeness, which accounted for nearly one-third of the summary offences prosecuted in the mid-Victorian period. (This figure can be obtained by examining the judicial statistics published in the British Parliamentary Papers; I have taken those for 1857, the first year of publication, and 1867.) These were, however, all offences relating to public, and therefore readily observable, behaviour. They are qualitatively different from drugs, obscene material, immigration, and even many sophisticated offences relating to fraud or corruption.

[21] Above, pp. 5–7.

reality of policing has far outgrown the pristine character of the office of constable. The contemporary policeman needs to be recognised for what he is: a public official exercising administrative or executive powers, albeit of a particular kind. Their special characteristics may in some instances require modification of the general principles and practices governing legal control of administrative action, but those modifications must be carefully crafted and specially justified, not merely assumed.

The process of creating an appropriate framework of public law for the police must begin by casting aside the shibboleth of the police officer as constable. The result is an escape from what may be termed the individualistic fallacy. The police officer can no longer be seen as a self-directed decision-maker answerable only to the law. Rather he is a person subject to organisational and occupational/professional rules and norms, like other employees. One question that immediately arises is, who is to make those rules or at any rate is to be ultimately responsible for their content? This is the fundamental question addressed throughout this study.

A second question is what status the policeman should occupy within the framework of public law. As constable, he has been held to occupy an office, which formerly meant that he enjoyed certain procedural protections in the event of dismissal denied mere employees.[22] This particular advantage has largely been erased by the advent of unfair dismissal legislation. In so far as a constable now enjoys greater procedural protection of job security than other public employees, this derives from the Discipline Regulations considered in Chap. 9. However, the police remain subject to certain disabilities imposed on few other employees, even in the public sector. They cannot join a political party or a trade union, and they are subject to a discipline code which can be used to regulate their off-duty behaviour to an extent other occupational groups would not tolerate.[23] Moreover, as was illustrated by *Evans* v. *Chief Constable of North Wales*,[24] vague notions such as "efficiency" or being "well conducted" are used by senior officers to make moral judgments about a police officer's private life.

---

[22] *Cooper* v. *Wilson* [1937] 2 K.B. 309. Note also *Ridge* v. *Baldwin*, [1964] A.C. 40.

[23] This Discipline Code is found in Sched. 2 of the Police (Discipline) Regulations (S.I. 1985 No. 518), discussed in Chap. 9.

[24] [1982] 1 W.L.R. 1155, H.L. This House of Lords found the procedure of dismissal wholly deficient, though some of their Lordships criticised the substantive decision as well, which was taken under reg. 16 of the Police Regulations 1971 (S.I. 1971 No. 156), governing probationer constables.

In that case, a probationer constable was dismissed because he had married an older woman who had formerly lived with his uncle, had purportedly lived with her a " 'hippy' life style," and kept an excessive number of dogs in his police council house. Onerous intrusions of this kind seem unnecessary to ensure impartial discharge of a police officer's duties; it would be sufficient to forbid active engagement in politics whilst at work, standing for political office, or striking.

The police perform an important public service to a particular community, which pays them. It would epitomise and reinforce their relationship to that community if they were treated as employees of its local authority, with the same contracts of service and rights under employment legislation enjoyed by all other employees. Such a change would not affect the constable's responsibility for peace-keeping and law enforcement, even if the proposals for greater local responsibility for policing put forward below were adopted. Nor would it alter his powers under statute or common law. It would, however, emphasise that the difficulties of ensuring that public officials serve their community, and of identifying and respecting those areas in which their independence from political control is genuinely necessary, are neither peculiar, nor peculiarly difficult in relation to, the police. Rather they are the critical problems of representative democracy in its relation to the state apparatus.

Chapter 3

THE STRUCTURE OF GOVERNANCE, 1829–1964

The contemporary controversy about the relationship between the police and democratic institutions of government takes place in a particular doctrinal and political context. It is dominated by the theory enshrined in the Police Act 1964, and the Court of Appeal decision in the first *Blackburn* case,[1] and imbibed like mother's milk by all police officers in their training. This is the doctrine of police independence—the view that the police, uniquely among public officials, should not be under the ultimate control of democratically elected representatives of the public. This theory does not entail police acting heedless of public feeling: after the Brixton riots and the Scarman Report it has been stretched to encompass consultative or liaison arrangements, which are now a statutory requirement.[2] In some politically sensitive areas, like Lambeth, the local police leadership has been willing to discuss, defend and accept criticism of policing and handling of specific cases in a way that would have been rejected outright a decade ago.[3] Nonetheless the doctrine insists that no political body shall have the power to direct or command those in charge of the police organisation to adopt or reject a particular policy or practice, and that in the end responsibility for policing rests with the chief constable. This theory is alien to Europeans, who find it incomprehensible,[4] and equally so to the United States, where commissioners of police are usually appointed by the elected head of local government.

Being different is not necessarily a vice, and police independence could be seen, like the absence of a written constitution and

---

[1] [1968] 2 Q.B. 118; see below, pp. 63–66.

[2] P.C.E.A. 1984, s.106; see below, pp. 89–94.

[3] See below, pp. 89–94 and see the papers in Brown (1985) by Alec Marnoch, the Commander in Lambeth; Canon Walker, first Chairman of the Consultative Committee; and Supt. Cansdale.

[4] A fascinating account of an attempt by the British occupation force in occupied Germany to impose a new police system headed by an "independent" chief is found in Ebsworth (1960), Chap. 9. The Germans regarded this independence as politically dangerous, giving excessive power to authoritarian-minded police, and asked plaintively how decisions requiring discretion and hence political choice, could possibly be exercised by someone not controlled by the responsible political authorities. They abandoned the experiment as soon as self-government was restored.

the importance of conventions, as a peculiar but valuable British contribution to the diverse forms of liberal democracy. One of the strongest arguments in favour of the theory, however, is the suggestion that it is a vital component of English liberty—in Geoffrey Marshall's caustic phrase, "a thing of antiquity with its roots alongside Magna Carta."[5] Marshall's impressive critique, published in 1965, argued that in reality the theory only crystallised around 1930 and was contrary to nineteenth century practice. His analysis, long ignored, has recently been criticised,[6] but in terms of practical effect on political and judicial elites, it might as well never have been written. In view of both the intellectual challenge and the practical indifference, it seems worthwhile to re-examine the evidence. There is a considerable amount of historical material Marshall did not discuss, which has been supplemented by research undertaken in the past two decades. The nineteenth century statutes also deserve more detailed scrutiny than they have received. Moreover, there are related themes, notably the shifting balance between local and central power over the police organisation, which command attention. This chapter will therefore look at the way the statutes establishing police forces, leading political figures, judicial decisions, and commentators on British government dealt with matters concerning the governance of police in the long period preceding the enactment of the Police Act 1964.

The Metropolitan Police

Peel's "New Police" were the product of a lengthy period of agitation, resistance and compromise, which was almost as much concerned with corruption among justices of the peace as it was with the inadequacies of law enforcement. The "trading justices" were attacked in a statute promoted by Pitt in 1792, which established seven "police offices" in various areas of the metropolis. These were manned by newly appointed justices, one of whose major duties was the appointment and control of a small band of paid constables.[7] In 1829 the Metropolitan Police were formed by establishing a new "police office" at Westminster, provided with two justices who, responsible to the Home Secretary, were to rule the organisation. These justices (who became one in 1856) were not styled commissioners until a decade later, and even today the Metropolitan Police Commissioner is appointed a magistrate upon

---

[5] Marshall (1965), p. 33.
[6] Jefferson and Grimshaw (1984), pp. 47–58.
[7] Maitland (1885), pp. 99–100.

taking up his duties. Despite judicial assertion to the contrary,[8] the commissioner is not a constable. Nor is he a chief constable, an official whose mode of appointment and dismissal and powers of office are specified in the Police Act 1964. Unlike every other chief officer of police, he holds office at the pleasure of his police authority, the Home Secretary; the dismissal of chief constables is governed by an elaborate statutory procedure.[9] Indeed the 1964 Act barely affects the Metropolitan Police, whose governmental structure remains largely that of Peel's Act.

The relationship between the Home Secretary and the commissioner is the central axis round which revolve questions of political authority and independence. The statute itself is unclear. The commissioner is empowered to perform the duties of a justice, as well as the duties specified in the Metropolitan Police Act 1829 and those which "as shall be from time to time directed by one of His Majesty's principal secretaries of state for the more efficient administration of the police."[10] Since the duties of a justice at that time included controlling constables, it appears that some structure of overlapping responsibilities was envisaged, and that no one felt the need for a clear legal division of powers. Certainly the valuable study by R. Plehwe[11] demonstrates that successive Home Secretaries repeatedly gave oral instructions to commissioners on a very wide and detailed range of matters. Thus in 1833 Lord Melbourne authorised the practice of exercising surveillance of political meetings in plain clothes, and even directed attendance at particular gatherings; in 1881 Sir William Harcourt issued a directive, which he announced in Parliament, forbidding the use of methods of entrapment without direct authorisation from the Home Office; in 1913 the commissioner was informed what attitude he should take toward whist drives. Plehwe concludes that "During the formative years of the Metropolitan Police Force neither the Home Office nor the Commissioners seem to have doubted that the Minister could issue instructions on operational matters" and that "It seems that at least until the First World War the practice of the Home Office was in accordance with Harcourt's view that it was for the Secretary of State to decide how far he should exercise his authority."[12]

---

[8] Notably Lord Denning's oft-quoted dicta in *Blackburn I,* below, pp. 64–65.
[9] Below, p.157. No doubt the principles of *Ridge* v. *Baldwin,* [1964] A.C. 40 would apply to the process of dismissal of a commissioner.
[10] Metropolitan Police Act 1829, s.1.
[11] Plehwe (1974), p. 316.
[12] *Ibid.* pp. 327, 330.

The reference to "Harcourt's view" also recalls perhaps the most famous instance in which the Home Secretary asserted his control over the running of the Metropolitan Police. The late 1880s were a bad time for London's police. Their handling of the Trafalgar Square riots, in which one demonstrator was killed on the first British "Bloody Sunday," and their inability to run to earth the Whitechapel killer later christened Jack the Ripper, subjected them to strong and widespread criticism—including a quietly barbed comment from the Queen.[13] When Commissioner Sir Charles Warren unsuccessfully sought the Home Secretary's support for any action, "however illegal," and was denied authority to offer a reward for information relating to the murders, he resigned.[14] It is startling to realise that an "operational" matter like offering a reward was one that even a notoriously high-handed commissioner understood to require approval from his political superior. Indeed in his brief time in office Warren had engaged in an almost continuous series of rows with the Home Office as he attempted to assert the commissioner's freedom from its supervision. This was trenchantly denied by the Permanent Secretary, Godfrey Lushington, who insisted that:

> " . . . for practical every day purposes the test of a Department being attached to the Home Office is whether it is subordinate to the Secretary of State. It is in this sense that the Commissioner denies that the Metropolitan Police is a department of the Home Office and it is in this sense that I maintain it is, just as the Prisons Department for instance."[15]

Warren's resignation occasioned a Parliamentary debate, in which the Conservative Home Secretary Henry Matthews and his Liberal predecessor, Harcourt were in full agreement on the fundamental principles. In Harcourt's words:

> " . . . There cannot be any doubt about the matter. It is not a dual control at all . . . [T]he Commissioner of Police is no more independent of the Secretary of State than the Under Secretary of State for the Home Department . . . Of course the Commissioner is the man who knows the Force under him, what is its work, and how it can best be accomplished; but for the policy of the police, so to speak, the Secretary of

---

[13] Critchley (1978), p. 161.
[14] *Ibid.* pp. 161–162.
[15] Quoted in Pellew (1982), p. 49. See pp. 47–50 for a good account of these conflicts.

State must be, and is, solely, responsible. For instance, whether public meetings are to be allowed or prohibited in the Metropolis, is not a question of police, but a question of policy, for the Secretary of State to decide."[16]

Simultaneously but independently of this controversy came the introduction of elected representative government in London. The establishment of the London County Council, which occurred in 1888, had long been resisted by Conservatives, and one of the key questions was what functions it would be permitted to assume from central government. To the dismay of some of the Radicals, policing was retained by the Home Office, and in March 1889 a Conservative writer thought the question sufficiently important to devote a long article to attacking the Radicals' position.[17] For present purposes, the interest of his argument lies in what it does *not* question. The level on which he confronted his opponents was that of *who* should govern the police, not of the limitations on that power of governance. For he did not think any such limitations existed. He characterised the Radical position in a purely descriptive sense as requiring that the Metropolitan Police "should be placed in the same position to the London County Council as the constabulary bear to the County Council of [other major cities.] In these the chief constables will be appointed by the County Council, in *whose hands also the sole control and organisation of the police will be placed* . . . The question is thus reduced to the very simple one: whether the *absolute control* of the Metropolitan Police shall pass from the Secretary of State to a Council chosen by the electors of the Metropolis" (emphasis supplied). And in passing he echoed Harcourt's view of the Home Secretary's power to "give direct instructions to the Commission of Police" in relation to mass meetings and public disorder.[18]

Thus whilst in later Victorian times the locus of political control was in serious dispute, the existence and extent of that control over police policy and operations in contentious areas was not. This consensus lasted well into the present century. Indeed the primary objection to local control of London's police was not the view that their "independence" would be threatened, but that the "Imperial" functions of the Force—notably protection of the Queen and the Houses of Parliament and preventing "the perpetration of dynamite outrages by Irish-Americans"—uniquely

---

[16] Parl. Deb. (*Hansard*) Vol. 330, Ser. 3, cols. 1162–1163.
[17] Evans (1889), pp. 445–461.
[18] *Ibid.* pp. 446–457.

required retention of a role for central government.[19] Otherwise the Metropolitan Police were considered no different from other urban forces, which were governed by elected watch committees.

The Borough Forces

Although establishment of a police force was not then made mandatory, the basic statutory structure for police in the boroughs was laid down by the Municipal Corporations Act 1835. Municipal corporations were to establish watch committees which were empowered to appoint "a sufficient number of fit men" and to make regulations for the running of the force. It was the committee, not its employees, who were responsible for policing. Although any two justices could suspend a constable, only the watch committee had power to dismiss, a power which covered the head constable, who had no special status and was not mentioned in the Act. The County and Borough Police Act 1856, which made creation of a police force compulsory in all areas, also stated in section 7 that constables were to obey the lawful commands of the watch committee as well as of the justices. This provision—which remained on the statute book until 1964—coupled with the power as employer in a legal regime in which employee rights were virtually non-existent, gave the watch committee—composed entirely of elected members—great powers of control over the police.

These powers were exercised regularly, and included sacking head constables when they resisted directions. Such occasions of conflict were relatively rare, for the extreme exercise of power was seldom necessary. This is illustrated by the well-documented incident in Birmingham in 1880, when the head constable was opposed to a resolution of the watch committee and appealed to the Home Secretary. The latter called his attention to the watch committee's powers of rule-making and dismissal, and refused to intervene. Faced with the alternative of a forced resignation, the head constable complied.[20] Head constables were often men who worked their way up through the force, and had learned compliance with the wishes of the watch committee as part of getting on: it is extremely doubtful that anyone thought likely to prove defiant would be appointed to the position of command.

In the early years of the new forces, the watch committees in

---

[19] See, *e.g.* the debate between Evans, *op.cit.*, and a Radical spokesman, Professor James Stuart, M.P., who replied in the next issue of the *Contemporary Review* (1889), pp. 622–635.

[20] Critchley, *op.cit.* pp. 131–132, see n. 13.

some areas were literally in day-to-day operational control. Michael Brogden's study of the Liverpool police reports that in its first eleven years, a sub-committee of the watch met daily to supervise the operations and issued on average one order each week in response to requests for services from local property owners concerning the disposition of officers.[21] The committee's role receded by the 1850s as the pattern of policing became routinised, but this does not indicate that the head constable was seen to be independent or that political direction was inappropriate. Rather, it shows that the politicians had established practices and procedures with which they were satisfied and no longer thought detailed supervision necessary. When, however, a politically contentious issue arose, explicit directions were issued and the head constable complied. This was clearly illustrated in 1890 when, as the culmination of a decade of campaigning by anti-vice crusaders, the watch committee by resolution ordered the head constable, Captain Nott-Bower, to bring prosecutions against all brothels rather than, as he had preferred, against those thought to be connected with other crimes. He objected that the drive was bound to be unsuccessful because the activities would relocate, and for other practical reasons. The proceedings were duly launched, though his predictions proved accurate. Brogden argues that his episode indicates that the balance of forces within the city's economy, rather than the watch committee, ultimately dictated policing policy, and that within this structure the head constable began to develop an operation of autonomy based upon technical expertise.[22] The real point, however, is that when the watch committee knew its own mind, or thought it did, its employee did its bidding. And the rather tendentious argument that the incident merely reinforced the duty of the police to uphold the law[23] simply cannot be squared with what both sides to the dispute actually did, nor with Nott-Bower's own reflections on the incident years later.[24]

The question of control over borough forces appears never to have become an issue for judicial decision. However, in yet another Liverpool matter, *Andrews* v. *Nott-Bower*,[25] Lord Esher M.R. observed that a resolution by the watch committee, directing the head constable to compile a report detailing information his

---

[21] Brogden (1982), p. 62.

[22] *Ibid.* pp. 66–71.

[23] Offered by Jefferson and Grimshaw, *op.cit.* pp. 41–44.

[24] Nott-Bower (1926), pp. 139–146.

[25] [1895] 1 Q.B. 888. The primary question raised was whether obedience to commands of the justices, in their capacity as licensing authority, made the occasion privileged for purposes of defence to a libel action brought by a publican.

force had gathered concerning the conduct of all public houses in the city, amounted to an order under section 7 of the 1856 Act which he was required to obey.[26]

It is difficult to see a place for the independence doctrine in any of this. The subordination of the police to elected representatives in the boroughs was part of common understanding. However, this emphatically did not mean that the police were seen as a political instrument of the ruling party, or as political actors. As Maitland wrote, "It has been the English policy to separate police from politics, therefore the paid policeman, be he Chief Constable or of the lowest rank, is subjected to political disabilities."[27] Strict rules were formulated to this effect: no constable could vote, seek to influence an election, or serve on a jury. That the Victorians did not share twentieth century pre-occupations seems readily explicable. Whilst there were complaints that some watch committees were unduly influenced by certain interests, notably brewers and licensees, policing seldom became politically contentious in the sense that it has become so in the past decade.

There was no way it could have done. Nineteenth century England was a political oligarchy. Not only did approximately two hundred families dominate the national political life of a country they also largely owned,[28] but the franchise was astonishingly restrictive even after three so-called Reform Acts. In the first decade of the twentieth century, of those states which had established representative institutions, the British electorate was smaller than anywhere except Hungary.[29] Only after the First World War was anything like universal suffrage established for men, along with the partial admission of women to the electorate. Recent research has yielded the convincing estimate that—over and above paupers, most of the military and live-in servants, all of whom were barred by law—almost half the industrial working class was excluded, largely as a result of the so called £10 lodger and occupation franchises.[30] Any one who was transient—the common condition of the intermittently unemployed, casual workers and seasonal workers—was also voteless. The "political nation" was thus comprised of the propertied and the respectable working class; and their consensus about public order and public decorum could not be disturbed by dissonant notes from the politi-

[26] [1895] 1 Q.B. 894.
[27] Maitland, *op.cit.* p. 114, see n. 7.
[28] Thompson (1963), *passim*.
[29] Matthew *et al.* (1976), pp. 723–724.
[30] *Ibid.* pp. 733–735. Much of the evidence is taken from Blewitt (1965).

cally voiceless.[31] Throughout the century the largest number of arrests were of drunks, vagrants, and "disorderly characters"[32]— categories that were co-extensive with poverty and homelessness and reflected an increasingly prim middle class view of propriety in public places.

Exclusion of the main targets of repressive police activity from political life ensured that on fundamental issues like the nature of order and acceptable public behaviour, local politicians, regardless of party, had the same standards and expectations. These were easily fitted into the substantive law, and came implicitly to define legality and order. Within this hegemonic structure, disputes about policing were over minor matters which threatened none of the dominant groups' economic or political interests.[33] Hence control over policing by elected representatives was acceptable to those who controlled British politics. This was particularly true of the urban areas, for the nineteenth century political elite was still a landed aristocracy, to whom municipal government remained largely alien territory.

The final angle from which one may view the governmental structure of nineteenth-century urban policing is that of contemporary writing on local government. No one thought to treat the police separately from other local institutions; there is no hint of the independence doctrine nor suggestion of a unique relationship between representatives of the public and police officials. The Webbs' treatise[34] merely treats the police unexceptionably alongside all other county borough or magistrates' administrative functions. Redlich and Hirst, however, writing in 1903, were in no doubt about where control of the urban forces lay:

> "The larger towns are divided into police districts . . . but there is no such thing as an independent director of police. On the contrary, the Chief Constable, who has as it were the military command of the force, is *entirely subordinated to the Watch Committee* (emphasis supplied). This form of organis-

---

[31] For evidence of hostility to the police among what may be called the lower or marginal working class, see Storch (1975; 1976) and Cohen (1979).

[32] Bailey (1981), p. 15.

[33] This is not to deny that there were on occasion bitter conflicts involving law enforcement, notably in relation to the Liberals' Licensing Acts and the Sunday Trading Acts. But although these aroused intense opposition of certain interests, notably brewers and traders, they did not challenge fundamental power relations or definitions of order.

[34] B. and S. Webb (1906–1908), *passim*

ation, founded by the Municipal Corporations Act 1835, has remained undisturbed ever since."[35]

As will be seen, that system came increasingly to be "disturbed"—by the accretion of power to the Home Office as centralisation and national uniformity became dominate twentieth century themes. But alongside it existed another system of police governance, one which came increasingly to provide the model for those seeking a uniform system whose centre-piece was the chief constable unconstrained by democratic control.

The County Police

The structure of police governance in the shires was always different. Until 1888 there was no democratic element in county government; executive power was in the hands of the justices, who exercised it, along with their judicial function, at Quarter and General Sessions. Unlike their municipal counterparts, they could not meet regularly over an extended period at one convenient point; geography and the way of life of a land-owning leisure class ensured that effective control of the county forces would have to be vested elsewhere. This could only be in its operational head.

The statute 2 & 3 Vict., c. 93, which has come to be known as the County Police Act 1839, gave the justices power to appoint a chief constable, who could only be dismissed at Sessions. This official was empowered to appoint other constables, with the approval of any two justices. And it was he, not they, who exercised the managerial prerogative of dismissing his subordinates at pleasure. Most striking of all, in section 6 he was granted "the general Disposition and Government of all the constables thus appointed subject to lawful orders of Justices."[36]

The chief constable thus held a statutory office and was a far more formidable figure than his borough counterpart. He was by no means an independent autocrat: the last clause of section 6 indicates that the justices retained powers of command. In the early years of newly established forces they often used them, but particularly after 1856 when all areas were required to establish forces, there was a notable tendency to appoint scions of gentry families, particularly those with military experience, as chief constables.[37] Men of social standing equal to the justices themselves

---

[35] Redlich and Hirst (1903), vol. 2, p. 305.
[36] Country Police Act 1839, ss.4, 6.
[37] Steedman (1984), pp. 47–49 analyses the social origins of chief constables appointed between 1856 and 1880. See also Critchley, *op.cit.* pp. 138–141.

could not be treated as menials, and conversely could be assumed to be "reliable." Thus their legal and social standing enabled constables from fairly early on to enjoy an effective autonomy that could later, when reinforced by a developing sense of themselves as possessors of professional expertise, be transmogrified into the ideology of constitutional independence. By the First World War, their position had crystallised into clear dominance over their police authorities.

The second sharply different characteristic of county forces was their relationship to the Home Office. This had two aspects. First, the justices' appointment of a chief constable was subject to the approval of the Home Secretary. Unfortunately, no one seems to have studied how this power was used, how often local choices were vetoed or withdrawn in the face of informal disapproval, and so forth.

Secondly, section 3 of the 1839 Act provided that all county forces should come under uniform rules concerning "Government, Pay, Clothing and Accoutrements of constables," to be promulgated by the Home Secretary. It is not clear why central government insisted upon a more dominant role for itself in policing outside the boroughs. It may, paradoxically, have been a response to the absence of democratic institutions in the shires: with ratepayers and electors without political voice, the Home Secretary—accountable to Parliament in the days before institutionalised party politics deprived that accountability of most of its bite—was the only element of responsible government available to check the actions of the justices. In any case, the practice immediately arose of direct contact between the Home Office and chief constables, bypassing the justices who were then dependent upon the chief constable for information about central government policy and crime patterns in their area. The formation in 1888 of Standing Joint Committees, evenly divided between councillors and magistrates, as police authorities, made little difference. Indeed by 1914 the Home Office had come round to the view that magistrates had no place on police authorities, and prepared a bill—apparently never introduced—to make their membership wholly elected.[38] This was shelved with the onset of war, and never revived.

Thus by 1914 there existed, apart from the Home Secretary's relationship to the Metropolitan Police Commissioner, two divergent models of police governance. Yet even county practice had not yet produced anything recognisable as the doctrine of police

[38] Critchley, *op.cit.* p. 291, see n. 13.

independence. Precisely how this developed remains a mystery which badly needs historical investigation. All that can be offered here in the present state of knowledge is a tentative theory, based on similarities to contemporaneous developments in other spheres of government and recent research in labour history which has almost inadvertently opened up new perspectives on the problem. What is clear is that, from being almost unimagined in 1914, the independence doctrine had achieved virtually unchallenged supremacy 30 years later. It seems that the critical period was the decade or so beginning in 1919. Unlike the Victorian period, which has yielded a rich historical literature, the inter-war years have largely remained uncharted territory. An important study begs to be written, and will no doubt modify the interpretation put forward here when grounded in a more solid factual base.

What *is* well documented is the changed role of the Home Office. Critchley, whose semi-official history is quite reliable so far as it goes, points to two causes of the emergence of "a new concept of the police as a service, an integrated system, rather than a collection of separate forces each concerned with its merely local requirements and personnel."[39] These were the War, which forced the Home Office for the first time to assume a co-ordinating role, setting up committees, issuing circulars and holding conferences where chief constables began exchanging information and ideas; and the aftermath of the police strikes of 1918 and 1919. The latter produced the Desborough Committee Report[40] which, in addition to recommending unprecedentedly high levels of pay and a police federation as an alternative to unionisation, led to two important structural changes. The first, embodied in the Police Act 1919, was the extension of the Home Secretary's power of making regulations to all forces. Thus pay, terms and conditions of employment, promotion and discipline were now uniform nationally, and determined by the centre. The second was the establishment of a permanent police department in the Home Office, with responsibility not only for the Metropolitan Police but for dealing with provincial forces as well. The Home Office thus achieved unprecedented legal power and administrative capability to influence the evolution of policing throughout England and Wales.

The uses to which these capabilities were put was determined by the heated political climate of the period. The fear in the minds of the Coalition Government that the Russian Revolution had set off a tidal wave of Bolshevism that imminently threatened to over-

---

[39] *Ibid.* p. 190, and generally on this period, pp. 176–195.
[40] Cmd. 574 (1919).

whelm British institutions now seems merely ludicrous. At the time it was anything but, and the Government responded with a well-calculated mixture of concession and repression in which the police played an important part.[41]

One of the first results of the 1918 police strike in London was the installation of a new commissioner, General Sir Nevil Macready. Macready acted in close liaison with the Home Office, prodding it into increasing the number of inspectors, which facilitated communication with county forces. Moreover, when Sir Basil Thomson, head of what is now MI5, began reporting every fortnight to the Cabinet on revolutionary agitation in Britain, he relied on information fed by local forces through Scotland Yard.[42] The Government engaged in a systematic campaign of what would today be called disinformation, seeking to discredit organisations of the unemployed, particularly the National Unemployed Workers Movement, as communist revolutionaries, not as protestors against worklessness and poverty.[43] As part of this effort, it exhorted local police to take a hard line against hunger marchers. It solicited accounts of public meetings of the unemployed from local C.I.D.s, and supported the police even when criticised by the courts for their brutality against peaceful demonstrators, as in Liverpool's Bloody Sunday of 1921.[44]

When dealing with a supportive police committee, as in Conservative dominated Liverpool, Home Office policies were accepted without conflict. But not all authorities were so complaisant, and it required little imagination to foresee that increasing numbers might not be. Here we return to the "franchise factor:" the full voting strength of the working class only began to be exercised at precisely this time, and soon produced local Socialist administrations which challenged the policies of central government. The best known of these is of course George Lansbury's Poplar, but many other areas collided with government policies in relation to income support.[45] Such local bodies could hardly be relied on to support violent police suppression of demonstrators

---

[41] For a study of the repressive apparatus developed in this period, see Desmarais (1970); a valuable analysis of the Emergency Powers Act 1920 is found in Morris (1979). An excellent account of the way state income support was varied depending upon whether the Government feared or felt it could contain opposition is presented by Gilbert (1970).

[42] Weinberger (1986), p. 6. I am grateful to Barbara Weinberger, of the Centre for Social History at Warwick University, for advanced sight of this article.

[43] *Ibid.* pp. 9–10.

[44] *Ibid.* pp. 10–14. Brogden (1982), pp. xi–xii contains a good contemporary description of this episode.

[45] Keith-Lucas (1962); Branson (1979), both *passim*.

against unemployment nor, perhaps more important in the long run, could their attitude toward the policing of strikes be regarded as reliable. This problem arose most acutely in South Wales where, even with magistrates comprising half the membership of the S.J.C. the miners were politically powerful and their repeated strikes produced perhaps the worst "police-community relations" in Britain. The chief constables of several of the counties took a particularly hard anti-union line and expressed their views openly. During the General Strike they insisted upon summoning extra police, although the extraordinary communal solidarity made picketing unnecessary and there was far *less* conflict with the police in South Wales than in traditionally less militant areas.[46] Soon afterward the Monmouthshire S.J.C., supported by the County Council, called for the resignation of the chief constable. Labour representatives in Carmarthenshire unsuccessfully sought to get their S.J.C. to follow suit.

The upshot was a pointer of things to come. Both chief constables ignored the criticism, and the Home Office withheld the 50 per cent. police grant from Monmouthshire until the resignation call was rescinded six months later.[47] In political conflicts over policing, the existence of the chief constable as intermediary was a godsend to the Home Office. It did not need to usurp traditional local government powers to ensure that important policies were carried out, as happened with the Poor Law. In that instance, the conflicts of the 1920s and early 1930s led to central government stripping localities of their powers of poor relief, abolition of Boards of Guardians and Public Assistance Committees, and the takeover of their functions by Whitehall.[48] This enabled benefit cuts to be imposed uniformly despite the wishes of areas with Socialist political majorities, and relieved business and landed ratepayers of financial burdens, therefore gaining the support of a substantial local minority.

This "nationalisation" option was foreclosed, even had the Home Office wished to control the police directly. The tradition of policing as a local service was far too strong.[49] It would also have

---

[46] Weinberger, *op.cit.* pp. 23–27.

[47] *Ibid.* pp. 24–25.

[48] Branson and Heinemann (1971), Chap.3, who also point out that not all the areas in conflict with the Government on treatment of these unemployed were Labour-controlled, though most were.

[49] This was illustrated graphically in 1919, when the Desborough Committee's recommendations that small borough forces be compulsorily amalgamated with surrounding counties, and that watch committees lose their powers of appointment and dismissal of constables to the Home Secretary, were killed by opposition from the boroughs and their parliamentary representatives.

required an enlargement of the central bureaucracy that would have been economically and ideologically impossible in an era of financial crisis and retrenchment. Almost fortuitously the presence of the chief constables made it unnecessary. Without requiring explicit dictation, they could be relied upon—by virtue of their social origins, the process of their recruitment and the inbuilt conservatism that is inherent in a professional preoccupation with regularity and discipline—to share the Government's views on the dangers of "extremists" and its definition of "order" in relation to anything regarded as politically dangerous, such as major strikes and demonstrations. This did not preclude local variations in dealing with such matters,[50] but these were variations in severity, not disagreements on the fundamental point that such behaviour was to be regarded as illegitimate and must be controlled. Chief constables could not only appear to be, but genuinely be, in command of their forces and not subject to direction from central government, which nonetheless could be certain that what was fundamentally important about policing would be carried out to its satisfaction. Intervention by meddlesome Socialist local bodies could be constitutionally precluded, yet the centre would not incur any opprobrium for politically controversial policing, since responsibility would rest with the independent chief constable. This must be one of the very few instances in which it actually proved possible to have one's cake and eat it.

It may be objected that this is a tendentious and distorted interpretation, that the great bulk of police work deals with politically uncontentious minor crime or street patrolling which enjoys the support of the great majority of the population regardless of political allegiance. This is true enough, but does not conflict with the view that the paramount concerns of politicians and civil servants are not necessarily those of the general public. Writing in 1928, Sir Edward Troup, who had been Permanent Under-Secretary at the Home Office in the immediate post-war years, stated that the Home Secretary's general supervision and direction of policing had become increasingly necessary with the greater complexity of society, easier communication and mobility. To this anodyne explanation he added, "when a difficult situation arises, the local authority, chief constable, magistrates and Home Office must work together; and the Home Office has no more essential duty than in consultation with others to prepare for united and consist-

---

[50] For example, police and miners in the North-east had generally enjoyed good relations in industrial disputes, in sharp contrast to conditions prevailing in South Wales: Weinberger, *op.cit.* pp. 17–18.

ent action."[51] For "difficult situation" in the 1920s read "strike"
and "demonstration," not street violence or theft; the "united and
consistent action" referred to mutual aid, military aid and con-
tingency planning—all measures designed to ensure that the
government had the capability to suppress any movement it perceived as a threat.[52]

The build-up of the position of chief constables[53] as independent
of local control could draw upon the long-established legal view
that the occupant of the office of constable was responsible to the
law, *i.e.* that the legality of any individual action could be the basis
of an action for damages in the courts. The difference in functions
between a chief constable and the ordinary constable was conveniently overlooked. It also harmonised with the increasing
detachment of the police from their specific community. Three factors help bring this about: broader changes in the structure of local
government, the growing tendency of the police to see themselves
as crime fighters, and an increasing number of parliamentary
enactments which gave constables wide-ranging administrative
powers independent of local authorities and magistrates in matters
ranging from weights and measures to explosives.[54] The more or
less explicit concept of the police officer as the servant of local
ratepayers, dominant in the mid-Victorian era, had been displaced.[55] It was relatively easy to turn him into the servant of the
Crown.[56] Moreover, it seems likely that the identification of the
police with the law had increased as they began to take responsibility for criminal prosecutions.[57] They could be seen to be in
charge of the criminal process, rather than merely acting as the
agents of a private individual.

The notion of police independence received an enormous boost
in 1930 from the High Court decision in *Fisher* v. *Oldham*

---

[51] Troup (1928), p. 16.
[52] Troup specifically mentions mutual aid and military aid as subjects of Home
Office Circulars to local forces; *ibid.* p. 12.
[53] The Police Act 1919 designated the heads of borough forces as chief constables
for the first time. The timing of this change supports the thesis put forward here,
but the point does not seem to have been studied by historians, and without sight
of Home Office files it cannot be stated with confidence that the measure was a
deliberate attempt to enhance their position symbolically.
[54] Steedman, *op.cit.* pp. 53–55 and 158–159, stresses the importance of this expansion of police responsibilities. As early as 1885, Maitland had remarked upon the
extent of this practice (*op.cit.* pp. 116–117).
[55] Steedman, *op.cit.* pp. 59–63 and more generally in Part II.
[56] See below, pp. 58–59. The ambiguity of the concept of "servant" will become
apparent.
[57] See above, pp. 27–28.

Corpn.[58] It gained widespread allegiance among politicians and officials so rapidly that, within two decades, it had become enshrined orthodoxy. Individual chief constables might become embroiled in disputes with their police authorities, but this was a rare occurrence. In the long period of quiescence and consensus that emerged during the Second World War, policing came to be regarded as non-political and, for a surprisingly long period, uncontroversial. This further enhanced the credibility of the idea of policing as above politics, and hence that control of policing by the political authorities was improper. This view extended even to the Metropolitan Police in its relations with the Home Office; according to a senior civil servant with long experience in the department, throughout the whole post-war period "nobody would have dreamt that the Home Secretary could tell the Commissioner to do a particular operational job."[59]

Thus when, in the early 1960s, the constitutional position of the police came to be examined by a Royal Commission, the conceptual boundaries of that inquiry were narrowly defined: the independence doctrine not only furnished the starting point but dictated the conclusion. It is hoped that the foregoing analysis has demonstrated that the view put forward by Marshall two decades ago is essentially correct: the doctrine is of recent origin, contrary to earlier practice and understandings and no part of the tradition of "English liberty." Rather its triumph was part of a general process of removal of control over several institutions previously governed locally when the long-delayed extension of the vote to working class people created challenges to important central government policies. The police were unusual only in that control was not transferred directly to the centre, but to a figure whose common law status gave him a unique position. The independence doctrine and the resultant accrual of power to chief constables was thus a part of the broad counter-attack against the perceived threat of bolshevism and socialism in the decade following 1919. Yet long after the Red Scare had faded, it maintained a powerful momentum and resonance of its own. This can be seen in the report of the Royal Commission and the ensuing legislation.

---

[58] [1930] 2 K.B. 364; see below, pp. 56–60.

[59] Interview with Mr. D.J. Hilary, Assistant Secretary, Home Office, September 1984. Interestingly, whilst Mr. Hilary had a vague idea of "Blackburn or someone," he was very clear that *Fisher* v. *Oldham* supported this view of "operational independence" of the metropolitan commissioner.

The Royal Commission and the Police Act 1964

From the 1920's, two dominant trends began to emerge in police governance: growing national control expressed in statute and supplemented by informal influence, and increasing freedom of action for chief constables. Both gains of power were achieved at the expense of local police authorities, particularly the borough watch committees. Yet the change, though pronounced, was never translated into formal law. At the end of the 1950's, watch committees retained the powers of discipline and dismissal over all constables (though subject to appeal to the Home Secretary), and of issuing orders which constables were bound to obey. Moreover, unlike their rural counterparts, they contained no magistrates but consisted wholly of elected members.

Their spasmodic attempts to use some of these vestigial powers had more than one important constitutional consequence. When the Brighton watch committee dismissed its chief constable, who had been tried and acquitted of corruption charges but whose conduct had been censured by the judge, Mr. Ridge challenged the procedure it had followed and so began the revival of natural justice.[60] And a row between the Nottingham watch committee and its chief constable, Captain Popkess, was the last of a series of incidents which lead to the appointment of the first Royal Commission in more than a century to receive a remit to inquire into the constitutional position of the police.[61] Briefly, Captain Popkess, on the advice of the Director of Public Prosecutions, called in the Metropolitan Police early in 1959 to investigate a number of persons, including members of the watch committee, on corruption charges. The results were submitted to the D.P.P., who advised no further action. Subsequently the committee, having received a report from the town clerk which suggested a lack of impartiality in the chief constable's attitude toward the investigation of committee members, requested a report. This Captain Popkess refused on the grounds that law enforcement was his preserve entirely, and no business of the watch committee. The latter then suspended him, but the Home Secretary wrote to the committee strongly supporting the chief constable's view of his independence,

---

[60] *Ridge* v. *Baldwin*, [1964] A.C. 40.
[61] On the immediate background to the appointment of the Royal Commission, see Critchley (1978), pp. 270 *et seq.*, from which the summary of the Popkess affair is taken. The last fully-fledged constitutional consideration of the police had been undertaken in 1839, under the influence of Edwin Chadwick.

and stating that he regarded the suspension as unjustified.[62] The story ended inconclusively with Captain Popkess being reluctantly reinstated but retiring at the end of the year.

With this episode very much in its collective mind, the Royal Commission delivered its Final Report at the end of 1962.[63] It covered a wide range of issues and produced no fewer than 111 recommendations, but discussion here will focus on its treatment of constitutional questions, and in particular on its proposals concerning the role of chief constables, police authorities and the Home Secretary.

Although the Report endorsed the accumulated judicial dicta about the independence of the constable[64] it understood that notion to have a restricted application—to what it termed "enforcement of law in particular cases."[65] Equating this with what constables do, it endorsed the need for constabulary independence, and suggested that consequently this left the police largely free from legal control. In fact this conclusion was more logically connected to the commission's acceptance of the view that the constable was really no different from the ordinary citizen, who could if he so chose perform the same tasks.[66] This view was barely plausible at the most formalistic level in 1962, before codification of constables' powers of arrest, search and seizure, but was unrealistic even then: members of the public did not enforce road traffic laws, grant bail, or maintain order at industrial disputes or demonstrations. It also ignored the reality of the individual constable's discretion, and of the vast range of his activities that go beyond simple law enforcement.

The absence of legal control was, in the commission's view, mitigated by the existence of a strict discipline code; hence apart from its recommendations on changes in the procedures for handling complaints by members of the public, it saw no need to suggest any alterations to the constitutional status of the ordinary constable. It then expounded the central tenet of its constitutional analysis: "The problem of controlling the police can, therefore, be restated as the problem of controlling chief constables."[67]

---

[62] The Home Secretary never clarified publicly whether he was writing in his capacity as the appellate authority to which Captain Popkess could appeal if he were to be dismissed, or whether he was impliedly threatening to withhold the 50 per cent. grant. His position was perhaps strengthened by leaving his precise role as vague as possible.

[63] Cmnd. 1728 (1962).

[64] See further below, Chap. 4.

[65] Cmnd. 1728, paras. 86 and 88.

[66] *Ibid.* paras. 30–31.

[67] *Ibid.* para. 102.

The commission observed that in respect of "general policies," disposition of manpower, management of resources, and the instructions given to the force as to the "manner" and "method" of handling political demonstrations or industrial disputes, chief constables were accountable to no one. However, it did not accept that in such matters it was necessary that they enjoy this "complete immunity from external influence."[68] Its conclusion, though, was that such influence should be located at the centre: local forces, suitably enlarged by amalgamations, should be maintained, but the legal responsibility for their efficiency should be vested in the Home Secretary. Police authorities would continue to exist, and would be entitled to receive an annual report from the chief constable, but their major function, exactly reversing the normal relationship between councillors and officers,[69] would be advisory, with final responsibility locally resting with the chief constable.

This approach was open to the trenchant objection, advanced by Professor A.L. Goodhart in a dissenting memorandum, that if local connections were unimportant in preserving liberty, (as the committee argued), and not to be trusted as the locus of control where control was required, the logical solution was creation of a national force.[70] It did, however, have the great merit of rejecting the fallacy of the seamless web—of seeing quite clearly that, at the highest level, policing decisions are matters of policy, and require that a political authority be responsible for them. How that responsibility could be meaningful in the absence of effective mechanisms of control is a problem which unfortunately the commission did not explore.

The response of the Government was even less coherent. R.A. Butler, the Home Secretary, quickly rejected the proposal that central government take primary responsibility for policing. He did not, however, propose to extend or strengthen the powers of police authorities to meet the need for control over chief constables identified by the Royal Commission. Indeed his successor, Henry Brooke, who was actually responsible for the legislation, accepted the recommendations in the Report which, taken together, stripped the borough authorities of their long-held if largely atrophied powers. And successive Home Secretaries of both parties acted vigorously upon the commission's encouragement of the formation of larger forces: so vigorously that the

---

[68] *Ibid.* paras. 89–91.

[69] *Ibid.* para. 166.

[70] *Ibid.* pp. 157–179. Goodhart did suggest that such a force might be administered regionally, but only for purposes of convenience, not reasons of principle.

number outside London declined by *two-thirds* in just over a decade to the present 41.

It did not require the gift of prophecy to foretell the result. Power, like nature, abhors a vacuum; and with the police authorities left enfeebled and the Home Secretary standing aside, the chief constables quickly stepped into the breach. Now, as individuals, commanding much larger organisations with rapidly expanding budgets and increasingly sophisticated equipment, they have, individually and collectively, enhanced their status as their numbers have reduced. Indeed their small number has greatly increased their ability, through the Association of Chief Police Officers (A.C.P.O.) to undertake forceful and united campaigns to influence national policy.[71] Home Office and other central influence remains powerful, particularly when exercised through informal extra-legal channels, but police authorities in 1964 were reduced to little more than a sort of supporters' club for their chief constables. For more than 15 years they accepted this with remarkable self-abnegation; only the embittered politics of the 1980s caused a few to attempt to exercise their powers or attempt to increase them.

---

[71] Another factor that has significantly increased the cohesion of senior policemen as a bloc is that nowadays almost everyone considered for promotion to A.C.P.O rank will have passed through the Senior Command Course at the Bramshill Staff College. The network of personal contacts thus built up makes collaboration much easier than would have been possible thirty years ago. The role of A.C.P.O. is discussed below, pp. 108–111.

Part III

Chapter 4

THE CASE LAW OF POLICE GOVERNANCE

The preceding chapter examined the evolution of the statutory structure of police governance with particular reference to the increasing power exercised both by central government and by chief constables at the expense of local police authorities. The analysis focused especially on the development of the independence doctrine which, it was argued, was quite contrary to nineteenth century practice and only achieved a statutory basis in the Police Act 1964. However, one important element in the evolution of the independence doctrine was omitted. That is the contribution of the judges, which in the past two decades has come to provide the primary ideological authority for those who oppose greater democratic control of policing. The case law on issues of police governance, though relatively sparse, is a confusing mixture of public and private law, statutory interpretation and common law adjudication. It has also been fundamentally flawed by the conflation, or identification, of the chief constable—the administrative head of the police organisation—with the ordinary constable exercising his legal powers in a particular factual setting.

The first case has been oddly neglected by all those who have commented on issues of police governance. Like so much else in police history, it arose out of a miners' strike. Under the Police Act 1890, which first created the formal structure of mutual aid (below, Chap. 8) a "police authority"—defined in that Act to mean the Standing Joint Committee (S.J.C.) or the watch committee—was empowered to enter into agreements, either on a one-off or permanent basis, with other authorities for exchange of men where necessary. It was also empowered to delegate these powers to its chief or head constable. The Chief Constable of Glamorganshire, unable to control the strike with a normal complement of men, requested reinforcements from several sources: provincial forces with which there was a standing agreement, others with which there was no prior agreement, and the army, via a request to the Home Secretary. The provincial police authorities sent the men requested, but the Home Secretary refused to send troops and, as police authority for London, sent instead a large battalion of Metropolitan Police. The chief constable entered into agreements with all the aiding authorities, including the Home

53

Office, for the assistance received. After the strike was over, the
S.J.C. refused to pay the bills tendered by various coal companies—
whose enterprises were of course the main beneficiaries of the
enhanced police presence—for feeding and housing the incoming
forces. It argued that it had not requested the assistance, and indeed
had expressly repudiated responsibility for, the presence of the
Metropolitan Police.[1] In *Glamorgan Coal Co* v. *Glamorgan S.J.C.*[2]
two of the companies sought payment from the S.J.C. and/or the
County Council.[3] In the High Court, the Judge expressly pointed
out that this was not a case "where the police were employed by a
Chief Constable contrary to instructions given him by his police
authority"[4]—implying that had such a conflict existed, his ruling
would have been very different. Instead, he found as a fact[5] that the
chief constable had acted as agent for the police authority, and held
that the latter had "ratified by action" the agreements he had
entered into. Notwithstanding the S.J.C.'s avowed attitude toward
the metropolitan police, the latter's continued presence during the
dispute was also held to constitute ratification.

The Court of Appeal reversed the ruling with respect to the
Metropolitan Police, but affirmed as to the rest. Two points of
importance emerge from its judgment. The first concerns the
influence of the Home Office. Some years previously, the Home
Secretary had issued a circular encouraging participation in mutual
aid agreements. Although the circular did not, indeed could not,
empower the chief constable to make agreements, Phillimore L.J.
treated it as radically altering the context of decision-making:
where an S.J.C., in appointing a chief constable, did not explicitly
forbid him to contract such agreements, in light of the Circular it
would be taken to have authorised him to make emergency agreements, simply by virtue of the appointment.[6] Thus the role of central government in the organisation of policing achieved important
legal recognition even before the statutes of 1919 and 1927 gave
the Home Secretary formal powers of promulgating regulations
and reviewing dismissals.

---

[1] The real point here was that the Army would be wholly paid for by central
government funds, whereas the cost of the Metropolitan Police would be shared
between the Home Office, as policy authority for London, and the Glamorganshire ratepayers.

[2] [1916] 2 K.B. 206, affirming but varying [1915] 1 K.B. 471.

[3] The subsidiary question of where liability lay as between the S.J.C. and the
council is not germane to the issues under discussion.

[4] *Glamorgan Coal Co* v. *Glamorgan S.J.C.* [1915] 1 K.B. 471, 484–485.

[5] Accepted by the Court of Appeal as the basis of their own decision: see [1916] 2
K.B. 214.

[6] *Ibid.* p. 221.

Secondly, it is striking that the chief constable is treated throughout as clearly subordinate to the statutory authority. His authority to enter into agreements is treated—to invert a hallowed phrase—as delegated, not original.[7] Phillimore L.J. was careful to state that his view of implied authority extended, "not to mak(ing) general agreements, or even agreements lasting beyond the next meeting of the Standing Joint Committee, but emergency agreements only."[8] The clear corollary was that where the chief constable's authority was withdrawn by the S.J.C., he lacked the power to make the agreements. Thus, since none of the judges accepted the trial court's strange distinction between objection to the presence of the Metropolitan Police in lieu of soldiers and at local expense, rather than objection to their "employment" by the chief constable, that part of the judgment was overturned. But where the S.J.C., by silent acceptance of an agreement known to its members, or by the actions of its sub-committee, could fairly be said to have acquiesced in a agreement (as was found to be the case with respect to all the other aiding forces) such agreement would be regarded as binding. The clear thrust of the Court of Appeal's approach is the emphasis on the paramount authority of the Standing Joint Committee, the politically representative body, and the limited and derivative powers of the Chief Constable.[9] The notion that the latter possessed an independent authority to direct law enforcement activities, or enjoyed "operational" autonomy from his police authority, seems not to have entered anyone's head. The relationship was treated as one of statute, and the Court simply acknowledged the primary responsibility of the police authority as laid down in the 1890 Act—which followed the pattern of the other nineteenth century statutes discussed in the previous chapter.

Although the House of Lords did consider one point relating to policing in the 1920s,[10] the next case relevant to the issues considered here arose in 1930. Though the decision of a single High Court Judge, it was subsequently cited by later judges, the Royal

---

[7] Below, p. 62.
[8] *Glamorgan Coal Co.* v. *Glamorgan S.J.C.* [1916] 2 K.B. 206, 221.
[9] See also the judgement of Pickford J. *ibid.* pp. 229–230
[10] *Glasbrook Bros. Ltd.* v. *Glamorgan County Council* [1925] A.C. 270. The question here was whether the police authority could charge for extra policing protection granted at the express request of the plaintiff coal company after the officer in charge had stated that he considered the number of men requested unnecessary. As there was no dispute between the S.J.C. or county council and the chief constable—all three brought a joint action to recover on the company's promise to pay—issues of governance were not considered.

Commission and other authoritative sources as though graven on tablets of stone. Twenty years ago it was subject to extensive, penetrating and to my mind unanswerable criticisms by Geoffrey Marshall,[11] but his comments seem to have made no impression at all upon the courts. *Fisher* v. *Oldham Corporation*[12] continues to demand careful dissection.

The facts of the case were quite straightforward. Fisher, the victim of mistaken identity, was arrested under warrant in London and taken to Oldham on charges which were dropped when the error was recognised. He instituted an action in tort claiming compensation for false imprisonment. Rather than sue the officers who arrested him—presumably for fear that they would be unable to pay damages—he proceeded against their employer, the Oldham Corporation and its watch committee. To bring the principle of vicarious liability into play on his behalf, he had to establish that the watch committee and the constables stood in the relation of master and servant, a term of art with a long history in the law of tort. This the defendants, who argued that the police acted on their own initiative, denied.

The result was virtually a foregone conclusion. Twenty-five years earlier, in *Stanbury* v. *Exeter Corporation*,[13] the Divisional Court had to determine whether a municipal corporation could be liable for the actions of an inspector who negligently detained the plaintiff's sheep by virtue of his powers under the Sheep-Scab Order of 1898. However, though appointed by the corporation, that appointment was dictated by statute, and the instructions which guided his work were issued by a Ministry of central government. Two judges invoked the analogy with the police. Wills J. said:

> "This case is, to my mind, almost exactly analogous to the case of the police officer. In all boroughs the watch committee by statute has to appoint, control and remove the police officers, and nobody has ever heard of a corporation being made liable for the negligence of a police officer in the performance of his duties. I think the reason why that is so [is that if] the duties to be performed by the officers appointed are of a public nature and have no peculiar local characteristics, then they are really a branch of the public administration for purposes

---

[11] Marshall (1965), Chap. 3. These criticisms continue to repay careful reading, and I would respectfully endorse them. I wish to incorporate them by reference into my own argument and will therefore not repeat them.

[12] [1930] 2 K.B. 364.

[13] [1905] 2 K.B. 838.

of general utility and security which affect the whole kingdom . . . "[14]

In *Fisher*, McCardie J. quoted extensively from the judgments in *Stanbury*, and also cited several Commonwealth cases. It is odd that, although there had been numerous Canadian cases (which in turn drew heavily on American jurisprudence) concerning municipal liability for police torts, the issue had not squarely arisen in England until 1930. Perhaps after *Stanbury* it had been regarded as settled, for although the Judges' comments strictly speaking were *obiter*, the directness and clarity with which they dealt with the issue would have made it difficult for a subsequent judge, certainly one below the level of the Court of Appeal, to decide it differently.

It is therefore important to realise how little support these authorities provide for any broad proposition of constabulary independence. As a study prepared for the Law Reform Commission of Canada points out,[15] early decisions in Canada which refused to hold municipal corporations liable for police negligence did so by adopting what might be called the national public function argument very like that expressed by Wills J. This had been formulated in previous decisions involving employees of a city fire department and ambulance service.[16] There may, or may not, be good sense in refusing to hold local authorities liable in tort for their employees' negligence in carrying out functions either mandated by a national or provincial statute, or of general public concern. The point is that the police are only one such occupational category, and numerous others for which no one ever imagined there existed a unique constitutional status have been treated in precisely the same way. *Stanbury* itself concerned an inspector of sheep disease.

A second strand in the *Fisher* judgement, which McCardie J. rather confusingly wove together with that just discussed, was that constables have a "definite and limited" legal authority conferred directly upon them, are not subject to the control of those who pay them, and therefore the principles of agency do not apply to them. The origin of this view is the Australian case of *Enever* v. *The King*,[17] which offered the analysis as an alternative to that of Wills J. in *Stanbury*, which was regarded as unsatisfactory. There are two difficulties with this view. The first is that its concept of the

[14] *Ibid*. p. 842–843.
[15] Stenning (1981), pp. 102–109.
[16] *Ibid*. pp. 102–105.
[17] [1906] 3 C.L.R. 969 (High Court of Australia).

powers conferred on constables is based on an oversimplified view
of police discretion—of its breadth, and of the restrictions imposed
upon it by the reality of hierarchical organisational control.
Secondly, there are many other public officials on whom powers
are conferred directly, and to whom the same principle would
apply. Thus Professor Street in his study of *Governmental Liability*[18] cites a later Australian case[19] in which the negligence of a
legal aid officer did not give rise to liability of the state employing
him because he was performing duties imposed on him directly as
the person holding that office. Yet no one draws extravagant, or
even modest, conclusions about the independence of legal aid officers from such decisions.

There are more fundamental analytical difficulties with drawing
constitutional conclusions from a case like *Fisher* v. *Oldham Corporation*. It is a matter of *non sequiturs*. Whether or not a person is
held for purposes of tort law to be in a relationship of master and
servant with whoever pays him is simply irrelevant to whether he is
a "servant" in the sense of someone who is bound to obey the
command of the paymaster. In Marshall's words, " 'servant' is
simply a curious protean term meaning nothing."[20] This is nicely
illustrated by the Court of Appeal decision in *Inland Revenue
Commissioners* v. *Hambrook*[21] in which a civil servant was held
not to be a "servant" for purposes of the common law action *per
quod servitium amisit*. Dicey's view that one of the hallmarks, and
strengths, of British constitutional law was the judicial development of principle through private law litigation seems rather
dubious in light of the *Fisher* case, and still more its subsequent
influence. There may, after all, be some value in maintaining a
clear distinction between public and private law, at least to prevent
analogies and corollaries from straying into inappropriate areas.[22]

However, McCardie J. did not restrict his analysis entirely to
tort law. He reviewed various statutes setting out the powers of
central government and local authorities in relation to police,
and—inaccurately as a matter of contemporary description but
quite prophetically—emphasised "the fullness of central administrative control." He was assisted towards this conclusion by a glaring error: in examining the powers of the local authorities, he

---

[18] Street (1953), p. 34.
[19] *Field* v. *Knott* (1939) 62 C.L.R. 660.
[20] In private conversation.
[21] [1956] 2 Q.B. 641.
[22] But not to create procedural straight jackets reminiscent of the early nineteenth
century, as in *O'Reilly* v. *Mackman*, [1983] 2 A.C. 237.

noted that the Municipal Corporations Act 1882 required that a constable shall obey such orders as he received from a magistrate, but "there is no such provision as to the order of the Watch Committee."[23] Apparently counsel had failed to draw his attention to section 7 of the County and Borough Police Act 1856 (see above, p. 37) which was precisely such a provision. He then considered some older cases whose applicability was in fact analytically dubious[24] and concluded, "a police constable is not the servant of the borough. He is a servant of the State, a ministerial officer of the central power, though subject in some respects, to local supervision and local regulation."[25]

On the face of it, this conclusion could have extraordinary implications. Depending upon how "servant" was used—and also the concept of "ministerial officer"—the judgment could have been invoked to support the view that constables were subject to whatever degree of control and direction the "central power" chose to exert—a position quite untenable historically and cutting across a broad grain of tradition and history which has much deeper roots than mere self-restraint by central government. More narrowly, in relation to tort law, it would seem to follow that the police could be held to be servants of the Crown for purposes of vicarious liability. Indeed the fear that *Fisher* might produce that outcome appears to have actuated the draftsmen of the Crown Proceedings Act 1947. Section 2(6) excludes from the definition of Crown servants those not directly or indirectly appointed by the Crown and wholly paid from central government funds. The main group excluded by this provision are the police, as was its precise intention.[26] Yet no one suggested between 1930 and 1947 that the Home Secretary had somehow acquired political or administrative control over provincial constables, or that the reason for his failure to do so was that the Crown was not then liable in tort. This point is critical, because at two places in his judgment, McCardie J. invoked a consideration of public policy of a constitutional nature in support of his ruling. What would happen, he asked rhetorically, if a watch committee passed a resolution ordering the release of a felon? His answer was simple: not only would the arresting officer be duty bound to disregard it, but the chief constable would

---

[23] *Fisher* v. *Oldham Corporation* [1930] 2 K.B. 364, p. 370.
[24] Marshall, *op. cit.* pp. 23–24 and 37–38, critically examines the relevance of *Mackalley's Case* (1611) 9 Co. Rep. 61 and *Coomber* v. *Berkshire J.J.*, (1883) 9 App. Cas. 61, respectively, and finds it wanting.
[25] *Fisher* v. *Oldham Corporation* [1930] 2 K.B. 364, 371.
[26] Wade (1982), p. 705; de Smith (1980), p. 631.

have to consider whether the members of the committee should be prosecuted for conspiracy to obstruct the course of justice.[27] And if a police authority were held liable for improper arrests, he argued, they would logically be entitled "to demand that they ought to secure a full measure of control over the arrest and prosecution of all offenders. To give any such control would, in my view, involve a grave and most dangerous constitutional change."[28] Yet if the constable is the servant of the central power, by parity of reasoning the Home Secretary could have been argued to have precisely this power—a grave constitutional change indeed.

At all events, the Judge's point is a great oversimplification. Were the police authority held liable for negligent arrests, they might indeed become more active in exercising their powers to insist upon adoption of procedures to ensure so far as possible that only persons reasonably suspected of crime were arrested. One would have thought this was precisely the sort of activity for which they were created. Exercising such responsibility is a wholly different matter from let us say using their "control" as suggested in McCardie J.'s hypothetical example or preventing the arrest of members of the authority or their relations. These would be plainly criminal acts, and hence *ultra vires*. To all but philosophical anarchists, the fact that a power can be misused does not mean it should not exist. That a police authority may exercise control within the bounds of the law neither authorises its members to violate the law nor prevents those under their lawful supervision from enforcing it against them when they do so. The supposed corollary simply does not follow from the premise.

Even more extraordinary, however, are the uses to which *Fisher* has been put. Undoubtedly authority for the proposition that the constable is not the "servant" (in the sense peculiar to tort law) of local government, it became the keystone of the principle that he is free from democratic control exercised by both local and central government. The result has been to deny elected representatives an effective role in determining policing policies. Further, a case involving law enforcement activity of a subordinate constable in relation to a specific suspect has been extrapolated into a doctrine applied unthinkingly to chief constables in their formulation and administration of broad policies of general application throughout their force. This extrapolation has been facilitated by the constitutional fiction, if not indeed absurdity, that the difference

---

[27] *Fisher* v. *Oldham Corporation* [1930] 2 K.B. 364, 372.
[28] *Ibid.* pp. 377–378.

between the most junior constable and his chief is merely one of rank. In Marshall's neat description:

> "For the doctrine that chief constables were not subject to control in law enforcement matters rested squarely on the proposition that they were constables at common law; and the notion that constables at common law exercised independent powers rested in turn upon the doctrine that they were not in a master and servant relationship with anyone for purposes of civil liability."[29]

It may be doubted whether *Fisher* alone could have borne so much conceptual and political weight. In fact, as it was reinforced it was expanded. This occurred along two avenues: statements by politicians and the Royal Commission[30] and further judicial elaboration. These cases must now be examined.

The Argument Turned Upside Down

As we have seen, *Fisher* and the numerous Commonwealth cases preceding it were all attempts to hold municipalities liable for the negligence of their policemen—attempts which foundered on the decision that the requisite master and servant relationship did not exist between municipality and constable. Very late in the day, yet another Australian case offered an imaginative, if fore-doomed, variation. A New South Wales constable, riding a tram-car, was badly injured by a negligent motorist. The Crown, his employer, sought to recover damages for loss of services. To succeed it would have to establish the existence of the master-servant relationship—*Fisher* turned on its head. Not surprisingly, two decades later, the Australian High Court would have none of it, and the Privy Council affirmed.[31]

The bulk of the judgment, delivered by Viscount Simmonds, concerned the ambit of the action *per quod servitium amisit*, which was the subject of a long historical and policy analysis. However, before addressing the main point in the case, he quoted with approval the remarks of McCardie J. in *Fisher* about the relationship between a constable and the watch committee, and the unlawfulness of any hypothetical attempt by the latter to interfere with an arrest.[32] These remarks were relevant in so far as the Attorney

---

[29] *Op. cit.* p. 98.
[30] The use made of *Fisher* by the 1962 Royal Commission has been noted above, p. 50.
[31] *Att.-Gen. for New South Wales* v. *Perpetual Trustee Co.* [1955] A.C. 457.
[32] *Ibid.* pp. 479–480.

General was the functional equivalent of the watch committee in New South Wales, and confirm that, for purposes of tort law, *Fisher* stated the law correctly on the master-servant issue.[33] If any constitutional significance is to be read into them it is that unlawful instructions need not be followed—a salutary principle which one would hope may be invoked by civil servants and local government officials generally. This is the very reverse, however, of the view that sees the police as unique. One passage in the judgment has been frequently quoted:

> . . . "there is a fundamental difference between the domestic relation of servant and master and that of the holder of a public office and the State which he is said to serve. The constable falls within the latter category. His authority is original, not delegated and is exercised at his own discretion by virtue of his office . . ."[34]

The important point about the final sentence is that it appears in a particular and narrow context. It explains why the constable is simply one member of the "category" of public office holder whose relationship to his employer is not that of master and servant. Any conclusion about the constitutional status of the constable drawn from this case must perforce apply equally to all others failing with the "category." This would include soldiers, who were explicitly stated to stand in the same relation to the Crown[35] but for whom no one would dream of claiming independence from political control. But such a conclusion would be in a quite different sense a category mistake, for the Privy Council was not engaged in an exegesis of constitutional principle. It was delivering the quietus to an implausible, if novel, application of a long-rejected theory of tort liability.

Enter Mr. Blackburn

Such was the case law at the time of the Royal Commission and the enactment of the Police Act 1964. The *Glamorgan* case had

---

[33] Early in his speech, at 478–479 Viscount Simonds noted that whilst *respondeat superior* and *per quod servitium amisit* are not identical concepts, very similar considerations apply, and throughout the rest of his analysis they are treated as identical.

[34] *Att.-Gen. for New South Wales* v. *Perpetual Trustee Co.* [1955] A.C. 457 p. 489. (The 1962 Royal Commission, para. 63, quoted the final sentence as strong authority for its acceptance of the independence doctrine.

[35] *Ibid.* p. 489.

been forgotten and, although they were eagerly and successfully pressed into service on behalf of the independence doctrine, the master-servant cases left most of the important constitutional issues untouched. Relationships between the police as an institution, the police authority, central government and the courts had barely received judicial scrutiny. That this soon changed was due largely to the labours of Raymond Blackburn, moral entrepreneur and litigator extraordinary. Mr. Blackburn perceived, quite accurately, that the Metropolitian Police were doing very little by way of enforcing the law against illegal gaming in London casinos. He discovered that the commissioner had issued a formal "policy decision" requiring his authorisation before inside observation of any club was to be conducted, an instruction based on the view that other demands on police time and the state of the law made it inappropriate to conduct observations except where cheating was alleged or the club was the centre of other criminal activities. He sought a mandamus against the commissioner seeking assistance in prosecuting clubs and withdrawal of the policy decision. He failed in the Divisional Court but, having abandoned the first request, received a very different reception in the Court of Appeal.[36]

The strategy of his argument was subtle.[37] Seeking mandamus, he had to show absence of alternative remedy against the commissioner. Citing neither statute nor case law, merely relatively recent statements by civil servants or junior ministers, he contended that the chief officer of police was responsible to no political authority. Therefore he had to be responsible to the law, *i.e.* to the courts: otherwise he would be responsible to no one—a constitutional abomination. The judges took the bait.

Edmund Davies L.J. stated the issue in terms of whether the police owed the public a judicially enforceable duty to enforce the law. If they did not, it "would mean that, however brazen the failure of the police, the public would be wholly without a remedy . . . The applicant is right in his assertion that its effect would be to place the police wholly above the law."[38] The inflated language conceals a failure to think through alternatives: as with every other service, if the public were dissatisfied, they could complain to the responsible political authority, in this case the Home Secretary. If the latter were persuaded of the need for more vigorous action, he would quietly ask and as a last resort instruct the commissioner to implement it. This is the common currency of

[36] *R.* v. *M.P.C., ex. p. Blackburn*, [1968] 2 Q.B. 118
[37] Reported, *Ibid.* p. 123.
[38] *Ibid.* p. 148.

responsible government. The spectre of the police being above the law can be made plausible only by assuming that they are above democratic institutions.

Counsel for the commissioner also pointed out that the matter was not so simple, particularly as the commissioner is governed by a quite different statutory regime from all other chief officers of police and is not attested as a constable.[39] The Court of Appeal did not listen very well.

A passage from the judgment of Lord Denning M.R. has become the Bible of those supporting the independence doctrine, and is quoted in virtually all legal writing on police. Despite its length, it requires quotation in full, because seldom have so many errors of law and logic been compressed into one paragraph. These are noted in sequence by the addition of letters, and the points are taken up below:

> "The office of Commissioner of Police within the metropolis dates back to 1829 when Sir Robert Peel introduced his disciplined Force. The commissioner was a justice of the peace specially appointed to administer the police force in the metropolis. His constitutional status has never been defined either by statute or by the courts.[a] It was considered by the Royal Commission on the Police in their report in 1962. I have no hesitation, however, in holding that, like every constable in the land,[b] he should be, and is, independent of the executive. He is not subject to the orders of the Secretary of State,[c] save that under the Police Act 1964 the Secretary of State can call on him to give a report, or to retire in the interests of efficiency.[d] I hold it to be the duty of the Commissioner of Police, as it is of every chief constable, to enforce the law of the land. He must take steps to post his men that crimes may be detected; and that honest citizens may go about their affairs in peace. He must decide whether or not suspected persons are to be prosecuted; and if need be, bring the prosecution or see that it is brought; but in all these things he is not the servant of anyone, save of the law itself. No Minister of the Crown can tell him that he must, or must not, keep observation on the place or that;[e] or that he must, or must not, prosecute this man or that one. Nor can any police authority tell him so. The responsibility for law enforcement lies on him. He is answerable to law and to the law alone. That appears sufficiently from *Fisher* v. *Oldham Corpn.*,

---

[39] *Ibid.* p. 125.

[and] the Privy Council case of *A.-G. for New South Wales* v. *Perpetual Trustee Co.*[f]"[40]

The first statement is very odd. The commissioner's constitutional status (a) is wholly defined by statute: the Metropolitan Police Act 1829, with minor subsequent amendments. As a creature of statute, it is difficult to see how or where else he could be defined. And had that statute been considered, it would have been plain that the commissioner is not a constable (b), that he may be subject to the orders of the Home Secretary (c) with whom he shares responsibility for the Force, and that (d) the Police Act 1964 has no application to the Metropolitan Police. As to (e), we have seen that Ministers have at times given precisely such instructions.[41]

The last four sentences (f) of Lord Denning's peroration are plainly meant to be definitive. Yet, if the analysis presented in this chapter has been at all persuasive, it is clear that *Fisher* and *Perpetual Trustee* give little support to the conclusions asserted in them. They had nothing to do with chief officers of police, nor with the kind of policy decision taken by the Commissioner. In constitutional terms, the big jump is the *Blackburn* case itself. And the conclusions reached there by Lord Denning and his colleagues[42] are best understood in light of the largely extra-judicial development of the independence doctrine over the preceding half century. They are its apotheosis, judicial imprimatur its final seal of approval.

The Court of Appeal's conclusions rest upon acceptance of Mr. Blackburn's argument that political controls normally governing public officials do not apply to the police. Since it was hardly in the commissioner's interest to argue for political restrictions on his powers, the sort of analysis suggested by Marshall and presented in these pages never received an adequate hearing.

Lord Denning's ringing phrases also embody an outlook that has cast a dismal pall over the discussions of police governance. It may be called the fallacy of the seamless web. This is the assumption that if democratic control is recognised as legitimate in any aspect of policing, it must inevitably extend to all. Hence those opposing the independence doctrine can be dismissed as advocating that politicians be given power to direct the police not to arrest their supporters. Crafting the precise boundaries between proper and improper democratic control is a difficult and sensitive task which

---

[40] *Ibid.* p. 136.
[41] Points (a) through (e) have all been canvassed in greater detail above, pp. 33–36.
[42] Salmon L.J. and Edmund Davies L.J.

is made all the more difficult by having to compete with sweeping statements whose appeal owes much to specious simplicity.

And what does "responsibility to the law" mean in reality? Lord Denning and Salmon L.J. discussed the issue in essentially similar terms.[43] The chief officer has a wide discretion in many areas in which the court would not interfere at all. This includes treatment of a particular case, disposition of manpower and use of resources. It also includes some policy decisions, *e.g.* not to prosecute for attempted suicide or sexual intercourse with girls under 16. But it would not include a decision not to prosecute for theft of goods under a certain value. Why? In Lord Denning's case, no answer was proferred; he apparently believed that the correctness of his value preferences was self-evident. Salmon L.J. attempted to base the distinction on the intention of the legislature: the age restriction on female sexual intercourse was meant as a protection against seduction but "unfortunately, in many of these cases today in which teenage boys are concerned it is they rather than the girls who are in need of protection," whereas gaming brings "grave social evils in its train" which may "threaten the whole fabric of society" if unchecked.[44] These brief quotations do not adequately convey the fulminating tone of his strictures on gaming. Yet why the particular fixation of judges, or their peculiar perceptions of the behaviour of those fifty years younger than themselves, or even their view of the utility of a statute Parliament chose to retain after more than one review of the law, should command greater authority than the judgment of those responsible to the electorate was never discussed, let alone treated as problematic.

The result, however, is not what Mr. Blackburn hoped for.[45] The much-vaunted answerability to the law has in practice meant leaving chief constables virtually a free hand. When Mr. Blackburn tried in 1973 to challenge enforcement practices in relation to the Obscenity Publications Act 1959 he achieved an equivocal success: the so-called disclaimer procedure was sharply criticised and subsequently abandoned by the Metropolitan Police, but the practice of seeking uniform prosecution policies by means of reference to the Director of Public Prosecutions and centralising decisions within the force was upheld.[46] Some years later, he was even less successful in attacking the prosecution arrangements then in force. Policies promulgated by the commissioner were upheld as a proper

[43] *R.* v. M.P.C. ex. p. Blackburn [1968] 2 Q.B. 118, 136 and 139, respectively.
[44] *Ibid.* pp. 139–140.
[45] As he acknowledged in a *cri de coeur* letter to *The Guardian*, February 25, 1984.
[46] *R.* v. *Metropolitan Police Commissioner, ex. p. Blackburn (No. 3),* [1973] Q.B. 241.

exercise of his discretion, and Lawton L.J. went so far as to say that the courts would involve themselves only if a chief officer made no attempt at all to enforce the law.[47] And in the C.E.G.B. case [48] the court abstemiously limited itself to a forceful statement of the substantive law, leaving it to the chief constable to deploy his men and issue lawful instructions.

Conclusion

Two main points emerge from a survey of the judicial contribution to police governance. First, the Court of Appeal in *Blackburn* has given its blessing to the doctrine of constabulary independence in undiluted form. It has been argued that the judgments there are replete with errors of logic and historical analysis, and marred by crude value judgments inappropriate to the judical function. Moreover, Marshall is surely correct in arguing that most of *Blackburn I* is mere dicta, since no question of the relationship between chief constables and police authorities was actually presented.[49] Yet however persuasive either or both these views may be, the reality is that *Blackburn I* has over nearly two decades embedded itself in the lore and learning of both judges and police, and it is inconceivable that, without parliamentary intervention, the courts would resile from the position they have reached.

Secondly, the various Blackburn cases also stand for the proposition that the judges will control the actions of a chief constable in relation to law enforcement. This, however, is largely theoretical: short of total, and open, non-enforcement of a particular law, in reality policing policies and practices will be treated by the courts as falling within the non-reviewable discretion of the chief constable.[50]

Case law, however, is of subordinate importance in the overall structure of police governance. Much more central is the Police Act 1964, which largely institutionalised the independence doctrine with respect to local authorities, but gave an expanded role to central government. Its provisions are examined in detail in chapters 6 and 7.

---

[47] *R.* v. *MPC, ex. p. Blackburn, The Times,* March 7, 1980 (C.A.).
[48] *R.* v. *Chief Constable of Devon and Cornwall, ex. p. C.E.G.B.* [1981] 3 W.L.R. 961; above, pp. 13–14.
[49] Marshall (1984), pp. 140–142.
[50] This emerges most clearly in the fourth *Blackburn* case, above n. 47, the importance of which, perhaps because it has never been fully and offically reported, has not been adequately recognised.

Chapter 5

JUDICIAL CONTROL OF POLICE DISCRETION

Traditionally, so long as a constable stayed within the bounds of civil and criminal law[1] the courts have stayed well clear of involving themselves in supervision of his functions. A great deal could, and should, be written about control of prosecutorial discretion, but as this has now purportedly been removed from the police,[2] it must be passed over here. However, analogous issues remain.

We shall see later in this chapter that, where a constable has exercised a statutory discretion, his action is now in principle subject to challenge under public law. Generally, however, this can only occur when he has actively invoked a legal power, as by arresting or searching someone. Where he has chosen not to do so, the legal consequences are much more hazy. We are brought back to Goldstein's point about the effective non-reviewability of low visibility decisions not to enforce.[3] Where the participants in the incident do not object, as in the example of the fight given in Chapter 1, the only problem arising—a serious matter of justice—is that of selective enforcement on other occasions. But where failure to invoke the law is a matter of grievance, as for example among victims of racist attacks, there is a fundamental difficulty in that the legal process has nothing on which to get a grip. It is very difficult to review a non-decision.

This is a problem familiar to administrative law, which has not coped well with it. Indeed until recently it remained caught in conceptual snares. As Professor Wade points out, formerly a sharp distinction was made between failing to exercise a power, and exercising it negligently: the latter was actionable but the former, although it might have even more severe consequences, was not.[4] Hence decisions like *East Suffolk Rivers Catchment Board* v. *Kent*[5]

---

[1] Civil and criminal liability for police misconduct is surveyed in Chap. 9.

[2] This is a deliberate oversimplification. Whilst the Crown Prosecution Service established by the Prosecution of Offences Act 1985 will have responsibility for carrying out prosecutions and may drop charges brought by the police, the initial decision to charge, and selection of charges, remains with the police. Thus the most important decisions will still be taken by them, rather than the Service.

[3] Above, p. 10.

[4] Wade (1983), p. 662.

[5] [1941] A.C. 74.

in which slothful conduct in repairing a sea-wall, resulting in an unnecessarily prolonged period of flooding, was held not to occasion liability, since the Board was merely empowered to undertake the repair. In *Anns* v. *London Borough of Merton*,[6] that decision was disapproved and the idea that failure to exercise a power is cloaked by an absolute immunity was firmly scotched. However, whilst inaction may now potentially give rise to liability, the paucity of reported cases in which it has done so suggests that the legal system remains habituated to thinking in terms of clear-cut actions and responsibilities.

This problem does not stand alone. The discretions not to investigate beyond any particular point, or to classify a reported offence so as to make it non-arrestable, or not to arrest a possible suspect, or to charge someone with one offence rather than another which might equally apply to his conduct, are not based upon statute. They are common law discretions, an animal rarely encountered outside the context of policing or the exercise of prerogative powers.[7] They antedate modern administrative law, which has developed primarily as a means of controlling the exercise of statutory powers, ostensibly to ensure that Parliament's intention is effectuated. One of the reasons that the *Blackburn* cases—which also presented the problem of common law discretion though at a different level of the police organisation—produced so little practical result was that the absence of administrative law doctrine to govern discretion of this kind left the Court of Appeal analytically without resources. Whilst insisting that the commissioner could not simply refuse *tout court* to enforce a law, the judges could do little more than issue stern adjurations: their doctrinal tool kit was otherwise empty.

The judicial approach to police discretion took an entirely new course with the House of Lords decision in *Holgate-Mohammed* v. *Duke*.[8] Lord Diplock, in one of those increasingly common single judgments of the House which bear the imprint of others who have heard the appeal as well as of the author,[9] enunciated the test to be applied to the decision of a constable to exercise a power of arrest. Under section 2 (4) of the Criminal Law Act 1967 (now section 24 (6) of the Police and Criminal Evidence Act 1984), a constable who reasonably suspects that an arrestable offence has been com-

[6] [1978] A.C. 728.
[7] Wade, *op. cit.* pp. 359–360, notes the rarity of the discretion, but in my view exaggerates the effectiveness of the review established in these cases.
[8] [1984] A.C. 437, All E.R. 1054.
[9] See Lord Diplock's comment on this development *Re Prestige Group plc* [1984] 1 W.L.R. 335, 338.

mitted, may arrest without warrant a person whom he has reasonable grounds to suspect has committed that offence. A constable reasonably suspected the plaintiff was guilty of burglary. He arrested and took her to the police station rather than question her at home in the hope, not in fact realised, that she was more likely to confess when questioned there. She sued for wrongful arrest and detention, and the county court judge, who well understood that the change of scene was a non-too-subtle form of psychological intimidation, awarded damages. This judgment was reversed[10]; the reasonableness of the constable's conduct was not to be measured by the judge's view of the facts (or indeed—by implication—by an objective test in the sense familiar to tort law) but by basic principles of administrative law. The constable exercises "an executive discretion" under the statute,[11] and therefore his actions were governed by the *Wednesbury* principles under which certain concepts of unreasonableness make an administrative act *ultra vires*.[12] Since the constable acted in good faith and did not take account of irrelevant considerations, the plaintiff's arrest was lawful.

The implications of this judgment will only unfold over several years, but are fascinating and potentially far-reaching. At one level, it marks an important breakthrough in realism about the police. For the first time, the constable was treated as an executive officer, subject to the same legal analysis as any wielder of discretionary power. The mythology of the citizen in uniform, which has so distorted public debate about the governance of police, was buried without ceremony. At another level, it is unclear whether Lord Diplock truly intended to extend the conception of constable as executive officer to its logical conclusion. He stated explicitly that the *Wednesbury* test would determine the lawfulness of a challenge to a constable's discretion under the Act in proceedings for judicial review.[13] This opens up a vast and hitherto unseen prospect, for no one seems to have imagined that police conduct could be challenged under the Order 53 procedure. It is by no means clear whether the availability of such challenges will secure redress where previously none was available. Yet there would appear to be many statutes under which constables exercise a similar dis-

---

[10] The Court of Appeal [1983], 3 All E.R. 526, overturned the judgment, but on different grounds from those enunciated in the House of Lords.

[11] *Holgate-Mohammed* v. *Duke* [1984] A.C. 437, 443.

[12] *Associate Provincial Picture Houses Ltd.* v. *Wednesbury Corpn.* [1948] 1 K.B. 223, 229–231. For a discussion, see Craig (1983), pp. 353–359.

[13] *Holgate-Mohammed* v. *Duke* [1984] A.C. 437, 443c.

cretion which may now have suddenly become reviewable in this way: to mention only two of the most important, the whole range of powers of search, seizure, detention and roadblock under the Police and Criminal Evidence Act 1984, and provisions in several statutes governing bail.

The *Holgate-Mohammed* case itself at least makes plain that private law rights have not been dislodged, and that persons who seek damages for police misconduct long recognised as tortious will not be turned away from the courthouse under *O'Reilly* v. *Mackman*[14] and *Cocks* v. *Thanet D.C.*[15]. What remains to be seen, however, is whether application of *Wednesbury* principles will alter the standard of legality applied in private law actions, which it will also govern.[16] On one view[17] it marks an advance in the protections available to the public, since bad faith or improper purpose could not before *Holgate-Mohammed* invalidate an arrest: all that was relevant was the presence of reasonable cause. Yet it could equally be said that since reasonableness, rather unusually, had been held to be a question of law,[18] importation of *Wednesbury* principles shifts the focus to the constable's state of mind, thus making the standards vaguer and less rigorous. Certainly to a public lawyer invocation of *Wednesbury* usually sounds a clarion call to judicial retreat; with but rare exceptions it is used to *reject* challenges to executive discretion.

Moreover, application of *Wednesbury* where liberty of the subject is infringed sits uneasily alongside the approach taken in the *Khawaja* case.[19] The House of Lords held that in such circumstances *Wednesbury* principles were insufficient and that more exacting standards were required. Although that deprivation of liberty was very much greater than generally results from police action—the appellants were in prison under the Immigration Act 1971 preparatory to expulsion from the U.K.—no attempt was made to limit the principle enunciated to its particular administrative context. Indeed Lord Scarman, after noting that it made no difference whether the case arose on *habeas corpus* or judicial review, stated without qualification that *Wednesbury* is inappli-

---

[14] [1983] 2 A.C. 237.

[15] [1983] 2 A.C. 286.

[16] Lord Diplock made clear, *Holgate-Mohammed* [1984] A.C. 437, 443c, that the *Wednesbury* test is to apply equally in proceedings for judicial review and in actions for damages for false imprisonment.

[17] Suggested by my colleague Professor C.J. Miller

[18] *Lister* v. *Perryman* (1870) L.R. 4 H.L. 521. This obviously makes the test of reasonableness an objective one.

[19] *R.* v. *Home Secretary, ex p. Khawaja* [1983] 1 All E.R. 765.

cable where "interference with liberty" is involved.[20] A "high degree of probability" is required before it can be accepted that an immigration officer can establish the factual basis of the conclusion that a person is an illegal immigrant.[21]

Applying *Khawaja* to police powers of arrest and search under the 1984 Act would of course have to take into account that what must be reasonable is the constable's suspicion—a lower standard than proof of guilt, but by no means a mere hunch.[22] Nonetheless the constable would be required to demonstrate objective factual justification for his suspicion. It is hazardous to predict what practical difference this standard would make in altering police behaviour, but it would surely facilitate judicial redress for victims of illegality. It is difficult to see why the salutary principle of *Khawaja* should not apply to what is likely to be the greatest invasion of liberty most British citizens will experience.

These conundra will be compounded in cases challenging common law discretions, as for the first time would now seem to be possible. In the case concerning Government Communications Headquarters (G.C.H.Q.), a majority of the House of Lords stated explicitly that all common law discretions (whether or not emanating from the prerogative) are in principle reviewable on, amongst other currently recognised grounds, *Wednesbury* principles.[23] This might indeed be the correct approach to non-enforcement decisions, where deprivation of liberty is not involved and proper consideration of relevant factors only is often the key issue. It is altogether unclear, however, whether the availability of *Wednesbury* would have affected the outcome of any of Mr. Blackburn's forensic forays.

Moreover, Lord Diplock's speech in the G.C.H.Q. decision raised the tantalising possibility that English administrative law might come to adopt the 'proportionality" principle found on the Continent.[24] If this occurred, the exercise of police powers (from whatever source) would come under significantly greater judicial scrutiny. The precise implications of such a development, however, must remain in the realm of futurology.

The foregoing analysis is not meant as advocacy of greater

---

[20] *Ibid*. pp. 781–782.

[21] *Ibid*. pp. 782–784 and 792 (Lord Bridge, joined by Lord Templeman).

[22] *Hussein* v. *Chong Fook Kam*, [1970] A.C. 742, 747–748 (P.C.); *Dumbell* v. *Roberts*, [1944] 1 All E.R. 326.

[23] *C.C.S.U.* v. *Minister for Civil Service*, [1984] 3 W.L.R. 1174, 1196 (Lord Diplock) 1203 (Lord Roskill). Lord Scarman agreed with both (1193).

[24] *Ibid*. p. 1196.

judicial review of police discretion. Quite the reverse. Recourse to the courts may be valuable in securing redress in cases where individual constables have acted in excess of their authority. It is very doubtful, however, whether *post hoc* judicial review can have significant inhibitory effect on police misconduct, and almost inconceivable that it could regulate inaction. Nor, in many instances, should it do so. One is inescapably led back to the conflict Lord Scarman identified between maintaining public tranquility and enforcing the law. His conclusion that the former is paramount is a political judgment, not a legal one.[25] A sitting judge, by the nature of his role and the source of its legitimacy, must reach the opposite conclusion. If, for reasons suggested above,[26] Lord Scarman is correct, it follows that the pre-eminence of peacekeeping must be secured through political rather than legal institutions. The consequent potential abuses, notably selectivity in enforcement or in its denial, must be controlled in the same sphere. The same applies to discretion at command level. Judicial review is at best a long-stop: a much more useful role for the courts is in ensuring redress for victims of tortious or criminal police conduct, a matter considered in Chapter 9.

---

[25] Its character would not be altered if maintaining public tranquillity were added to the list of constables' statutory functions, like arresting suspected offenders. Though both functions could then be formally described as legal, their inevitable conflict would simply be highlighted rather than transformed, for the decision about priorities would remain intractably political.

[26] Pp. 22–23.

Part IV

Chapter 6

CHIEF CONSTABLES AND POLICE AUTHORITIES

The Police Act 1964 created a new and radically altered legal structure of police governance. Its allocation of powers, functions and duties to chief constables, police authorities and the Home Secretary underpin the constitutional and political controversies that have emerged, after a fifteen-year period of quiesence approaching the comatose. The statutory provisions, and the practices which have grown up round them, may be most conveniently studied by looking first at the local elements—chief constables and police authorities—and then separately at central government in the following chapter.

Chief Constables

Perhaps the most significant innovation of the 1964 Act was section 5(1), which declared that each police force shall be "under the direction and control" of its chief constable. This language is not found in any of the earlier statutes, and is quite different from the definition of the position of other directors of local government services. Thus the Education Act 1944[1] establishes a local education authority with the duty to secure sufficient schools for adequate educational provision, to which end it must appoint a fit person to be its chief education officer. Similarly, the Local Authority Social Services Act 1970[2] requires all local authorities to appoint a social services committee to which all matters related to the authority's discharge of its functions under the Act shall be referred. For purposes of these functions the authority is required to appoint a director of social services, who holds office at its pleasure.

The language of the Police Act is quite distinctive. In the other instances the locus of responsibility rests on the authority, with the director a functionary appointed to carry out its purposes. This comparison suggests that Parliament well knew how to subordinate the chief constable to the police authority, but chose not to do so.

Marshall's contention that the language of section 5 "merely

[1] Education Act 1944, ss.6, 8 and 88.   [2] L.A.S.S.A. 1970, ss.2, 6.

describes the existing situation" (in the relation between the police and the local authority) seems unsustainable.[3] He argues that chief constables always exercised immediate direction and control of their forces, and that the important question—whether they are in any sense subject to control by the police authority—is left unanswered. "Immediate" is, however, an ambiguous word, and as we have seen and as Marshall himself suggests, historically watch committees exercised considerable detailed management of their forces. Moreover, the nineteenth century statutes established a very different structure of authority. They designated justices, or created committees, with responsibility for policing. These then appointed head or chief constables. The 1964 Act sets up police forces (s.1), police authorities of specified composition and functions (ss.2–4) and a chief constable with the power defined in section 5. This structural change seems significant, and intentionally so. Although political reality had been moving in this direction for 50 years, 1964 was the first time that the supremacy of the chief constable was enshrined in statute.

The chief constable and his assistants are appointed by the police authority, but only with the approval of the Home Secretary and subject to Regulations promulgated by him.[4] These provide in effect that the short-list of candidates must be approved as well; hence no one unknown to or disapproved of by Home Office civil servants can ever become a senior police official. How such evaluations are formed has never been publicly discussed. It appears that great reliance is placed on judgements made by the inspectors of constabulary, supplemented by evaluation of performance on the senior command course at the police staff college at Bramshill, passage through which has become a *de facto* requirement for promotion to the highest ranks. The Regulations also forbid the appointment of anyone as chief constable who has not served for at least two years in another force at the rank of superintendent or above. This rule is purportedly justified by the need to avoid parochialism and dependence on the favour of local politicians, but it may also prevent senior police officials from developing the roots and commitment to an area indispensable to a sensitive and realistic "community" style of policing.

Once entrenched in post, a chief constable is almost impossible to remove. Corruption and misconduct aside,[5] a police authority

---

[3] Marshall (1965), p. 98.

[4] Police Act 1964, ss.4(2) and 6(4). See the Police Regulations 1979, as amended, S.I. 1979/1470, reg. 15.

[5] Below, p. 157.

may call upon him to retire on one ground only, "the interests of efficiency."[6] According to information received from the Home Office, this provision has never formally been invoked, "although a number of early retirements have probably been negotiated with it in the background." The crucial term "efficiency" is remarkably vague, and has never been construed by the courts. However, in one context it has acquired a traditionally accepted and well understood meaning. Since 1856, local forces have had to be certified as "efficient" by the Inspectorate of Constabulary before they can receive the Home Office grant.[7] Here efficiency has a technical connotation—ability to solve crimes and maintain order, use of equipment and technological aids at reasonable cost, availability of adequate numbers of persons trained in the whole range of police skills. In recent years it has been given a strongly economic emphasis, with central government insisting on ever-increasing cost consciousness and use of financial accounting procedures. On this understanding it would not encompass questions of policies, priorities or attitudes which may create profound disagreement between the authority and the chief constable, nor would it include refusal to co-operate or provide adequate information to the authority apart from the annual report prescribed by the Act,[8] absence of which would leave the authority incapable of intelligent discussion, let alone effective influence. "Efficiency" understood as a technical criterion reinforces the paramount position of the chief constable.

A broader interpretation would be sustainable, however. It is increasingly accepted in official circles that public co-operation is essential if the police are to make any headway in controlling crime.[9] If controversial policies adopted by a chief constable resulted in growing hostility between important sections of the public and the force, such co-operation would be jeopardised. This could be said to threaten efficiency, in the same sense in which

---

[6] Police Act 1964, s.5(4).

[7] The power to pay the grant is now contained in Police Act 1964, s.31. The instrument by which efficiency is monitored and evaluated is HM Inspectorate of Constabulary, whose importance is discussed in the following chapter.

[8] Police Act 1964, s.12, discussed below, p. 78.

[9] This can be seen most clearly in Home Office Circular 8/84 on Crime Prevention, unusually sent out jointly with the DHSS, Department of Environment and the D.E.S. to all chief officers of all local authority service departments as well as chief constables. It also informs the approach taken by Sir Kenneth Newman in his attempt to create "a new social contract" between the public and the Metropolitan Police. This is elaborated most fully in his Annual Report for 1983, Cmnd. 9268, Chaps. 1 and 3.

Lord Scarman declared that local consultation is a prerequisite of efficiency.[10]

However, the final decision concerning dismissal does not lie with the police authority. It requires the approval of the Home Secretary.[11] The practical reality is therefore that a chief constable can ignore his police authority if he wishes to do so provided he can count on Home Office support. Where conflict has occured in recent years between some police authorities with Labour majorities and chief constables, the latter have always been able to rely upon the safety net provided by a Conservative Home Secretary. Hence even those authorities which have passed motions of censure have not gone so far as to seek approval for compulsory retirement, well knowing it would not be forthcoming. The riposte of Mr. Kenneth Oxford, chief constable of Merseyside, when faced with a resolution inviting his departure—"I have every Christian virtue except resignation"—nicely expresses the security of his position.[12]

Indeed it is even possible that if, as a result of continual irritation and policy disagreements, a police authority sacked its chief constable with Home Office approval, the latter might successfully challenge his removal in the courts on the basis that it was on grounds other than "efficiency." Although where the responsible political authorities at both local and national level have followed fair procedures and reached a common view the scope for judicial review may well be limited, it is by no means certain that even a police authority and Home Secretary of one mind could dislodge a chief constable on policy grounds alone.

The process of dismissal may also operate in reverse. The Home Secretary may require the police authority to call upon the chief constable to retire in the interest of efficiency.[13] Since he would otherwise also be the appellate authority, he is required if he invokes this procedure to establish an inquiry, whose membership must include at least one person who is neither a police officer nor a civil servant, and must consider any report it produces.[14] This provision appears to have been inspired by suspicion of localism, and enables the central power to remove a chief constable notwithstanding that the police authority are satisfied with his performance. However, it has yet to be used.

[10] Cmnd. 8427, paras. 5.62–5.64.
[11] Police Act 1964, s.5(4).
[12] For a summary of the Merseyside saga, or at least its most recent chapter, see The Guardian, May 20, 1985.
[13] Police Act 1964, s.29(1).
[14] *Ibid.* s.29(3).

The only explicit statutory duty the chief constable owes his police authority is that of submitting an annual report. Additionally, the authority may "require" that he furnish a written report on any matter pertaining to policing of the area,[15] and some authorities have done so in the wake of controversial incidents. However, this provision does not enlarge their jurisdiction, for the chief constable may refuse to make such a report if he believes it would contain information, disclosure of which would be contrary to the public interest or is not required for the police authority to discharge its duties. The authority can then only appeal to the Home Secretary, who has the final word.[16] No information is available about how often chief constables have refused requests, or indicated informally that they would do so, but apparently an authority has only once asked the Home Secretary to compel submission of a report—without success.[17] The unsatisfactory, indeed somewhat ludicrous, result is that police authorities are entirely dependent on their chief constables for information, making their ability to offer effective criticism subject to the co-operation of its primary target. And the position of the Home Secretary as ultimate arbiter quietly emphasises the power of central government in policing matters.

The contours of the chief constable's powers have never been precisely mapped. Some of the controversies in which chief constables have encountered attempts by police authorities to influence decisions, raising the issue of delineation to the level of urgency, will be discussed in later chapters. Here it is necessary to signal two important points. The first is that a consensus has emerged that chief constables have "operational" control of their forces. This phrase is heard repeatedly and from all sides—Home Office officials, the police themselves, and even reputedly "radical" police authority members, who deny they wish to invade this preserve. This term appears nowhere in the legislation, and has no legal provenance. Yet the power of this conventional understanding is immense. It was suggested earlier[18] that the notion is analytically unsound and far too restrictive as a definition of the areas from which democratic control should be excluded.

The second point is that, probably because its framers never foresaw the problem, the Police Act does not address the question

---

[15] *Ibid.* s.12(2).
[16] *Ibid.* s.12(3).
[17] *Hansard*, April 15, 1981, col. 142 (W.A.). This unilluminating response said nothing about which authority and chief constable were involved, the subject of the report sought, or why the Home Secretary supported the chief constable.
[18] Above, pp. 20–22.

of how far the chief constable's autonomy extends to financial matters. "Direction and control" requires taking decisions that involve expenditure, yet clearly does not include the power to provide funds, which remain in the hands of the police authority. Can the latter then use its power to veto particular expenditures, and indirectly exercise control over, for example, purchase and use of weaponry or deployment of manpower? The conjunction of increasingly stringent central government financial controls after 1983 with the expensive demands of the miners' strike thrusts this previously marginal question onto centre stage of the controversies concerning police governance.

Police Authorities—Composition and Structure

As an institution of local democracy, police authorities are unique in their composition and in their relationships with other elective institutions, central government, and those directing the service with which they are involved. Prior to 1964, the watch committees were composed entirely of councillors, whilst half the members of the shire standing joint committees were magistrates. When S.J.C.s were created in 1888, their composition was defended by reference to the previous absence of any elected local government at all in the shires, although what the Conservative Government of the day claimed was a necessary precaution against "inexperience" of the new councils is more realistically to be seen as a concession to the country landowners and squires who were the major pillar of its support. The Conservatives three-quarters of a century later required that one third of the all police authority members be magistrates[19] on the grounds that the county councils favoured their retention and that the presence of members familiar with police matters was desirable. The latter point seems specious, particularly because the identification of magistrates—in their own minds and in public perception—as supporters of police interests can only weaken confidence in the impartiality of their adjudication. Critics on the Left, both in 1888 and 1964, saw the real reason as distrust of elected members[20]; if so, Conservative Ministers' premonitions have been realised, though hardly in a manner they would have appreciated. Magistrates, along with Conservative councillors, have come to be seen as uncritical followers of the police line. Hence in Merseyside and Greater Manchester at least the Labour majority has treated the two as one bloc and limited

[19] Police Act 1964, ss.2(2) and 3(2).
[20] On the debates in 1888, see Critchley (1978), pp. 133–139; for 1964, see Marshall (1965), pp. 94–96.

the number of Conservatives so as to ensure a Labour majority over their combined votes.[21] In view of the continuing predominance of middle-class whites of Conservative sympathies as recruits to the magistracy, this response is hardly surprising.[22]

The presence of magistrates on the police authority is fundamentally misconceived, both because it places judicial figures in a political role that may immerse them in great controversy and because it gives political power to persons who are unchecked by political responsibility. This can hardly produce restraint in expenditure of public funds, and magistrates' presence may be one reason for the uncritically open-handed attitude to police budget requests often taken by police authorities even in times of stringency. It is true that other local authority committees may have co-opted members—up to one-third for spending committees and one-half for education committees—with full voting rights.[23] However, education apart, this supplementary membership is not mandatory; the elected representatives decide whether they wish to be assisted by others. They also select the particular co-optees, thus ensuring that experts or representatives of recognised interest groups are at least not hostile to their declared policies. Magistrates, on the other hand, select their police authority contingent themselves, rather like the members of an exclusive club. Their guaranteed presence on police authorities, if not simply an affront to democracy, is an indefensible anachronism.

Outside London, there are three types of police authority. The most common is the authority for a county, which functions as a committee of the county council and is usually called the police committee. It is unlike any other committee in one critical respect: its decisions cannot, except on matters of finance, be overruled by the full council. This follows from its position as a statutory authority, as opposed to a creature of the full council which could abolish it at will. By contrast, for all other activities like education or social services the authority is the full council which, for convenience or under legal compulsion, delegates primary responsibility to a committee.[24] Indeed the council as a whole has only the most

---

[21] Information supplied by the chairwomen of these authorities, respectively Margaret Simey and Gabrielle Cox.

[22] Burney (1979), Chap. 4 documents the existence of this bias.

[23] Local Government Act 1972, s.102(3); Education Act 1944, Sched. 1, Part II. Education committees are required to include "persons of experience in education and persons acquainted with the educational conditions prevailing in the area."

[24] In urban areas, only education and social services are compelled by statute to be directed by a committee and not merely the full council. Shire counties are also required to establish committees concerned with national parks and fisheries.

limited means of access to information about policing. During council meetings, questions may be put to a specially designated member of the police authority (generally its chairman) who is also a councillor, about matters relating to the discharge of its functions.[25] Yet if a matter has been treated by the police authority as being wholly within the purview of the chief constable, the designated member may be unable to answer any questions, thus foreclosing any discussion. Moreover, a survey undertaken in 1976 by a Working Party of the Association of County Councils and the Association of Metropolitan Authorities revealed that only one-third of councils received full police committee minutes; the majority made do with reports or extracts, and six did not even receive regular reports.[26] On some councils, rulings by the clerk that a given matter was "for information only" has prevented any discussion by the full council, notwithstanding significant public concern.

The second type of authority is the combined police authority, of which there are ten. These exist where police forces serve more than one county, *e.g.* Thames Valley, Avon and Somerset, or Northumbria. They consist of councillors and magistrates from each county, the numbers from each locality prescribed by the terms of the amalgamation order creating the force.[27] The problem of political "oil and water" arises relatively infrequently, because most combined police authorities exist in rural areas where all the constituent councils have conservative majorities. The exceptions, however, like Avon and Somerset—basically Bristol, Bath and West Country hinterland—do require one organisation to police radically different social, geographical and ethnic terrains.

Combined police authorities are wholly independent of the constituent councils, upon which they levy a rate which the latter have no power to reject or even question. The justification for combined police forces is that they achieve economies of size in providing services. It is arguable that this view reflects a bureaucratic outlook, generally characteristic of the 1960s, dangerously undervaluing the importance of community relations based on trust growing out of contact lost in large and remote structures. Inevitably, the authorities for such forces are rather unwieldy bodies, and one large step further removed from political accountability

---

[25] Police Act 1964, s.11.

[26] The results are reported as an appendix to a publication of the Merseyside Police Authority, *Role and Responsibility of the Police Authority* (1980).

[27] Police Act 1964, s.3(2).

than their county equivalents. This is most apparent in relation to
finance. A police committee will contain councillor members of
other committees who are aware of competing demands for
shrinking resources, and the requirement that the council as a
whole approve the budget at least potentially ensures that the
police claims on resources are weighed against those of other services. Combined authorities are not constrained by any choice
among priorities, and when their natural wish to provide as fully as
possible is allied to their notable tendency to follow chief constables blindly[28] the result is a strong tendency to sign blank
cheques which the constituent councils have to pay. No one has
ever studied whether the latter—subject in recent years to a series
of exotic and increasingly severe Department of Environment
financial controls—have been forced to reduce other services in
consequence, but the potential for being forced to do so is clearly
present.

The most bizarre police authority of all exists at time of writing
only on paper and in the minds of ministers, but its structure can at
least be sketched. The metropolitan county councils were with one
exception co-extensive with the police forces that served them.
The abolition of those councils, supposedly on grounds of their
cost and remoteness from the electorate, left the Government with
the problem of transferring their various functions. It chose a
variety of solutions: some services will be taken up by district
councils, others by statutory bodies, and yet others by joint
boards.[29] It is the latter that have replaced police authorities.

The membership of joint boards, known as metropolitan county
police authorities, consists of nominees of the constituent district
councils. The abolition legislation lays down the number of
appointees each council may nominate.[30] It further requires that,
so far as practicable, appointments shall reflect the balance of the
political parties.[31] No doubt the Government's decision to abolish
the metropolitan councils was entirely unrelated to the fact that
they were all Labour controlled, but the political arithmetic of this
proportionality rule of appointment suggests that, unless the 1986
local elections significantly strengthen Labour at district level, a
coalition of Conservatives and magistrates would have a working

---

[28] See, *e.g.* the account of a meeting of the Thames Valley Police Authority in Kettle (1980). This account could be replicated throughout the country, for this
authority is in no way atypical.
[29] White paper, *Streamlining the Cities,* Cmnd. 9063 (1983), enacted substantially
unchanged in the Local Government Act 1985.
[30] Local Government Act (L.G.A.) 1985, ss.29, 30 and Sched. 10.
[31] L.G.A. 1985, s.33.

majority on four of the new authorities.[32] Two of them would cover Merseyside and Greater Manchester, where some of the most vigorous attempts at using existing police authority powers, and some of the most highly-publicised disputes between the authority and its chief constable, have occured.

Joints boards are not a novelty in local government. They have been used, formally and informally, in relation to public utilities, recreation and the arts, passenger transport and land use planning. A study of these arrangements conducted by researchers based at the Institute of Local Government Studies of the University of Birmingham concluded among other things that:

> "The presumption in the White Paper as to the effectiveness of joint action with regard to accountability of performance is not borne out by the historical evidence. Joint boards and joint committees have been widely viewed as being in conflict with principles of local democracy. Joint boards have in the past tended to operate as "independent" officer-led authorities . . . Study of more recent examples of joint boards confirms that their members have retained only the loosest of links with parent authorities . . . The conditions under which joint action would take place in 1986 are not those which are conducive to effective joint action."[33]

The result will almost certainly be a decreased ability, and perhaps willingness, to challenge police behaviour and policies, and correspondingly greater unchecked freedom of action for chief constables in urban areas where distrust of the police has been particularly marked. This development will be materially compounded by the fact that even the joint boards will be virtually agents of central government for the first three years of their operation, during which their budget, precept and manpower levels will require approval of the Secretary of State.[34] This degree of national control is unprecedented in the history of provincial policing. Finally, after this probationary period, it will be possible for "break-away" authorities to be formed. The Home Secretary may grant permission to authorities or groups of authorities to secede from the joint boards and assume responsibility for policing their area if he is satisfied that they would provide more effective administration and that the service elsewhere in the metropolitan

---

[32] This analysis is drawn from the GLC publication, *Policing London*, No. 17, April/May 1985, p. 33.

[33] Flynn and Leach (1984), paras. 6.3–6.6.

[34] L.G.A. 1985, s.85.

area would not be adversely affected.[35] Birmingham City Council
have already announced their intention to break away from the
West Midlands force, currently the second largest in England and
which its highly-respected former chief constable had publicly
declared to be excessively large. Since the result would be to sever
the geographical link between the Black Country and all of the
West Midlands east to Coventry, the consequences could be quite
disruptive for the organisation of the policing of several million
people. The most that can be said about joint boards at this stage is
that their operation is likely to increase the alienation already felt
by those who believe the police are unresponsive to community
needs, and are unlikely to prove a more effective supervisory body
than the authorities they have replaced. Their existance may, however, increase the importance of the new statutory consultation
machinery.[36]

Powers and Functions of Police Authorities

All police authorities are under a duty to secure the maintenance of an "adequate and efficient" force for their area.[37] True to
form, the Act leaves these terms undefined. Towards this end,
police authorities are empowered:

  (1) to appoint a chief constable, his deputy and assistants, sub-
      ject to the approval of the Home Secretary[38];
  (2) determine the overall establishment, and the number of
      each rank, of the force[39];
  (3) provide vehicles, clothing and equipment[40];
  (4) determine the overall budget of the force, subject however
      to the requirement that costs incurred under authority of
      central government Regulations, or any statute, must be
      met.[41]

The meaning of this duty has never been judicially considered,
and there must be grave doubt whether it is a justiciable question.
Statutes of the post-war era have frequently created this sort of
duty, described by Professor Wade as "of a general and indefinite
character . . . perhaps to be considered as political duties rather

---

[35] *Ibid.* s.42(1)(a).
[36] Below, pp. 89–94.
[37] Police Act 1964, s.4(1).
[38] *Ibid.* ss.4(2) and 6(4).
[39] *Ibid.* s.4(2).
[40] *Ibid.* s.4(3).
[41] *Ibid.* s.8(4).

than as legal duties which a court could enforce."[42] It is a duty owed to the public within the police area, and not to any specific person, raising questions of *locus standi*. Even more important, the duty itself is of such a vague nature that it could only be the subject of legal enforcement if the judges were to make technical evaluations of policing needs, adequacy of provision, and quality of performance. These are matters which one would hope even the most ardent advocate of judicial review would recognise as well outside the competence of courts. This preliminary point is a critical one, because in some of the controversies arising from the miners' strike, legal action was threatened against police authorities which attempted to control expenditure by measures that met with central government disapproval.[43] It is very difficult to see how, without usurping political power, the courts could entertain such actions under the present statute.

In evaluating the effectiveness of police authorities, the only sensible bench-mark is the performance of other local authority committees. Two key points stand out. The first is that democratic control of the police cannot functionally be separated from democratic control of local government. It is a common complaint that officers are often able to lead inexpert part-time councillors by the nose. The diverse factors that have led town halls to be widely seen as the home of unresponsive bureaucracies—limited competence of councillors, their inability to gain access to necessary information, and officialdom's conviction that experts know better than mere politicians—are neither more nor less severe with respect to the police. The second point is that all authorities inevitably delegate a great deal of decision-making—involving day to day detail, broad policy, and power to spend substantial sums of money—to their officers. The police as an institution may present particular problems of democratic control, but any authority that has not confronted the wider issues in relation to all its services is unlikely to begin to exercise even its present power more effectively.

The extent and limits of the police authority's financial powers will be considered in Chapter 8. The power of fixing the establishment, though it may occasionally be useful to restrain over-enthusiastic chief constables, is otherwise of very limited value. It is difficult to believe that a threat by a police authority in conflict with its chief constable to cut the establishment would be politically viable. It is now clear from authoritative research that increases in police manpower have little impact on improving

---

[42] Wade (1982), p. 625.
[43] See pp. 120–123.

crime prevention or detection.[44] Whilst there is almost certainly some scope for reductions in the establishment—which increased nationally by 20 per cent. in the decade 1974–1984—without reducing effectiveness in crime control, no one can tell where the danger point would be reached. It is in any case doubtful whether the public would be convinced, especially with the chief constable issuing dire warnings. As a negotiating tactic such a threat would lack credibility. This leaves the power to provide vehicles and equipment, which is more controversial and important than may first appear. After the Brixton riots, a number of forces, encouraged by the Government, purchased considerable quantities of CS gas, plastic bullets and other military equipment. A number of police authorities, which had by standing orders delegated the power to purchase equipment to the chief constable, discovered they could do nothing to prevent these purchases, to which the majority was strongly opposed. Other subsequently amended their standing orders to require prior authorisation by the police committee on full council before any expenditure over a certain (fairly low) sum would be lawful. In such forces—Derbyshire is a prominent example—no more of such equipment was purchased and existing stocks were run down in training.

However, the unresolved problem is what sanctions are available to an authority if the chief constable chooses to ignore the limits imposed upon him. Such behaviour would not amount to a disciplinary offence, and we have seen that the power to dismiss requires the approval of the Home Secretary. This raises the question of whether police authorities should have the power to dismiss their chief constable.

Whilst other local authority committees have this power over their chief officers, it is seldom exercised because of policy conflicts. Senior officers either find it degrading to draw their salaries while being ignored and move or negotiate early retirement, or alternatively ostensibly accept but only minimally comply with the policy. Councillors may then attempt to bypass the chief officer by working through his senior assistants. These tactics are all worked out inside a structure within which councillors have the final responsibility for policy; it is this, rather than threat of the sack, that is crucial. However, the power to dismiss remains a necessary reserve sanction. More important to a police authority which had

---

[44] See especially Clarke and Hough (1980 and 1984). For a good summary of this research in this area, see Reiner (1985), pp. 116–122. Obviously we are talking about incremental or marginal effects above a certain indeterminate (perhaps indeterminable) point: no one suggests that abolition of the police would not result in a immediate increase in crime.

effective policy and management control would be freedom from
Home Office interference in the process of hiring senior police
officials.[45] It would thus be able to appoint people sympathetic to
its approach but who, like chief officers generally, would inevitably have substantial latitude in carrying it out, and would be
expected to initiate policies of his own in the context of agreement
on fundamentals.

In the nineteenth century, the watch committee was the most
prestigious of municipal corporation committees,[46] but the
modern police authority is largely the preserve of the inactive and
the conventional. Bereft of power to make policy, to direct
officials or even discuss substantive matters on the assumption of
equal responsibility or to intervene actively on behalf of aggrieved
constituents[47], this is hardly surprising. In the one authority that
received extensive study, the members were disproportionately
elderly and viewed their work as entirely non-partisan and apolitical.[48] Even commentators who reject the need for increased police
authority powers accept that most have failed to make full use of
their present ones.[49] It would seem that the attitudes and character
of individual councillors and the legal structure reinforce each
other, for if a committee has feeble powers, councillors concerned
to represent their constituents effectively and make their mark
politically will rationally choose to concentrate their energies elsewhere. At all events, with a few well-publicised exceptions, most
police authorities are pliant bodies whose members view themselves as a sort of cheerleader corps for their force.

Information is a valuable currency of power, and one of the
more serious obstacles to the effective working of police authorities is the law concerning access to information. Particularly
unhelpful is the Court of Appeal decision in *R.* v. *Lancashire
Police Authority, ex p. Hook.*[50] Briefly,[51] the Chief Constable of
Lancashire had been dismissed after accusations of corruption and
favouritism and the police authority, at the suggestion of the
D.P.P., commissioned a special enquiry by a retired chief constable, Sir Douglas Osmond. Subsequently, Mr. Hook was elected

---

[45] Above, p. 75.
[46] Steedman (1984), p. 43.
[47] This is because the statutory complaints procedure governs cases of individual
grievance. See Chap. 9.
[48] Brogden (1977).
[49] Notably Regan (1983). For several years this was Margaret Simey's view as well,
enunciated on public platforms and in Simey (1982).
[50] [1980] Q.B. 603.
[51] This account is taken from Birkinshaw (1981).

to the county council and chosen to be a member of the police committee. He was dissatisfied with the authority's handling of the matter, alleging that not all the charges, involving several influential local people, had been fully aired before it. He sought to examine the full Osmond Report, but was denied access by the chairman of the authority—subsequently supported by a vote of the committee—on the grounds that it contained many unsubstantiated allegations. He was supplied with a bowdlerised version. Mr. Hook challenged the Chairman's decision on the basis that he could not adequately perform his duties as a member of the committee. He lost before a divided Court of Appeal, Lord Denning M.R. dissenting. The majority held that the decision could only be challenged on *Wednesbury* grounds, and that in view of the material purportedly involved—it was never shown to the court— caution and restricted distribution were readily understandable.

Hook's Case is dangerous because it enables the majority party on an authority effectively to shut out its opponents from offering informed criticism of decisions it has taken out of public view.[52] However, it may in considerable measure have been overruled *sub silentio* by the House of Lords in *R.* v. *Birmingham City Council, ex p. O.*[53] There Lord Brightman, for a unanimous House, set out the principles that should govern access by councillors to confidential information in the possession of a local authority. Members of the relevant committee will almost always be able to command access to information concerning matters within its purview, for such documents are prima facie necessary for them to do their jobs,[54] but non-members can be excluded unless they can demonstrate a "need to know," a question ultimately to be determined, not by the courts, but by the council itself.[55]

This decision leaves unanswered some questions unique to the police governance. The peculiar composition of police committees, and their tangential relation to the full council (recognised most clearly by the limited "answering service" provided by section 11 of the Police Act 1964)[56] suggests that they, rather than the full council, will decide if a non-member councillor can gain access to confidential material concerning policing. In instances where a non-member councillor seeks to assist a constituent with a

---

[52] This, apparently, was at the bottom of the dispute between Mr. Hook and the chairman of the authority, who were of opposing political parties.
[53] [1983] 2 W.L.R. 189.
[54] *Ibid.* p. 198.
[55] *Ibid.* p. 199. The council's decision, said Lord Brightman, would only be judicially reviewable on *Wednesbury* grounds.
[56] Above, p. 81.

grievance or complaint of police misconduct, about which the authority alone will have the relevant information, he will be wholly dependent on the authority's support if he is to offer any useful assistance. The same would be true of a councillor concerned about expenditure wishing to determine the factual basis of a committee's approval of a particular item, which may well have been based primarily on documents provided by the chief constable but never made public. Yet more frustrating is the position of a councillor whose area in served by a combined police authority: he is not a member of that authority—which is wholly distinct from its constituent councils—and hence has no more right of access to the documents than any member of the public. Both examples further highlight the incongruities caused by the treatment of police authorities as separate entities rather than committees of their local authority.

By virtue of the first provision of the Police and Criminal Evidence Act 1984 to come into force, police authorities have moved into new territory. Section 106 requires all authorities to "make arrangements" for obtaining "the views of people in that area about matters concerning policing of that area" and as well as "their co-operation with the police in preventing crime." What is generally called police-community consultation or liaison has, following a recommendation in Lord Scarman's Report,[57] been placed on a statutory footing, although it should be noted that there is no requirement that new or formal machinery be established. It remains open to the police authority, upon whom the responsibility rests, to determine whether such machinery is required. In many rural or even suburban areas, where policing has remained uncontentious and officers have already regularly attended parish council meetings, the police authorities may conclude that prior arrangements are satisfactory.

Although consultation became a matter of statute with the 1984 Act, pressure from the Home Office and the Inspectorate of Constabulary ensured that most forces had established some sort of consultation methods by the end of 1984. The form these took has been surveyed by Morgan and Maggs[58] whose thoughtful analysis of the underlying purposes of the enterprise and of the mechanisms that have been created is an authoritative examination of this subject. They identify four aims of formal consultation that have emerged: expression of public opinion; education of that opinion

---

[57] Lord Scarman's discussion of the role of liaison committees outside London is found in paras. 5.55–5.66 of the report.
[58] Morgan and Maggs (1984).

by the police; establishing public acceptance/legitimacy or at least giving the appearance of trying to base police activity on community co-operation; and mobilising the public to assist in crime prevention. This last objective, they argue, is the key element in Home Office thinking. With the police finally coming under financial constraints similar to those imposed earlier on other services, and with mounting evidence of the limited impact the police working alone can have on controlling crime, Home Office Circular 8/84 on Crime Prevention signalled the importance of establishing mechanisms to involve the public in crime control activities. This also requires that it be provided with a forum to articulate its concerns.

However, the context of policing in a Cotswold market town is worlds away from, for example, the political and social conflicts surrounding policing in Brixton or many mining districts. The latter require a radically different concept of community liaison, the purpose of which is to gain or regain the trust of alienated sections of the community. This function would be served by provision of a forum to express dissatisfaction in public and—much more important—to enable the police to submit their plans and policies for public consideration, and to be seen to be influenced by critical responses. This objective of reconciliation animated Lord Scarman's view that "a police force, the Chief Officer of which does not discuss, or allow his senior officers to discuss, matters of policing policy openly and responsively with the community, is certain in the long run to find its efficiency undermined by loss of community support."[59] In the long run it may be hoped that reconciliation will lead to greater and more effective community involvement in crime prevention, but in the short run the practice of consultation will be far more demanding and contentious where the more difficult objective is sought. In particular, it is here that the balancing act Lord Scarman thought possible will be put under the greatest pressure: permitting "community involvement in the policy and operations of policing" without abandoning the now-reigning view of police independence. The recent Home Office Guidelines on consultation outside London emphasise the importance of this element of consultation.[60] It is equally possible that experience will demonstrate that consultation capable of leading to changes responsive to genuine grievances is inherently incompatible with the independence doctrine.

Thus the objectives of consultation in a particular locality will

[59] Scarman (1981). para. 5.64.
[60] Home Office Circular 2/85, para. 4.

dictate the essential features of its machinery: the size of the group; whether its membership is open or fixed; composition of the invited membership—particularly the relative number of police, councillors and M.P.s and representatives of statutory services compared to delegates of specific organisations from which nominations are sought; conduct and location of meetings and whether they are open to the public; finally and most important, the content of the agenda and how and by whom it is formulated.

It is beyond the scope of this book to examine in detail the workings of the committees that have been established and alternative models that have been proposed.[61] The most important influence on evolving practice seems to have been the initial Home Office Guidelines in Circular 54/82, sent to all police authorities and chief constables in June 1982, long before legislation was even introduced. The constitutional question posed by their emergence is how they relate to the police authority. In London this has a particularly sharp edge, because advocates of an elected police authority see liaison committees as an attempt by central government to outflank them by providing a non-elected structure which would nonetheless go some way toward satisfying the demand for public participation. Hence both the Greater London Council and several boroughs have refused to co-operate, although the Guidelines envisaged the borough as the geographical unit for the new arrangements. Although in the rest of the country the committees function under the aegis of the police authority, there remains a distinct possibility that, where conflict arises with the chief constable, he will use supportive opinions expressed at consultation meetings as evidence that he is in closer touch with popular feeling than authority members, whose views he may therefore legitimately ignore. Yet those who participate in such exercises may not be at all representative of those for whom they purport to speak and, even more likely, may represent only a narrow segment of the population.

Indeed the consultative committees raise fundamental questions of democratic theory and institutional practice. There are obvious objections to interposing a non-elected body between officials and elected representatives who are supposed to articulate the views and interests of the public. The objections become considerably more pointed when the scope of the powers of those representa-

---

[61] This is done in depth by Morgan and Maggs, *op. cit.* Several short but useful contributions by persons involved in consultation in various localities were presented at a colloquium held at Cranfield Institute of Technology in September 1984 and published by the institute as Brown (1985).

tives is itself a matter of controversy. It is doubtful whether any local authority committee can lawfully share and delegate any of its powers to self-selected voluntary bodies.[62] It is certainly undesirable than an elected police committee with full powers should do so, particularly because well-documented studies of political participation suggest that such bodies will contain a disproportionately small number of working class, young and ethnic minority persons.[63] Since these are precisely the people who are most estranged from the police, it is possible that one influence consultative committees could have on police priorities and practices would to be aggravate the conflicts between the police and the politically marginal.

On the other hand, no one could plausibly claim that existing structures of local government are the ideal manifestations of local democracy. Some police officers have argued that liaison bodies, covering a much smaller area than the police authority, can express local feeling on policing and crime more genuinely than councillors who are responsible for a much wider range of concerns and geographic area, particularly if the ward is strongly dominated by one party so that elections produce little real debate and a low turnout.[64] This is not mere opportunistic rhetoric from those shrewd enough to see the possibilities of deflating the movement for greater democratic control. One may doubt whether the police, or any public servants for that matter, are the right persons to take upon themselves the task of curing the ills of representative democracy,[65] but there is real substance to the argument. Indeed it points the way out of the dilemma.

A democratically governed police authority can view consultative arrangements as an adjunct to its powers, a way of exercising them more effectively and an extension of the conventional political process. Provided it retains active control, it can use consultation mechanisms to reach the politically voiceless and to counteract the disproportionate influence of the politically articulate middle-aged property owners who tend to dominate politics at

---

[62] s.101(1) of the Local Government Act 1972 permits delegation only to a committee, sub-committee or officer. A liaison committee could not be a "committee" or "sub-committee" of a local authority in the statutory sense because of the requirement (s.103(3)) that at least two-thirds of its members be councillors.

[63] *e.g.* Newton (1976), p. 231 and sources cited; Verba *et al.* (1978). Since ethnic minorities are disproportionately working class and young, their absence is particularly likely, quite apart from any specifically ethnic factors that may influence behaviour.

[64] This view emerged from several thoughtful police contributions in sessions of the Cranfield colloquium, above, n. 61, which the author attended.

[65] On the constitutional implications of police politicisation, see pp. 168–169.

all levels. Conceived in this fashion, consultative arrangements can be regarded as analogous to the devolution of housing functions to tenants' organisations and local offices, and other decentralisation initiatives that have been taken by a few radical local authorities in recent years.[66] Even within the present structure it is possible for police authorities to use consultation for this purpose. Merseyside has organised a series of open meetings, some of which have attracted well over a hundred people, in preference to formal groups with limited membership. The Chairwoman of the Greater Manchester Police Authority has described her conception of liaison panels as relating to the Authority "in much the same way as sub-committees do." However, it is difficult to resist her conclusion that "community panels are anathema to some sections of the community because they are seen as powerless and ineffectual; and that in itself is a reflection of the perceived position of the Police Authority. It may be, therefore, that a fully effective consultative/liaison structure will not develop until we have a more democratically accountable system of policing in this country."[67]

In the short run, however, consultative groups may acquire an importance in certain areas for reasons quite unconnected to the circumstances which gave them birth. In those conurbations in which policing has passed to joint boards, they will be the only institution with more than tenuous ties to the people being policed. Many of these areas contain large numbers of the young unemployed, major ethnic minority populations, or mining communities, If police-community co-operation is to be established or re-established in these areas, liaison bodies will perforce be the only machinery available to step into the breach. In this respect their position will in reality by analogous to consultation committees in London, where no elected forum exists.

The introduction of consultation arrangements is a concrete expression of the importance of local interest, needs and feeling in relation to policing. However, by definition it excludes those who are not "local" but who are nonetheless affected by policing decisions in a particular area. The clearest example is that of people who come to demonstrate at a particular site *e.g.* Greenham Common or Molesworth, but other groups, like gypsies, may even be more alien to the locality yet subject to its policing. This tension between the importance of local participation and control, and the need to respect the rights of outsiders who may arouse great local hostility, is inescapable and poses a severe challenge to

[66] For an account of one such initiative, in Walsall, see Seabrook (1984).
[67] Gabrielle Cox, in Brown (1985), p. 54.

democratic values. At this point it is sufficient to flag on the problem, to which we shall return to in Chap. 10 when considering policing issues in the context of democratic constitutionalism.

A final point is that consultative arrangements are not entirely in the hands of the police authority. The Home Secretary retains power to oversee the arrangements put into effect, and if he does not believe they are "adequate," he may require the authority to submit a report on them. After considering that report, he may require the authority to review the arrangements and submit a further report to him.[68] Strictly speaking this does not amount to a formal power to order changes, but the capacity for moral and political pressure is virtually overwhelming. This provision, and the influence of the Circular, epitomises one of the major themes in the development of police governance: the shadowy but increasingly dominant role of the central power. This is the subject to the next chapter. Before it is considered, however, the Home Secretary's direct responsibility for policing must be discussed.

The Home Secretary as Metropolitan Police Authority

Central government's most direct responsibility for policing is found in the Home Secretary's role as police authority for London. This derives from Peel's Act of 1829, which made the Secretary of State responsible for approving the size of the force and the regulations governing it, and empowered him to direct the justices (later commissioners) in command of the force to execute specific duties. It must be remembered that in 1829 elected local government institutions did not exist and in any case the electorate was a tiny fraction of the male population. Since monolithic party government and the whip system also did not exist, individual ministerial responsibility to the House of Commons was a meaningful concept. Thus the provisions of the 1829 Act were designed to ensure the maximum accountability that the political system was capable of constructing at that time.

Some would argue that such a degree of effective accountability has never been equalled since. There is much force in this view, but the question of the governance of London's police raises issues that have no parallel elsewhere. This is due to the sheer size of London's population and area, but even more to the fact that the Metropolitan Police perform, and have always performed, many functions which are national in scope and for which purely local

---

[68] P.C.E.A 1984, s.106(10) and (11).

accountability is not appropriate. These include affording royal and diplomatic protection and patrolling demonstrations over national issues—both of which reflect London's position as the capital of a remarkably centralised state; special branch and related work concerning national security[69] and a large number of forensic services, computerised intelligence, criminal records and co-ordinating facilities which the Metropolitan Police provide to other forces. Moreover, there are a number of crimes, for example, fraud and those coming under the purview of the Fine Art Squad, which though physically occuring within the metropolis are little more related to the lives of most of its inhabitants than to those of Caithness.[70]

Before the advent of representative institutions elected according to a genuinely democratic franchise, it mattered little whether responsibility for such matters was combined with that for public order and crime control affecting London's residents. Yet whilst at least some of these matters are of such national concern that it would be wrong to permit a political majority elected from one particular locality, however large, to determine policy, the others are of critical importance to Londoners and it is equally unacceptable to deprive them of the normal rights enjoyed by citizens of a democracy. It seems wrong too that Londoners alone should have to bear the rates burden incurred by the various functions of national importance or benefit. Thus the question of control is at present entwined with that of function or jurisdiction in a way that has no parallel elsewhere.

Two points are seldom made in discussions about retention of the Home Secretary's police authority function, but almost certainly weigh very heavily in the thinking of the Home Office. The first received its clearest public expression in the article by Sir Edward Troup (quoted in Chap. 3) whose importance as a guide to the very influential Home Office view has never been adequately recognised. Writing in 1928 after retirement from forty-two years in the Department, the last fourteen as Permanent Under-Secretary, Troup declared:

> "The central government should have complete control of the police in the seat of government. It would be intolerable that

---

[69] National security is a concept often grossly and dangerous overused by governments to combat political opponents. Nonetheless it has a narrow area of validity in relation to spying and other acts by people working on behalf of the interests of a foreign state, and some form of police organisation is needed to counter it.

[70] For a complete list of the national and co-ordinative functions performed by the Met., see GLC (1983), para. 172.

the legislature or executive should be at the mercy of a police force controlled by a municipal authority which might come into violent conflict with the national authority."[71]

Though such a fear might seem to most people paranoiac, or merely bizarre, it is the sort of consideration that administrators of the central state, concerned above all to ensure its paramountcy, would find compelling.

Secondly, there is the critical role of the Met. in relation to mutual aid. This system, under which various forces may call upon each other's assistance when their chief constables believe their own manpower is inadequate, is discussed in Chapter 8. In relation to London, however, "mutual" aid is a distortion of language. The Metropolitan Police force does not receive assistance from any other force, even at times of greatest pressure, as during the Brixton riots. It has, however, always been the main provider of assistance to other forces, a pattern established in the early years of its existence when many areas still lacked an organised force, and reinforced in late Victorian times when successive Home Secretaries grew increasingly reluctant to authorise the use of troops. This heavy reliance on London's police for national public order functions continues—almost one-third of the police drafted in during the miners' strike came from the Met.[72] Were the Home Secretary to cede his direct responsibility for their deployment to a body for which specifically London concerns were of predominant importance, it is highly unlikely that it would agree to arrangements so inequitable and on such a scale. Reluctance to accept this possibility, and the fear of political vulnerability expressed by Sir Edward Troup, may go a long way towards explaining the tenacity with which an elected institution of government for London's police has been resisted.

How the Home Secretary performs his police authority function depends primarily on how his civil servants are organised. The numbers involved are surprisingly small. Only one high level official, a senior principal, devotes full time to this work; the assistant secretary to whom he reports, and two officials who assist him, have other responsibilities as well. None of the seven police divisions within the department is responsible for the Metropolitan Police as such, although since they are organised on functional lines a substantial proportion of their work will involve the country's largest force. The result is that the superintendence of

[71] Troup (1928), p. 9.
[72] The figure was provided by Mr. Martin Ennals, formerly head of the GLC Police Committee Support Unit.

this massive organisation, which employs 42,000 uniformed and civilian staff, is left entirely to the commissioner. He does not even have to open his force to evaluation by HM Inspectorate of Constabulary. Because HMI was established in 1856 to ensure that the newly-formed forces were sufficiently up to scratch to merit central government grant, their brief never included the Met. which was always heavily funded by the Exchequer. The Met. has its own inspectorate, but they report only to senior management. This does not, however, preclude substantial discussion and 'guidance' between Home Secretary and commissioner or between civil servants and equivalent ranks in the police hierarchy. The result seems to be that the Home Secretary exercises greater influence— though not control—over broad policies and identification of problems to be addressed by the police themselves with respect to the Met. than other police authorities do over their forces.

This is not to say, however, that this degree of authority is adequate, or that a Cabinet Minister with a wide range of other responsibilities is the appropriate instrument to exercise it. Indeed on day-to-day policing issues, the kind that give rise to the greatest antagonism with sections of the public—the handling of specific demonstrations, tactics to be adopted in a particular neighbourhood, or treatment of suspects in a particular police station—the Home Office will not be consulted in advance and will be as ignorant and dependent on the police themselves for information in the event of complaints as any other authority. Moreover, it is by no means certain that within an organisation long diagnosed to be suffering from elephantiasis, senior officials at Scotland Yard will be aware of, or able to control, conduct of their subordinates at ground level. This problem was an important motivating factor in the major administrative changes announced late in 1984, devolving decision-making powers to district commanders and away from central management in New Scotland Yard. It raises the question whether it is necessary to maintain a force anything like the size of the present one, particularly if its national functions are hived off.

The Home Secretary does indeed have a formal accountability to Parliament, in that he will be more forthcoming in answering questions about policing in London than in the provinces. M.P.s will periodically debate policing in London but only occasionally will policing elsewhere be considered. However, this arrangement is several removes from providing an effective means for ensuring that the needs and dissatisfactions of people in particular areas or communities are met and are acted upon. It was to remedy this defect that Lord Scarman so strongly emphasised the need for community consultation. Nonetheless, for reasons offered earlier,[73] consultation/liaison is not an adequate substitute for democratic institutions of control; if taken as a general constitutional principle we would have to dispense with elected representative government entirely. However, in this respect Scarman was caught in a trap of his own making, for he had previously committed himself to the proposition that "there are good reasons for the national accountability of the Metropolitan Police"[74] without saying what these were. If one does not start chained to that assumption, it becomes possible to examine alternative local governmental structures, to which consultation would be a valuable but subordinate adjunct.

The inadequacy of consultation as a complete substitute for elected institutions is seen most clearly in relation to finance. At present the commissioner submits a proposed budget for the Home Secretary's approval; this is by no means automatic, and the Metropolitan Police were subjected to cash limits in 1984 for the first time in their history. However, London ratepayers, who pay a substantial proportion of the more than £800,000,000 involved[75] have no say in determining either the total or the amount spent on individual items. The Metropolitan Police Receiver simply issues a precept upon all the boroughs, which they are bound to pay. Non-elected neighbourhood or other locally-based liaison bodies could not constitutionally be clothed with powers of approving expenditure or allocating funds, and in any case an agency operating on a much wider basis is required for reasons of efficiency and genuine economies of scale. Equally important is the need for an institution which can evaluate area-wide priorities and choose among competing demands for resources.

It is easier to identify the need for an alternative than to design it. The abolition of the Greater London Council has eliminated the obvious London-wide elected alternative, but such a limited transfer would in any case have left the problems of size, remoteness and unmanageability unaffected. A thoughtful paper produced for the GLC some years ago canvassed a series of options, but it assumed continuation of the Metropolitan Police as one

---

[73] Above, pp. 92–93.

[74] Scarman (1981), para. 5.68.

[75] The financial relation between the Met. and the Home Office is difficult to unravel. Total expenditure and sources of income are printed as an appendix to the Commissioner's Annual Reports. These do not, however, separate block grant from the Home Office grant, nor do they indicate the particular items, *e.g.* computers, for which the Home Office pays the entire cost. The police rate accounts for about 25 per cent. of the entire expenditure, substantially lower than for provincial forces.

organisation, and its rather unwieldly proposal for a two-tier authority also assumed, not unnaturally, continued existance of the GLC.[76] The organisation of electoral politics requires that the borough be taken as the basic unit, just as it is for Parliamentary constituencies.[77]

One attractive option would be to split the Met. into several more manageable segments, each comprising three or four boroughs. The result might be seven or eight forces of about 3,000 constable each. This change might in turn stimulate similar fractionations in places like the West Midlands and Greater Manchester, which have suffered badly from excessive amalgamation. There would be obvious problems of co-ordination between forces; for example, a march to Westminster or Hyde Park might pass through two or three police areas, as would car thieves or fleeing robbers. The creation of separate forces and authorities would involve considerable administrative cost, but even if it were possible to estimate this reliably, that argument should not be allowed much weight save in extreme cases: democracy costs money.

A less radical alternative along similar lines is for the new forces to conform to the present four areas into which the Met. is at present administratively divided. These areas seem to have been designed purely on geographical lines, and contain boroughs which are economically, socially and ethnically highly diverse. Indeed any splintering would have to face the problem of which boroughs would make an appropriate unit, a choice in which political judgments of many kinds would loom large.

One point, however, seems unarguable: the present bailiwick of the Metropolitan Police—a fifteen mile radius from Charing Cross, reflecting the distance that horse patrols could reasonably be expected to cover—makes no more rational sense than almost any proposed alternative. Whatever form an elected London authority took, it would not take over responsibility, political or financial, for the national functions presently performed by the Met. These would remain with the Home Secretary, or with the body that took over his present responsibilities for provincial policing, a matter taken up in Chapter 10.

---

[76] GLC (1983), *passim.*

[77] Small bits of Surrey, Hertfordshire and Essex have remained within the Metropolitan Police district. These could easily be absorbed by their respective county forces. There is also a strong argument for making policing of Heathrow Airport, where most Special Branch officers are assigned and deal with offences far removed from normal policing, the responsibility of central government.

Chapter 7

THE ROLE OF CENTRAL GOVERNMENT

Study of the influence of central government on provincial policing is a paradigm case of the need for an empirical, rather than merely formal, study of the constitutional allocation of power. The ever-strengthening centripetal force—the steady accretion of power to the centre—is only imperfectly reflected in statute, has eluded judicial consideration and has never fully been acknowledged by those involved. This gap between paper and practice is a well-documented characteristic of the working of political institutions, but seems unusually wide in respect to police governance. Some of the key institutions have no statutory existence, while others have unaccountably escaped the attention of researchers. Above all, practice in this area embodies to an extreme degree a notable feature of British politics: its informality and preference for behind the scenes influence, quiet words in ears, and careful selection of key people who can be trusted to share fundamental norms.

Because so little has been written, what follows is based primarily on interviews with officials of the Home Office, the Inspectorate of Constabulary (HMI) and a former Home Secretary,[1] and in part on inferences from particular incidents. Analysis may best proceed by looking first at the statutory powers of the Home Secretary, which largely relate to the division of power between central and local political authorities, and then at what may be termed working relationships, which covers primarily the relations between the Home Office and chief constables.

Statutory Powers

The Home Secretary is enjoined to exercise his powers "under this Act" in ways he believes best calculated to "promote" police efficiency.[2] These powers are specifically enumerated and he does not have a generalised residual control or veto power. In numer-

---

[1] With Rt. Hon. Merlyn Rees, M.P., Home Secretary 1976–1979, Mr. D. Hilary, Assistant Secretary, Home Office (both September 1984); telephone interview with Mr. B. Gange, Principal, Home Office, May 7, 1985; Mr. S.C. Vessey, Assistant to the Chief Inspector of Constabulary and Sir James Crane, former Chief Inspector of Constabulary (both September 1985).

[2] Police Act 1964, s.28.

ous other contexts[3] the relevant ministry is equipped with default powers in respect of local authority functions. Perhaps the best known example is in education, where the Secretary of State can give a direction to a local education authority if he is satisfied the latter has used or will use its powers unreasonably.[4] Even more drastically, if he believes the authority is failing to perform some function adequately, he may take over the administration himself or put it in the hands of another authority.[5] Another, more recently created, instance enables the Environment Secretary to take over a council's functions in relation to selling council houses if he believes tenants are having undue difficulty in exercising their right to buy.[6]

The nearest analogue in relation to policing is far less direct, though in practical terms perhaps equally powerful. Along with the requirement that a full-time police force be established, the County and Borough Police Act 1856 also contained a sweetener, in the form of a 25 per cent. subvention of the cost of the operations from central funds; this was increased to 50 per cent. in 1874 and remains at that level today. However, receipt of the grant is conditional upon the Secretary of State being satisfied of several matters, most importantly that the area is being efficiently policed, that the force receives efficient and proper maintenance, equipment and administration, and that it provides adequate co-operation to other forces.[7] However, the sanction is withdrawal of the grant, not issuance of directions or taking over the authority's functions.

The grant is of course a carrot to cajole local authorities to conform to central government standards, and was designed and used precisely for this purpose from its inception. Under the 1856 Act no borough with a population under 5,000 was eligible for grant, an exclusion intended as an incentive to amalgamate with the surrounding county force.[8] The grant provision has always been

[3] For a full list taken from *Hansard*, see [1984] P.L. 485–486 (Current Survey).

[4] Education Act 1944, s.68. Use of this section produced the *Tameside* litigation: *Secretary of State for Education and Science* v. *Tameside M.B.C.* [1977] A.C. 1014.

[5] Education Act 1944, s.99. This is so drastic a measure that it has never been used in England, and only once in Scotland. See Freeman, L.A.G. Bulletin, March 1980, p. 64.

[6] Housing Act 1980, s.23(1). The Secretary's use of this power was upheld by the Court of Appeal in *R.* v. *Secretary of State for the Environment, ex p. Norwich C.C.* [1982] Q.B. 808.

[7] Police (Grant) Order 1966, S.I. 1966/223, as amended, Article [*sic*] 2.

[8] Steedman (1984), p. 26.

bound up with the working of the Inspectorate, created in 1856 as the Home Secretary's eyes and ears in determining whether particular forces had reached the level of efficiency necessary to qualify for central funds. The early inspectors used their position as gatekeepers to the Exchequer to encourage construction of lockups and other improvements they thought desirable.[9]

The police grant is perhaps the major survivor of an earlier era of central-local financial relations, in which grants in aid were standard practice and local authority expenditure was subject to pervasive central control.[10] Since the Local Government Act 1958, the trend has been toward greater local autonomy, with grants earmarked for specified purposes being replaced by block grants to be allocated as the recipient authority determines. Even the constrictive controls of recent years, which have been directed at the size of total spending, have not sought to reverse this trend. Critchley, writing in 1978, reported that threat of withholding grant had been made on average once every two years since the war, but the power has never actually been invoked.[11] Although there is an analogous general provision which enables the Environment Secretary to reduce rate support grant where a local authority has failed to carry out *any* of its functions to a reasonable standard, it is used, not as a direct threat, but as the basis of central government "advice" to local authorities on a range of matters.[12] The grant is thus a more important instrument of central control with respect to police than to any other service. It is also one which a police authority is peculiarly ill-placed to resist. It could not replace the lost sums, which would amount to millions of pounds even for the smallest authority, because the rate increase involved would be politically suicidal in itself and also might well result in the imposition of ratecapping or additional financial penalties.[13] It could only maintain its resistance to the Home Secretary's wishes if it were prepared to scale down its operations by fifty per cent. To put it at its lowest, it would take a very determined authority in a

[9] *Ibid.* pp. 26–27 and 38–41.

[10] Garner and Jones (1985), p. 376.

[11] Critchley, *op. cit.* pp. 193–194; Gange interview. A conflict of evidence exists on this point. Brogden (1982), p. 112 reports that 1965 was the last time withdrawal of grant was threatened, and that on 17 occasions since 1922 (presumably up to the War) it was actually withheld.

[12] Local Government Act 1974, s.5; Garner and Jones, *op. cit.* p. 391, see n. 1.

[13] On one reading of the *GLC Fares* case, *R.* v. *Greater London Council, ex p. Bromley L.B.C.* [1982] 2 W.L.R. 62, such a rate increase might be held to be a breach of the authority's fiduciary duty if challenged by a ratepayer, though most probably only if it resulted in a loss of rate support grant.

political position of virtual invulnerability to accept this conse-quence. It is thus finance, rather than legal powers of compulsion, that is the most potent weapon possessed by central government.

Of the powers which the Secretary of State does possess, much the most important is that of making regulations concerning the "government, administration and condition of service of police forces".[14] Acquisition of this power—which he possessed over county forces from their inception but which was only extended to borough forces until 1919—was a major step in curtailing local autonomy and imposing uniform practices throughout the country. It is valuable because it prevents any force from exploiting its con-stables by paying poor wages or insisting upon onerous conditions of work, given that they are barred by law from going on strike[15]; it also ensures a necessary common standard of discipline. Yet there is a vital difference, which has never been properly recog-nised, between maintaining minimum standards and insisting upon rigid uniformity. The former is necessary to prevent an unaccept-able deterioration in the quality of service provided, the standards of conduct required and the conditions offered to employees. Above all it is necessary to ensure that the freedoms of political or social minorities in a particular locality are not trampled upon in the name of ruthless populist majoritarianism.

However, this is a far cry from saying that variations based upon local needs or policy preferences should not be permitted. For example, the current uniform pay scales, rank and promotion cri-teria make it impossible for a police authority to reward those con-stables who perform particularly well as community policemen with extra pay or promotion. Like every other bureaucracy, the police suffer from the absurdity that anyone who does well in deal-ing with the public can only improve his living standard by doing something else, usually administrative and quite possibly less well. A force which wishes to encourage and reward community polic-ing skills ought to be able to offer pay increases over the maximum scale rate for a P.C. and/or promotion based on good performance in this field, without need to satisfy the standard criteria. It may also wish to impose additional probationary conditions, such as

---

[14] S.33 (1). Sub-section 2 contains a long though not exhaustive list of matters to be covered by this power.

[15] There is no provision explicitly prohibiting a constable from striking. Instead, the result is reached by a combination of the effects of s. 47 of the Police Act 1964, barring trade union membership; s. 53, which makes it a criminal offence to induce or attempt to induce a constable to withdraw his labour; and provisions of the Discipline Code requiring obedience to lawful orders. See Morris (1983), pp. 71–72.

absence of behaviour and attitudes that give rise to a reasonable inference of racial discrimination or prejudice.[16]

These are merely examples. The important point is that the present structure of centrally-imposed uniformity is unnecessarily inflexible and prevents desirable local initiatives. Yet it would also be wrong to advocate complete local autonomy. We shall repeatedly return to this critical issue in police governance: how to maintain the balance between central and local control that makes use of what is most valuable in each.

The Home Secretary may also require a report from a chief constable on any policing matter.[17] Such requests are frequently made, often in response to questions in the House of Commons. Thus although the Secretary of State is not formally responsible for provincial policing in the same way as he is for the Metropolitan Police, M.P.s can at least indirectly raise complaints about practices in their constituencies. However, since the reports are never made public, neither the M.P. nor those dissatisfied may know whether their representations have had any effect. Less frequent is use of the power under section 32 to set up a local inquiry into policing matters in a given area. It was under this provision that Lord Scarman's report on the Brixton riots was commissioned, and also his report on the Red Lion Square demonstration in which one student died.[18] Setting up such an inquiry is entirely within the Secretary's discretion and where he remains adamant in his refusal to do so—as with the policing of the Southall demonstration in April 1979 in which Blair Peach was killed—nothing can be done. There may be dispute about when a section 32 inquiry is appropriate; Merlyn Rees was of the view that it should only be used "to look at a whole area, not just a specific incident," yet it is precisely those sorts of controversial incidents involving claims of serious misconduct, as at Southall or at the Manchester University demonstration against Home Secretary Leon Brittain and alle-

---

[16] Racially discriminatory conduct is now an offence under the Discipline Code (see Police and Criminal Evidence Act 1984, s.101(1)(b) and the Police (Discipline) Regulations 1985, S.I. 1985/518, Sched. 1, para. 9 made thereunder), but must be proven in the normal way, beyond a reasonable doubt. (See further Chap. 9). An authority with a large ethnic minority population might well decide to impose a more rigorous standard than simply absence of a proven complaint of discriminatory behaviour on its probationer constables, perhaps based on evaluation of a senior officer (Chief Inspector or above) after informal consultation with community representatives.

[17] Police Act 1964, s.30(1).

[18] Cmnd. 5919 (1975).

gations of subsequent police persecution of the demonstrators,[19] where the need for a section 32 inquiry is greatest. Internal investigations, even if conducted by officers of another force, will be seen as rigged by those aggrieved, and the issues are sufficiently grave to merit evaluation by a person of stature and indisputable independence.

Working Relationships

The key paradox is that, whilst the Home Office exercises enormous influence over policing, it does so without directly infringing the independence of chief constables, which it genuinely respects. As one civil servant remarked, "It would be a sad day when chief constables could no longer tell the Home Office to get lost." Yet the fact that direct command is never used does not mean that influence is not exerted. Perhaps the most important instrument is the Circular—a form of regulation in public law which deserves more study than it has received,[20] which because it is not technically subordinate legislation, receives no Parliamentary scrutiny. Indeed, circulars concerning police matters are often not publicly available, nor sent to libraries that can otherwise receive all government documents. They are nevertheless treated as though they were binding law by chief constables, even though they are no more than strong declarations of government policy. This was illustrated most poignantly by the aftermath of the shooting of a constable by a bank robber in Essex in August 1984. In the previous year, following the shooting of an unarmed victim of mistaken identity, Steven Waldorf, by two Metropolitan Police detectives, the Home Office issued Circular 47/83 on the circumstances of issuance and use of firearms by police. After the later incident, the Chief Constable of Essex publicly complained that the guidelines in the Circular put his men in an impossible pos-

---

[19] See *The Guardian*, July 22, 1985, for a report of the evidence submitted to an unofficial inquiry into police conduct in these matters established by Manchester City Council and chaired by Mr. John Platts-Mills Q.C. An unofficial inquiry, chaired by Professor Michael Dummett, a philosopher, produced the only coherent public account of the events surrounding the death of Blair Peach.

[20] Its use is not of course limited to policing and in some areas, notably education and the National Health Service, it is a major instrument of government policy. For over a decade, for example, the sole official expression of the policy of creating comprehensive schools was a D.E.S. circular.

The Home Office also issues what are termed "Guidelines" to the police, which are publicly available and may be accompanied by a press release. An example is the Guidelines on the work of Special Branches, issued in December 1984.

ition, because it required them not to shoot until fired upon.[21] What made this response so extraordinary was, first, that the chief constable had simply misread the Circular, which contained no such requirement,[22] and, secondly, that he nonetheless felt bound to instruct his force to follow it, notwithstanding his objections. The idea that he could assert his independence as a chief constable and ignore the Circular seems never to have occurred to him.

One reason for the attitude of chief constables towards Circulars may be that they are often the product of a process of consultation which may range broadly or narrowly but will invariably include solicitation of the views of the Association of Chief Police Officers (A.C.P.O.), which includes all chief constables. Indeed, they may result from working parties which include Home Office officials and A.C.P.O. representatives. The process of decision is often a sort of loop circuit, and a document which has the imprimatur of both the Home Office and A.C.P.O. is one only the most strong-willed chief constable could resist.

Some Circulars, however, may signal a firm Home Office policy which, though not interfering with specific "operational" matters, determines a general approach or ethos and is expected to be followed uniformly. Much the most important example is Circular 114/83 on manpower, efficiency and economy in the police service. This was a clear statement that, after years of expansion of numbers and unparalleled open-handedness in making funds available for various technological devices, the police would have to operate under the same financial constraints that had long applied to other services. A new management style was ordained, value for money became the watchword, and senior police officers were told to give priority to ensuring that their limited funds were spent in the most cost effective way. They were also enjoined to set specific goals for their forces each year, and to monitor their attainment.

The mechanism by which the message of this Circular was disseminated, its impact monitored and assistance with compliance given, was and is the Inspectorate of Constabulary. It is this body which occupies the critical space between central government, chief constables and, on occasion, police authorities. Although its statutory function is sparsely described as inspecting and reporting

---

[21] *The Times*, August 24, 1984.
[22] Para. 6 of the circular states only that, unless impracticable, a warning should be given to the intended target before a firearm is used.

to the Secretary of State on the efficiency of provincial forces[23] it is in fact the lynchpin of the tripartite structure.[24] It is simultaneously the eyes and ears of the Home Office, a conduit for disseminating its policies, a repository of advice for chief constables, headhunter of the next generation of police leaders, and the major source of professional advice to civil servants. The seven inspectors are all former chief constables of high professional reputation, thus able to speak with chief constables on at least an equal footing. Their standing as individuals has become increasingly important in recent years, as chief constables have decreased in number and increased in power, eminence and prominence of public visibility. Their annual visits to each force, the culmination of considerable and regular communication, involve the application of a series of questions under twenty four topic headings which reflect Home Office concerns, which themselves may alter year by year. Although technically the purpose of the inspection is to ensure that the force can be certified "efficient" so as to remain eligible for grant, in fact this regulatory function is a residual concern. Save where resistance to amalgamations was involved, withdrawal of grant has never even been threatened in the post-war era. It is the shaping and co-ordination of policing practice throughout the country that is the Inspectorate's dominant role. However, although its expertise commands considerable influence, the policies it promotes, and the ends it serves, are ultimately those of the Home Office.

In so doing it may in effect compel chief constables to organise their forces in a particular way, or adopt priorities they might not have chosen themselves. An example is found in the Annual Report of the chief HMI for 1984, which stated, "Chief Constables have also been advised that HM Inspectors of Constabulary will place increased emphasis on the work of their drug squads during future inspections."[25] This forecloses the possibility that a chief constable might decide that a special drug squad was unnecessary in his area, or that its work was not one of his major emphases. However sensible HMI's priorities may be, they clearly make sub-

---

[23] Police Act 1964, s.38(2). Sub-section (3) also enjoins the inspectorate to "carry out such other duties for the purpose of furthering police efficiency" as the Home Secretary may direct.

[24] No systematic study of the inspectorate has been undertaken. The only available printed material is a brief though useful handout it produces, plus the Chief HMI's Annual Reports, published as House of Commons Papers.

[25] H.C. 469 (1985), para. 1.19.

stantial inroads on the supposedly sacrosanct independence of the chief constable.

The Inspectorate may also serve as the line of communication of messages from the Home Office to chief constables that are not meant for public consumption. During the miners' strike, for example, it was the Inspectorate which made it clear that there would be no limit to the resources central government would make available to ensure that the picketing was "adequately" policed. It also disseminated the warning, almost certainly erroneous,[26] that a working miner whose access to work was blocked by pickets might successfully bring an action against the police force for the area, to ensure that he received the assistance necessary to gain entrance to the workplace.

One unsatisfactory aspect of the Inspectorate's work is its relationship with the police authority. In those relatively infrequent instances where there is a political dispute between the authority and its chief constable, it would feel bound to support the latter, at least publicly. Although inspectors during their visits are willing to discuss their general evaluation with authority members—a facility that it not always taken up—their reports are never made available to the authority. The basic reason for this is that they contain evaluations not always flattering of the chief constable and his assistants, and the Inspectorate do not trust councillors to respect their confidentiality. Clearly a shift in the balance of governance towards localism will require a significant change of attitude on the part of the Inspectorate if its expertise is to be put to effective use.

The other actor on this rather crowded stage meriting mention is the Association of Chief Police Officers (A.C.P.O.). Some have seen this organisation as a tremendous and undesirable influence,[27] whilst others have been more sceptical.[28] Here it is necessary to distinguish between its role in relation to central government and to public debate. A.C.P.O. clearly has an important influence on policy formulation, since it is automatically consulted on relevant issues and is assured of a place on working parties. To some extent this is both inevitable and desirable, since the views of the most senior police officers on such matters

---

[26] See the analysis of the courts' approach to attempts to compel chief constables to allocate their manpower resources in a manner requested by the plaintiff; above, pp. 66–67.

[27] A great deal was heard about A.C.P.O. during the campaign against the 1984 Act and during the miners' strike. Brogden (1982), Chap. 6, presents the most fully developed statement of this view.

[28] Particularly Kettle (1985), pp. 31–32.

obviously should command a serious hearing, and some formal mechanism for their articulation is convenient for everyone. Much more questionable is its overtly political role as a lobbying organisation, attempting to influence legislation and public debate, invariably to urge ever-greater police powers. This is a relatively recent development, and part of the emergence in the 1970s of the police as a political pressure group, a constitutional innovation of great significance.[29] However, it is not a case of what A.C.P.O wants, A.C.P.O. gets; the final version of the P.C.E.A. 1984 fell well short of what it sought, and the right of constables to legal representation in disciplinary hearings was granted despite its opposition. Moreover, it is never certain that a position taken by A.C.P.O. will be accepted by all chief constables. Former Home Secretary Merlyn Rees deprecated its influence because "a lot of Chief Constables take no notice of A.C.P.O."[30]

The position of A.C.P.O. became particularly controversial during the miners' strike because of its relation to the National Reporting Centre.[31] This organisation, housed in New Scotland Yard, co-ordinated the movement of constables sent on mutual aid from all around the country to the centres of large-scale picketing.[32] Though liaising closely with the Home Office public order desk and the Chief Inspector of Constabulary, the N.R.C. was throughout the strike under the direction of successive presidents of A.C.P.O. That such power should rest in the hands of the representative of an organisation with no statutory existence, who took decisions with major implications for policing in both receiving and sending areas independent of any democratic authority, central or local, is constitutionally unprecedented and cannot be justified in a democratic polity. It has emerged, however, not from a police conspiracy against democracy but because the Home Office established the structure which uses A.C.P.O. in this way. The N.R.C. was established after mass picketing forced the closure of the Saltley coke depot in 1972 because the Home Office was determined that never again would inability to assemble the requisite manpower result in what it saw as a "defeat" for law and

---

[29] Described fully in Kettle (1980) and Reiner (1983). Its implications are discussed below, pp. 168–169.

[30] On the other hand, some treat it with great respect. One chief constable told me that if he received an A.C.P.O. recommendation on some particular matter, he would feel bound to follow it even if he personally disagreed with it, because it represented the collective judgment of chief constables.

[31] Kettle (1985), *passim* gives a good account of this body.

[32] See the following chapter for a detailed study of mutual aid.

order.[33] In the absence of a truly national police force—one actively directed by an arm of central government—*some* person or organisation would obviously be needed to take charge of co-ordinating the movement of thousands of men. The principle of politically responsible government would dictate that the task be entrusted to the Home Secretary, acting through his civil servants, but that solution would fall foul of the traditions of locally-based policing and would thrust the manner of policing the picketing onto the centre stage of political controversy, thus undermining the myth of the apolitical nature of policing. Some may regard these consequences as desirable, but that is not a view the Home Office could be expected to take. Hence, placing the running of the N.R.C. in the hands of the president of A.C.P.O. gets the Home Office off the political and ideological hook, whilst ensuring achievement of the end it seeks. The constitutional objections to this manoeuvre are compelling, but reducing the power of A.C.P.O. in this respect can only be done as part of a general con-sideration of the balance of local and central power over police matters, a question pursued in detail in Chapter 10.

A.C.P.O. also plays a major role in law enforcement practice. It drafts and publishes recommendations on a wide range of matters, such as the circumstances and procedure relating to checks on criminal records of potential jurors,[34] or the manner in which racial attacks are to be investigated. It is also involved in more contentious matters. During the trial of fourteen miners on charges of riot at the Orgreave coke plant—ending in the acquittal of all defendants—defence counsel quoted sections of a manual prepared by A.C.P.O. entitled "Public Order Tactical Oper-ations." According to the *Observer* account,[35] this document has been concealed from police authorities and not even shown to policemen below A.C.P.O. rank. Its suggestions for methods to control pickets include "running at the crowd in pairs to disperse and/or incapacitate," accurately described by counsel as an incite-ment to police officers to commit criminal offences.

The matter is worrying enough, but the manner raises the more

---

[33] Unfortunately Arthur Scargill interpreted the same incident as a great "victory" and seems to have assumed that mass picketing could be equally successful twelve years later. Moreover, as Reiner (1985a), p. 142 points out, it was not that the police were incapable of keeping the gates open at Saltley; a political decision was taken not to assemble the requisite numbers and use the necessary force. The Home Secretary, Reginald Maudling, believed this could be done, but with unacceptable long-term consequences for social stability.

[34] East (1985), pp. 525–526.

[35] *Observer*, July 21, 1985.

fundamental questions. Almost certainly the document was prepared after consultations with the Home Office, with whom A.C.P.O. always works in close liaison. Sending it out under the auspices of A.C.P.O. however, allows the Home Office to avoid direct responsibility and any resultant public outcry. It also furthers concealment from public view and yet again helps perpetuate the myth of the apolitical character of law enforcement. Blurring of responsibility becomes irresponsibility. The need for open public scrutiny and the location of the final determination of policing policy firmly in the hands of democratically elected bodies is made most clearly manifest in these circumstances.

A National Police Force?

During the miners' strike, there was a great deal of critical comment from the Left about the emergence and danger of a national police force, or, more precisely, of effective though not formal central government control of policing. A related charge was that the police had become overtly politicised, in the sense of becoming agents of the Government's policy of defeating the miners. The impression that has come through strongly in the course of the present research is that the critics were wrong. Chief constables, and senior police generally, are a crusty and independent lot who resent "interference" from any source. As one person interviewed put it, "They are no more sympathetic to Tory politicians than to Labour politicians, though they are to Tory policies." They genuinely believe that they are engaged in the non-political task of maintaining law and order, and suspect the motives of those who question this. For this reason, some are known to be unhappy about the Government's attempt to make law and order a political issue. Their close identification with the Government's position during the strike was, in the words of the same person, a case "of getting messages they wanted to hear." Thus, in practical terms it was irrelevant whether the National Reporting Centre was directed by A.C.P.O. or the Home Office, as each sought the same immediate ends, and would use the same technical means if thought efficient, though not necessarily for the same purposes.

The trouble of course is that policing is inescapably political, and a public servant's resentment of "interference" by elected representatives is experienced as, at best, professional arrogance and, at worst, political usurpation. And there remains a large unanswered question: what happens when the police get from the political authorities messages they do not want to hear? This raises the fundamental constitutional question, of designing institutions

of governance for law enforcement and order maintenance appropriate to a liberal democracy

of governance for law enforcement and order maintenance appropriate to the philosophy and practice of a liberal democracy. That issue is addressed in the final chapter.

Chapter 8

THE TRIPARTITE STRUCTURE:
THE CASE OF MUTUAL AID

The three-cornered relationship between the chief constable, the Home Office and the police authority is generally known as the "tripartite structure." The triangle so formed is not a structure well designed to take the heavy weight of conflict, as it depends upon there being a consensus between the participants about the extent of the others' responsibilities, and about the goals towards which all three are supposed to be working. In the words of a Home Office official, "the whole system depends upon everyone being reasonable." This is a fair reflection of the expectations of those who framed the legislation of the early 1960s, and of the way the system operated universally for the ensuing fifteen years or so, and in most places still operates. But what happens when "reasonableness" becomes an essentially contested concept, when, for example, one side adheres to a different set of political values than the others? These questions, and the legal uncertainties attending their solution, were highlighted with unprecedented clarity during the miners' strike of 1984–1985, particularly in relation to the controversies surrounding mutual aid. Mutual aid certainly presents its own special, and specially grave, problems, but it may be taken as a case study, for in many respects the problems are simply an intensified version of the issues that arise when consensus breaks down.

Although decisions about priorities and the deployment of manpower were an important element in the controversies, even more central was the question of finance. The control of police authorities over the expenditure of their force, and the role of central government in the subvention of provincial policing, are logically and statutorily quite distinct from the provisions governing mutual aid. However, during the strike they became intertwined in a way that was impossible to disentangle, and as that crisis was the first real test of the extent and utility of police authority financial powers, the two issues may profitably be discussed together.

The analysis in this chapter relies heavily for its factual base on the research of Sarah Spencer into the actions of police authorities during the strike.[1] It is not concerned with the rights and wrongs of

[1] Spencer (1985), pp. 34–53.

that dispute, nor even with the way it was policed. Its focus is directed solely to the question, who decides?

The fundamental issues can be put succinctly. First, what role if any does the police authority have in relation to inviting or sending constables to and from its area? In other words, can it make its voice heard in relation to mutual aid? Secondly, one of the few responsibilities clearly allocated to local bodies by the 1964 Act in section 8 is that of financial control. Subject to enumerated exceptions, approval of the county council or combined police authority is required before payment can be made out of the police fund, which must be kept separately from other council monies. When the chief constable's exercise of his power to direct his force leads him to take decisions with financial implications, can the police authority reverse that decision by virtue of its financial powers? As a supplementary to this—and the precise way the issue arose during the strike—even if it be accepted that the chief constable's powers extend to complete freedom to spend within the limits of the budget agreed with the authority, where does the power of decision lie when the two disagree about where cuts should be made when the budget limit is reached? A third question raising a different set of legal issues is what actions, if any, may be taken by the Home Secretary if he is dissatisfied with the manner in which the police authority exercises its financial powers? Finally, what role is there in this context for the Attorney General in his capacity as guardian of the public interest?

The Legal Structure of Mutual Aid

The police authority's statutory power in relation to mutual aid is if anything, even more attenuated than in ordinary policing matters. Mutual aid is the system under which a police force which needs additional manpower to cope with a particular emergency— usually a strike, demonstration, or riot, but the need may also arise through any unusual event, such as the Pope's visit—calls upon other forces to supply additional constables. The system first acquired a statutory basis in the Police Act 1890, which made police authorities responsible for any agreements.[2] When that Act was repealed in 1964, it was replaced by the current provisions which specify that the chief constable shall decide what assistance his force will provide at the request of another chief constable[3]

---

[2] Police Act 1890, s.25. This provided the statutory context for the *Glamorgan* case, discussed above, pp. 53–55.
[3] Police Act 1964, s.14(1).

whilst leaving it to their respective authorities to agree payment.[4] Moreover, if a chief constable were to refuse a colleague's request, the Home Secretary possesses the unusual though not unique power to order the chief constable to provide whatever assistance he determines.[5]

Thus the police authority has explicitly been deprived of any voice in the decisions whether, and to what extent, mutual aid should be requested or granted. It merely picks up the tab. Those chief constables who told their police authorities that they had no say in the disposition of their force during the strike were legally quite correct; all the authority could require was an ex *post facto* report.[6] Yet how are they to discharge their legal responsibility for the adequacy and efficiency of the police force for their area? There is no doubt that reported crime rose and detection rates fell substantially throughout the country during the strike, as communities watched their manpower being drained away a hundred miles or more. Training and community policing initiatives, which are highly labour intensive, were delayed or suspended.[7] An authority which cannot put a stop to measures which obviously impair the performance of its force cannot fulfil its legal duty. The Police Act has deprived it of the means to do so. The unprecedented scale and duration, and hence intensity of its effects, of the strike of 1984–1985 exposed inherent tensions and contradictions within the structure established by the Act. These previously had been concealed by the assumption that all elements in the tripartite structure would be pulling in the same direction.

Scope of the Authority's Financial Powers

Under the Act, a county council must, subject to three exceptions, approve all expenditure out of the police fund. This enables competition among priorities to be publicly debated and determined by councillors responsible for or concerned about the whole

---

[4] *Ibid.* s.14(4). This subsection also empowers the Home Secretary, in default of agreement between the two authorities, to determine the appropriate contribution owed by the receiving authority.

[5] *Ibid.* s.14(2). A similar power is found in s.13(5), permitting the Home Secretary to order a chief constable or police authority to enter into a collarboration agreement with another force.

[6] *Ibid.* s.12, discussed earlier at p. 78.

[7] See the survey of both effects conducted by the *Sunday Times* on September 23, 1984. An example from a specific police area, Thames Valley, is reported in the *Oxford Times,* July 6, 1984. H.M. Chief Inspector of Constabulary acknowledged the effect of the strike on training and policy initiatives, though not on crime rates, in his annual report for 1984: HC 469 (1985).

range of locally-provided services. In sharp contrast, no such constraints exist on combined police authorities, which are responsible only for policing and not subject to direct check by their
constituent councils. This absence of accountability to other councillors, over and above their remoteness from the electorate, is the
gravest defect of combined police authorities, for their unchalleng-
able decisions may result in forced cuts in other services or the
imposition of financial penalties by central government.

It should be noted, however, that the cost of policing to local
authorities is substantially less than with any other major service.[8]
The Home Office pays 50 per cent., and the remainder, included
in a council's total budget, attracts the normal rate support grant.
Assuming the latter is also 50 per cent., the local authority is
responsible for only one-quarter of the expenditure on its policing.
Viewed from a different angle, if it were not spending at the level
where penalties would attach, an extra pound on policing would
attract three from central government, whereas an equal amount
spent elsewhere would attract only one, and produce a total sum
only half as great. Whether this stimulates a more permissive
attitude towards proposed expenditure on policing is an empirical
question on which no research has been done, but at the least it
would seem there is substantially less disincentive to this form of
spending than any other.

The three exceptions to the requirement of prior council approval are where the expenditure is necessary to give effect to Regulations made under the Act, to satisfy a court judgment, or is
directed by an enactment.[9] These seemingly innocuous provisions
in fact remove the vast bulk of police expenditure from local control. Police salaries and pensions are negotiated nationally and
promulgated by the Home Office Regulations. Since nationally
over 85 per cent. of all provincial police expenditure comes under
this head,[10] the extent of local decision making is clearly quite
limited. Moreover, police salaries since 1979 have been governed
by the formula of the Edmund-Davies Report which guaranteed
inflation-proofed salaries,[11] a cushion enjoyed by no other public

---

[8] There are some specific expenditures that receive full grant in aid (for a list see
Garner and Jones (1985), pp. 376–378) and a few miscellaneous others, like
"immigrant assistance" grants under s.11 of the Local Government Act 1966,
which similarly receive double subvention from central government. But policing is the most heavily supported by central government of all the major items of
local authority expenditure.

[9] Police Act 1964, s.8(4)(a), (b) and (c), respectively.

[10] Report of H.M. Chief Inspector of Constabulary 1984, HC 469, para. 2.1.

[11] Committee on Training of the Police, Cmnd. 7283 (1979).

sector employees, and one which inevitably puts heavy pressure on the level of salaries a local authority can afford to pay teachers, social workers, environmental health officers and others who are increasingly being asked by the police to co-operate in a "multi-agency approach" to crime. Here again, national regulation produces a distortion of local priorities.

In exercising its powers under section 8, the police authority can exert as tight or as lax a control as it chooses. It can simply set an overall total for the chief constable to spend as he wishes, it may fix maxima for certain categories of expenditure and leave the particulars to his discretion, or it can specify that prior approval is required for expenditure on any item over a specified sum. The latter approach has been used by some authorities to prevent acquisition or replacement of certain equipment, particularly paramilitary hardware such as CS gas and plastic bullets. This financial power is allied to the authority's responsibility for provision of equipment for its force,[12] and however much a chief constable may claim this is an "operational" matter, that term, whatever it may mean, is not found in the statute. The authority's decision has not interfered with the "command and control" of the force, which is the realm of his statutory responsibility.

The financial powers may be used or extend the authority's influence still further. For example, a chief constable wanting to computerise the records his force has kept will, unless he has been given complete carte blanche, have to seek approval of his police authority either to spend money already allocated to the force generally or for supplementary funds. The authority, whilst recognising the value of computerisation for purposes of crime detection, may be concerned about misuse of the data, *e.g.* by giving access to private security firms staffed by retired policemen; about its reliability; or about whether some of the information has been collected as a form of persecution of the politically unpopular or of those who have criticised the police. It may therefore require the chief constable to accept certain restrictions or guiding principles to govern retention, collection and use of the data before agreeing to provide the funds.[13] One can imagine other instances—*e.g.* purchase of surveillance equipment or newly-developed anti-riot technology—where the financial power is virtually the only leverage

[12] Police Act 1964, s.4(4).

[13] This example is fairly close to what has in fact happened on Merseyside. As of writing, the police authority has refused to provide additional funds until the restrictions it thought the chief constable had accepted were honoured. My information about this question derives from a conversation with Margaret Simey, chairwoman of the authority.

the authority presently can use to try to ensure that very important interests and values are protected. This is not to assume that senior police officers will always be insensitive to the kinds of consideration the authority might wish to raise,[14] but like any occupation or profession, they are bound to put their own immediate job-related concerns first, and to assume that civil liberties questions are secondary.

The major difficulty with this back-door approach to influencing policing policies is that there exists no satisfactory mechanism to ensure that the police live up to their side of the agreement. The police committee can complain and publicise violations, but in the absence of powers to discipline or dismiss, words are its only weapon once the money has been granted. It could of course approve the expenditure only in stages, subject to performance monitoring, deny funds for further development in the event of non-compliance, or threaten to refuse future unrelated financial requests. However, institutionalised suspicion or bluff and counter-bluff are hardly to be commended as the best methods of ensuring open and effective review and implementation of important policies.

The supposedly co-ordinated powers of chief constables and police authorities came into head-on conflict during the miners' strike. The strategy chosen to police the dispute in all localities meant that a massive number of police gathered at any pit with a substantial presence of pickets.[15] Several forces were affected, but the main areas—Nottinghamshire, Derbyshire, South and West Yorkshire—could only maintain that strategy with the help of thousands of reinforcements. Nearly every force in England and Wales

---

[14] Or that the authority will always be more sensitive to them; many will not.

[15] I do not mean this statement to be tendentious or a hit-and-run criticism. It is the case, however, that compared with the policing of earlier industrial disputes, for example the steel strike of 1980–1981, the police more clearly identified themselves with the employer, for instance by operating from inside the picketed areas, which they had never previously done. Similarly unprecedented was the use of literally thousands of constables to accompany lone individuals across picket lines, as occurred at Cortonwood in November 1984 (Reiner, 1985a, p. 146). This supported the Coal Board's strategy of breaking the strike by financial attrition. I do not suggest that in earlier strikes picketing would have gone uncontrolled, but the abandonment of the previous policy of visible neutrality, and of any notion of manpower and other resource capacity as a limit to the commitment to policing the pickets, were a real departure from past practice. These points are made in the final report of the independent group, initially established under the auspices of the N.C.C.L., on the policing of the strike. I am grateful to Dr. Sarah McCabe, a member of this group, for the benefit of her insights into these matters, which I have found wholly persuasive.

sent men[16] to Nottinghamshire and South Yorkshire. Mutual aid is expensive, for both sending and receiving authorities, and the unprecedented, and unforeseen, scale of the operations meant that every area had major additional expense. Without going into the intricacies of the different classifications of mutual aid and the implications for sending and receiving authorities of each,[17] even authorities far removed from the dispute had to find very large sums, primarily for overtime, both for the men sent and those who had to cover for them at home. Millions of pounds were involved: the Home Secretary, after months of havering with various authorities, agreed to pay all expenses over three quarters of a penny rate. For the West Midlands, for example, this still meant raising £3 million.[18] Chief constables insisted that police must be provided; some authorities insisted that they could not afford the provision. Many found themselves placed in an intolerable predicament. The extra expenditure might bring them up against Department of Environment financial penalties, and in the case of authorities already visited with that affliction, the possibility of rate-capping might then arise. Hence considerable pressure developed to cut expenditure elsewhere, either from the police budget or from other services. The prospect that education or the caring services, already subject to years of financial stasis if not actually decline, should be further debilitated because of an industrial dispute aroused great bitterness, particularly in deprived areas unconnected with it. Hence the police budget became even more obviously the place to search for the necessary savings. It was at that point that three issues came to prominence.

The first was the peculiar position of councils served by a force covering more than one county. As has been seen[19] a combined police authority is wholly independent of any of its constituent councils, to which it simply issues mandatory precepts after formulating a budget. Thus when the Thames Valley police were granted an additional £500,000 for overtime payments, Oxfordshire County Council were landed with a bill for £74,000 with no apparent way of raising the money that would not result in government penalties and further revenue loss.[20] Possibly because voters and

---

[16] Women are not sent on mutual aid duty, nor are CID officers.

[17] There are three levels of classification of mutual aid, set out in Home Office Circular 134/73. The implications of the classifications for particular authorities during the strike are set out by Spencer, *op.cit.*, pp. 37 *et seq.*

[18] Details of the various positions taken by the Home Secretary, and of the cost to the authorities involved, are found in Spencer, *op.cit.* pp. 36–39.

[19] Above, pp. 81–82.

[20] *Oxford Times*, September 28, 1984.

ratepayers do not understand the separateness of the police authority and the council they elect, there has been surprisingly little
protest from these areas, which are the most effectively disenfran-
chised in Britain relating to policing.

Matters did, however, become very contentious in other police
authorities, particularly those where financial stress, antipathy to
police conduct on the picket lines and sympathy for the aims of the
strikers were combined. The best-known instance was that of
South Yorkshire, whose attempts to limit its expenditure raised
but did not resolve two important constitutional issues.

One concerns the powers of the Home Secretary in relation to
the police authority. At one stage, the police authority asked its
chief constable to present a list of priorities for cuts. He suggested
manpower reductions, which went contrary to the county council's
policy of no redundancies. As part of a package which included
late recruitment of civilians, reduction in the number of police
vehicles and deferral of repairs to premises, the authority
announced its intention to eliminate one half of the dog section,
and the entire mounted section, which had been involved in the
televised charge into the picket line at Orgreave coke plant. The
RSPCA remained silent, but the Home Secretary threatened to
take the matter to court. In fact the announcement was part of a
chess game whose object was to put pressure on the government to
meet with the authority's representatives and increase its contribution to the cost of mutual aid. This strategy was successful to the
extent that the authority decided it could avoid major cuts and the
issue faded away.[21]

The intriguing question is the basis on which the Home Secretary thought he could sue. Although he has a statutory responsibility for the efficiency of policing generally, that responsibility
does not *add* to his statutory powers, which are specifically enumerated.[22] None of these powers gives him control of the finances,
establishment or equipment of local forces—all of which are explicitly the responsibility of the police authority.[23] He could of course
declare that a threatened cut would jeopardise a force's efficiency
and threaten to withhold its grant, but that would hardly be an
effective device when his aim is to maintain the force's repressive
capacity. In the specific instance, the Home Secretary's threat to
take legal action may also have been a bit of bluff, but the more
general conclusion is that it was one he was fortunate not to have

---

[21] Spencer, *op.cit.* pp. 40–41.
[22] Police Act 1964, s.28 above, p. 100.
[23] By ss.8, 4(2), and 4(4) respectively of the 1964 Act.

had called. It may well be that the Home Office reached the same conclusion, because having threatened to sue Nottinghamshire Police Authority when it stated it would leave the Regional Crime Squad to save money, it did nothing when the authority persisted.[24]

To judge from the comments of an assistant secretary in the police department, the stance of the Home Office (though not necessarily of its political masters) during this protracted saga reflected its traditional conception of the tripartite structure. He thought that a "sensible" police authority and a "sensible" chief constable "would sit down together and determine where the least dangerous cuts can be made." He added that whilst it would "take a lot" for the Home Office to get involved in a police authority decision to cut expenditure, "the South Yorkshire horses are considered to be quite a lot"—presumably because of their use in controlling large-scale picketing.

Yet another incident illustrated the boundaries of the Home Office view of its proper activity.[25] One of the steps taken by Greater Manchester police authority to lessen its financial burden was to order the disbandment of the force band, which it discovered to its amazement consisted of a substantial number of full-time officers. The chief constable regarded this direction as an encroachment on his domain of command, but abandoned his resistance after the Home Office refused to support him. Its view, apparently, was that the band was not an "operational" matter, and therefore outside the legitimate sphere of the chief constable's autonomy, or conversely, within the legitimate sphere of the police authority's powers. Whatever one may think of this view, it seems deeply ingrained and adhered to with consistency.

The second issue arose in an earlier episode in the South Yorkshire negotiations. The authority had instructed the chief constable to obtain its prior approval for all expenditure within its jurisdiction. He complied, and requested payment of various housing and related costs of constables from other forces on picket duty. The authority refused to pay, and sent the requests to the Home Office. The next day, the Attorney General initiated legal action, which again was aborted when the Government accepted greater responsibility both for immediate payments and future mutual aid expenses, and the authority agreed to pay the bills.[26]

---

[24] Spencer, *op.cit.* pp. 39–40.
[25] The ensuing discussion is based on an interview with Mrs. Gabrielle Cox, chairwoman of the Greater Manchester Police Authority.
[26] Spencer, *op.cit.* pp. 40–42.

The Attorney General stands on a very different footing from the Home Secretary. He is the legal embodiment of the Crown's traditional, presumably inherent, power of *parens patriae*, from which has been deduced a sort of roving commission to ensure the protection of public rights.[27] Consequently he has been granted virtually limitless access to the courts to correct misuse of powers of public authorities. In precise terms this means ensuring that they have not acted *ultra vires*. Most of the cases, which date from the early years of this century, seem to involve determination of whether they have exceeded the precise wording of their powers.[28] To adopt Lord Diplock's useful classification of the heads of judicial review,[29] they present the question of "illegality," or incorrect understanding of the law governing the decision maker's powers. In the present context, this could only mean that a refusal to approve particular expenditure was an interference with the chief constable's power of command and control of the force, or that it was a failure of the authority to exercise its powers to maintain an adequate and efficient force.

On the first interpretation, it is difficult to see what public rights are involved. The person affected is the chief constable, and it is doubtful whether anyone but he could bring legal action to vindicate his powers under section 5 of the 1964 Act. In any case, to hold that a refusal to approve expenditure infringed section 5 would be both to nullify the police authority's financial powers under section 8 and hand each chief constable a blank cheque for all aspects of his force's work. The structure of the legislation cannot sustain this interpretation.

The second point would, as has already been noted,[30] require the courts to decide what constituted an adequate and efficient force. This seems a determination of a character at once technical and value-laden and hence highly unsuitable for an inexpert and politically detached body to make. It would be quite wrong to rely on the evidence of purported experts, such as an Inspector of Constabulary, because although neither political appointees nor civil servants as such, the inspectors are perhaps the most important

---

[27] For a thorough analysis, see de Smith (1980), pp. 432–33 and 450–55 and Edwards (1964), pp. 286–292.

[28] Notably *L.C.C.* v. *Att.-Gen.*, [1902] A.C. 165 and *Att.-Gen.* v. *Fulham Corpn.* [1921] 1 Ch. 440.

[29] Presented in *Council of Civil Services Unions* v. *Minister for Civil Service* [1984], 3 W.L.R. 1174, 1196.

[30] Above pp. 84–85.

mechanism for influencing provincial forces to adopt Home Office policy.[31] Though their expressed opinions would no doubt be honestly held, their position makes it impossible to treat them as impartial experts in a suit brought by a member of the Government. Moreover, where the decision challenged is one to reduce expenditure, it is obvious that some aspect of the organisation's performance will suffer to some degree. The extent of the injury may possibly though doubtfully be treated as a matter on which a factual judgment, or prediction, may be made, but which area can be sacrificed with the most bearable damage—the question of priorities—is precisely the "balancing exercise" of weighing competing policy considerations that Lord Diplock identified as the hallmark of non-justiciable questions.[32] It therefore seems that a decision like that provisionally taken by the South Yorkshire Authority could not be challenged on grounds of illegality.

The other head of judicial review that must be considered is that of "irrationality" or "*Wednesbury* unreasonableness."[33] This may be broken down into two categories. The first is what might be called the primary *Wednesbury* criteria, of failing to take account of relevant considerations or taking account of irrelevant ones in reaching a decision. If it could be shown that the decision to sell the horses was taken in retaliation for their use against the Orgreave pickets—not because the authority believed that they were unnecessary and intimidatory, but because its members were sympathetic to the picketing and were alarmed at the effectiveness of the horses as a legitimate means of crowd control—then an action by the Attorney General would, on commonly recognised principles, be entitled to succeed. Additionally, the equally well-settled principle that decisions taken for improper or ulterior purposes are unlawful would support his case, as indeed would the invalidity of decisions taken in bad faith, if that is an independent category.[34] Everything, of course, would turn on bitterly disputed factual questions of intention and purpose—the authority would obviously explain its actions on quite a different basis.

More worrisome is the possible invocation of what may be termed the residual *Wednesbury* test, that of something "so

---

[31] Above, pp.106–108.

[32] *Council of Civil Service Unions* v. *Minister for Civil Service* [1984] 3 W.L.R. 1174, 1197.

[33] This again is Lord Diplock's terminology, above n. 29. The reference of course is to *Associated Provincial Picture Houses* v. *Wednesbury Corpn.* [1948], 1 K.B. 223, *per* Lord Greene M.R.

[34] Wade (1982), pp. 395–397 casts doubt on whether bad faith is a separate head of invalidity.

124 *The Tripartite Structure: the Case of Mutual Aid*

unreasonable that no reasonable authority could ever have come to it"[35] or in Lord Diplock's reformulation, a decision "so outrageous in its defiance of logic or accepted moral standard that no sensible person who had applied his mind to the question to be decided could have arrived at it."[36] It would require a long article on the evolution of administrative law to evaluate whether this category, originally understood as a very rare longstop, has gained ground in recent years as more highly charged issues have found their way into the courts. Unfortunately, in the inflammatory circumstances of the miners' strike, with the strikers identified by the Prime Minister as "the enemy within," one cannot be confident that the courts would have refrained from assuming that their "moral standard" and "logic" were definitive, and, moreover, that these consisted of supporting whatever the police and Home Secretary thought appropriate. The judgment of the Lord Chief Justice, upholding unprecedentedly restrictive bail conditions imposed on persons arrested for picketing offences—despite absence of any evidence that most of the individuals thus restricted had engaged in violence and in effect rewriting the law to make mass picketing illegal— indicates that decisions based on precisely such assumptions were a real possibility.[37] This prospect is a compelling objection to the breadth of judicial power opened up by the residual *Wednesbury* test, an objection not limited to the area of police governance.

The danger of judicial usurpation of political decisions is exacerbated by the fact that the Attorney General need not even incur the political opprobrium caused by his inevitable identification with government policy, of bringing such an action. He need only grant his fiat to enable a ratepayer to bring a relator action, and in such politically highly-charged circumstances there would be no shortage of litigants. Indeed it is not even certain whether the Attorney General's fiat is required; it is possible that a ratepayer might proceed via an application for judicial review, subject to leave of the court.[38]

---

[35] *Associated Provisional Picture Houses Ltd.* v. *Wednesbury Corpn.* [1948] 1 K.B. 223, 229–230.

[36] *Council of Civil Service Unions* v. *Minister for the Civil Service* [1984] 3 W.L.R. 1174, 1196.

[37] *R.* v. *Mansfield J.J., ex p. Sharkey* [1984] 3 W.L.R. 1328.

[38] Wade, *op.cit.* pp. 530–533 at 590 suggests that this route may be available to the private litigant.

Conclusion

The tripartite structure is a very lopsided thing. The miners' strike exposed almost cruelly the powerlessness of police authorities to carry out their statutory duties. If power without responsibility is the prerogative of the harlot, responsibility without power is the prerogative of the eunuch. Taken with the long term steady flow of power to central government, and the growing importance, stature and political prominence of chief constables, the diminution of the police authority has radically reshaped, not to say badly distorted, the structure over the past two decades. It is now necessary to redesign that structure with emphasis on rebuilding two elements which have been allowed to deteriorate badly: democracy and localism. This is considered in the final chapter.

Chapter 9

CONTROLLING POLICE MISCONDUCT

Most of the analysis presented so far has looked at policing in relation to policies and institutions. This is inevitable when policing is considered as a matter of public law and government, of the structures through which state power is exercised. However, most people aggrieved at specific police conduct or critical of the police generally do not do so for reasons of constitutional principle, or even of disagreement with a particular practice, but because they or someone they know have been treated by a constable in a manner they feel involved injustice or abuse of power. In any encounter with a member of the public, the unstated possibility of the use of force is always in the background, for the legitimate use of violence on behalf of the state is what makes the police unique as an institution of government.[1] The potential for abuse of power felt directly and immediately by the victim is therefore particularly great, but one should not conclude either that the police are more likely than other agents of government to exceed their authority, or that the consequences of their doing so are necessarily worse.[2]

The discussion that follows assumes that a particular grievance or category of complaint is valid, *i.e.* that misconduct has in fact occurred. The police are of course highly vulnerable to false complaints, because discrediting them may deflect attention from or minimise the alleged victim's own criminality. That fact does not, however, imply that allegations of police misconduct by offenders should be deemed *prima facie* false, or that they formally or in practice require more substantive proof than where a "respectable" person is involved. Much police misconduct does indeed involve lawbreakers, but the judicial process exists to impose sanctions upon them and they do not otherwise forfeit their liberties. It simply means that the mechanisms for adjudicating misconduct must employ a process of fact-finding not unduly weighted in favour of either complainants or constables.

---

[1] Compare one of the leading sociological definitions of the "police mandate" (Bittner 1974, p. 18). This conception of the uniqueness of the police assumes, perhaps too readily, that the army is used only against foreigners, which has been largely true of twentieth century Britain, though not of course of the United Kingdom.

[2] This point is pursued further below, pp. 147–148.

The approach taken here to the problem of police misconduct is seriously incomplete. That is to say, it reflects the law's traditional emphasis on redress for the victim and punishment of the wrong-doer. This legal outlook is inherently negative, individualistic and orientated towards sanctions. Rewards and incentives, and measures devoted to altering misguided group values and solidari-ties which reinforce objectionable conduct are beyond its capabi-lites. It does not concern itself directly with the organisational context which stimulates misconduct.[3] Almost certainly the most effective way to reduce racism, brutality, falsification of evidence and what the Discipline Code calls generically "abuse of auth-ority" is for those in charge of the organisation to change its ethos and working atmosphere, career rewards and disincentives, so that its members come to identify their interests, individually and col-lectively, with the desired behaviour. Training and effective man-agement supervision to reinforce its strictures would be a central element in any reform strategy.

All of this has very little to do with the legal process, whose impact on organisational change is likely to be at best marginal. Nonetheless traditional legal methods serve important values. The victim of misconduct deserves compensation; it is neither just nor healing for him to learn that internal changes make it less likely in future that others will suffer similar ill treatment. Nor is it accept-able, as some commentators at times seem near to suggesting, that organisational changes be treated as wiping the slate clean in rela-tion to malefactors within it. If policemen who have committed acts which would result in members of the public having to pay compensation or to undergo significant punishment are in effect absolved from responsibility on the dual grounds of organisational pathology and the paramount importance of its cure, we will have dishonoured the fundamental value of equality before the law in its simplest, formal liberal sense that is at the heart of the rule of law. A liberal democratic state cannot accept such a rule without jeopardising its moral legitimacy, particularly when the institution involved is itself devoted to law enforcement.

The existing mechanisms for controlling police conduct span the full range of legal institutions. Private law contributes various actions in tort, which can be said to "control" police behaviour only in the attenuated sense that their existence may deter unlaw-ful conduct. This is an empirical question no one has researched,

---

[3] The concept of "organisational police deviance" (Shearing, 1981) is very useful in understanding police illegality, as is the related notion of an occupational sub-culture (Reiner, 1985, Chap. 3).

though there are good grounds for scepticism. At present, however, they are the only means by which compensation may be obtained. A second category may be called forensic: various ways in which the judicial process, usually in the context of criminal prosecution, allows the legality of police conduct to be adjudicated. Finally, there is the complaints and disciplinary procedures, which are largely internal to the police organisation, although the external element purportedly has recently been enlarged. There is a partial overlap between the last two in the influence of the Director of Public Prosecutions (D.P.P.).

However, permeating all of these is an innovation of potentially great significance introduced by the Police and Criminal Evidence Act 1984.

Codes of Practice

Codes of Practice are a relatively recent and increasingly popular form of sub-legislation. They now govern, or at least guide, areas of great importance, such as picketing and good employment practices under the Race Relations Act. These are now dwarfed in sheer volume, and perhaps constitutional gravity, by the codes issued under the 1984 Act.[4] Written by the Home Office after lengthy consultation and revision, they replace the Judges' Rules and cover a vastly wider field—detention, treatment and questioning of suspects, identification and search and seizure. Though there may be nice technical distinctions, in effect they are subordinate legislation which has been debated on the floor of the House of Commons and approved.[5]

What concerns the present study is less the substance of the Codes than their enforcement. They regulate in complex detail police performance in these areas, and include many restrictions on the use of their powers. To take one particularly important instance, the critical concept of "reasonable suspicion"—the legal prerequisite for a stop and search—in subject to five paragraphs of explanation which include the following:

> "Reasonable suspicion cannot be supported on the basis simply of a higher than average chance that the person has committed or is committing an offence, for example because he belongs to a group within which offenders of a certain kind

---

[4] P.C.E.A., s.66.

[5] The complete texts, together with useful commentary and discussion of the legislative background, may be found in Zander (1985), pp. 93–104, 261–308.

are relatively common, or because of a combination of factors such as these. For example, a person's colour of itself can never be a reasonable ground for suspicion. The mere fact that a person is carrying a particular kind of property or is dressed in a certain way or has a certain hairstyle is likewise not of itself sufficient. Nor is the fact that a person is known to have a previous conviction for unlawful possession of an article."[6]

Clearly the intention of this instruction is to warn officers against stops and searches based on racial bigotry or a generalised hostility to street people. It, and many provisions like it in the Codes, are a major improvement in the rules governing the treatment of people subject to police control.[7] The key issue is whether these rules will remain paper pronouncements only.

Unfortunately the Act's handling of the matter of enforcement is not wholly adequate. A police officer who fails to abide by the Code "shall be liable" to disciplinary proceedings: regulations provide that any Code violation is a disciplinary offence.[8] Provided that mid-level superiors—inspectors, chief inspectors and superintendents—are prepared to take the Codes seriously and insist that they be followed, this will be an important sanction in contexts where breach of the Code is apparent or readily detectable within the organisation. This may be particularly applicable to detention and questioning, although that will depend critically on the attitudes and responses of those persons designated custody officers and review officers under the Act.[9] Even here, however, invocation of disciplinary proceedings is wholly discretionary. Some discretion is unavoidable, because breaches may be trivial or the result of a misunderstanding of a provision due to faulty training, making disciplinary sanctions inappropriate. Nevertheless, the discretion can equally well be misused by superior officers either not committed to making the Code effective, or manipulat-

---

[6] Code of Practice for the Exercise of Powers of Stop and Search, para. 3. (Zander, op. cit. p. 304).

[7] Although Eldon Griffiths M.P., Parliamentary spokesman for the Police Federation, claimed during Standing Committee discussion of the Codes that they merely represent existing good practice: Official Report, Standing Comm. E, March 1, 1984, 43rd Sitting, col. 1567.

[8] P.C.E.A., s.67(8)

[9] P.C.E.A., ss.36–40. Although custody officers are required to have reached at least the rank of sergeant (s.36(3)), a constable of lower rank may perform his function if a custody officer is not available (s.36(4)). These are precisely the people likely to be most resistant to attempts to control overbearing practices in relation to detention and questioning.

ing it as an excuse to victimise an individual they dislike for other reasons. The worst abuses here might be avoided by a requirement that all decisions not to bring proceedings be reviewed by someone at least of the rank of Chief Superintendent.

A more important problem is that many, and perhaps the most serious, failures to follow the Codes or indeed the Act itself will occur in the presence of no one but the citizen and the officer(s) concerned. The disciplinary process can then only be set in motion by a formal complaint; in other words, enforcement of the Code stands or falls with the effectiveness of the complaints procedure generally. For reasons that will be set forth at some length,[10] this is open to serious question.

Even more murky are the forensic consequences of Code violations. In the Standing Committee debates on the Bill, the Home Office Minister in charge of its passage, Mr David Mellor, described the purpose of the Codes as providing "a clear touchstone against which performance of the police can be measured so that it can be put to officers and deployed in any aspect of a criminal case whether they have behaved properly and in accordance with a code which they are deemed to know and operate," and also protecting them from allegations of misconduct if they had complied with it.[11] The difficulty is determining what its "deployment" in a criminal—or indeed civil—case will actually mean. The statute simply says that any Code is admissible in evidence, and if its provisions seem "relevant" to any question arising during the proceedings, a court or tribunal shall "take it into account."[12] This must be read alongside the limited discretion in section 78, under which evidence can be excluded only if it affects the fairness of the proceedings.[13] This reinforces the conclusion that breach of any Code provision is not meant to result in exclusion of the evidence thereby obtained, although in a statement noteworthy for its opacity, the Minister seemed to suggest that a police officer's credibility in giving evidence against a defendant might somehow be diminished if he were shown to have violated the Code.[14] Presumably this means that whilst the evidence would be admitted, the fact of the violation may influence the jury against the prosecution emotionally. It would thus provide a sort of informal exclusionary practice based on lay persons' sense of appropriate police

[10] Below, pp. 146–150, 153–158.
[11] Offical Report, above, cols. 1539–1540
[12] P.C.E.A., s.67(11).
[13] Discussed below, pp. 143–146.
[14] Official Report, above, col. 1565.

conduct. Whether this in fact occurs would be well worth empirical study, although the methodological difficulties would be formidable, since the situation to be compared is one of absence of any Code and hence little possibility of alerting the jury to police misconduct.

The other possible effect of the Codes is in relation to civil actions. The Act states explicitly that breach of any Code does not of itself create civil (or criminal) liability.[15] Moreover, they govern matters to a depth and with a concern for good practice substantially in excess of the minimum standard that might emerge from the law of tort.[16] They also cover areas, such as identification parades, into which that law would probably never venture. Nonetheless, some activities, notably searching of premises and seizure of property, which are subject to the law of trespass[17] are also covered by a Code, and the relationship between the two is quite uncertain. Since breach of the Code is not itself actionable, it can only be "relevant" in so far as it alters or elucidates the existing torts. In an action for trespass to the person or goods, the trespass is generally admitted, but lawful exercise of statutory powers is pleaded as justification. If violation of a Code provision was "taken into account" as one element in determining legality, or indeed treated as automatically negativing legality, the scope for defence of such suits would be significantly narrowed. If the Codes are treated as modifying common law in this way, civil actions could become an increasingly effective influence on police behaviour.

Anything written about Codes of Practice under the 1984 Act must inevitably be couched in the conditional tense. Analytically and practically, they can be examined from two distinct perspectives. The first is their effect on ensuring that the police act with due regard for the liberty of the subject. This translates at one level into questions of training, supervision, commitment of supervisors and their willingness and ability to insist upon compliance. No textual reading, however meticulous, will enable one to gauge the likelihood of this happening. Rather more can be said about exclusion of evidence for this purpose. It is very unlikely that the limited discretion in section 78 will be exercised often, and so, subject to what has been said about the possible effect on juries, there seems little prospect that the Codes will have any deterrent effect

---

[15] P.C.E.A., s.67(10).
[16] For example, the treatment of juveniles and the mentally handicapped, and the taking of evidence from body samples.
[17] Below, p. 135.

in this way. The second question is whether individual victims of police breaches of the rules will be able to secure redress. Here it is possible to be more hopeful, though the optimism depends entirely on the assumption that the courts will interpret the Codes as modifying traditional tort law.

Tort Actions

In constitutional theory, the police are subject to the same restrictions of tort law as any private person; the absence of any special privileges or immunities is a prime example Dicey might have chosen to illustrate his concept of equality before the law had he considered the police at all. However, since the boundaries which define police powers are increasingly those of statute law, the critical legal issue in most actions is not whether the tort has been committed, but whether the general defence of statutory authority has been made out. Thus since any touching of the person except perhaps the most trivial constitutes an assault, the defence will generally turn on whether the constable used reasonable force in making the arrest or trying to prevent an offence; similarly, actions for false imprisonment will be met by an attempt to show that the defendant reasonably suspected that the plaintiff had committed an arrestable offence.[18] A legal analysis of the relevant torts can therefore be presented relatively briefly.

(a) **Malicious Prosecution.** This is perhaps the most difficult tort to establish. The plaintiff must prove two elements: malice, and the absence of reasonable and probable cause. These elements must be kept quite distinct: the second is not to be inferred from the existence of the first.[19] The difficulties facing a potential plaintiff—perhaps someone who has been acquitted on a charge he feels was brought for illegitimate reasons—are illustrated by the leading case, *Glinski* v. *McIver*.[20] The plaintiff had been arrested for conspiracy to defraud, but charges were dropped when witnesses failed to pick him out at an identification parade. Soon after, he gave evidence on behalf of someone who, presumably as a result, was acquitted on a serious charge. The police began perjury inquiries, and then reactivated the original charge; Glinski alleged that McIver had told him that he would not have been prosecuted had he not given the evidence. After an acquittal on the conspiracy charge, he brought his tort action, and was awarded

[18] P.C.E.A. 1984, ss.24–25; see also n. 32 below.
[19] *Glinski* v. *McIver*, [1962] A.C. 726, 745, *per* Viscount Simonds.
[20] [1962] A.C. 726.

damages by a jury, which presumably believed his version of what McIver had said, both for malicious prosecution and for false imprisonment, from which the defendant did not appeal.

On these facts, which can be taken as established, Glinski was plainly a victim of a misuse of the police power to prosecute.[21] A similar problem exists with respect to problems of selective prosecution discussed in Chapter 1: a person may have committed an offence, but if he alone of those equally guilty is prosecuted for extraneous reasons, justice has been perverted. Moreover, the problem can have a nasty political dimension if those whom the police, individually or institutionally, define as opponents, or whom they may dislike for racial or cultural reasons, are more likely to face prosecution than those whose conduct or characteristics they approve.[22] Yet a unanimous House of Lords composed of a panel of unusual stature whose views are unlikely to be overturned[23] decided that the jury's verdict was wrong in law. It was held that, so long as the defendant honestly believed that the plaintiff was guilty of the charge brought, the question of reasonable and probable cause to prosecute should be decided by the judge alone; on the facts there was ample evidence of reasonable cause, thus making it impossible for the plaintiff to prove his case.[24] That McIver had been actuated by an improper purpose was therefore so to speak surplusage, or at most went only to the question of malice.

The practical result of this case is that, apart from prosecutions based on fabricated evidence—an important residuum—the tort of malicious prosecution has all but ceased to exist. Policy considerations explicitly dictated this result: their Lordships were intent that the police should not too readily suffer liability at the hands of an acquitted person.[25] Unfortunately they sent the pendulum swinging wildly the other way. Yet even had the verdict been

---

[21] A touchstone of the value of the establishment of the Crown Prosecution Service independent of the police would be whether in a case involving facts similar to these, the prosecutor would be willing to exercise his authority and drop the charges.

[22] The problem is primarily an institutional rather than individual one, *i.e.* the main concern is not the aberrations or prejudices of particular officers, but of an organisational ethos or "custom and practice" that produces such results.

[23] The five who heard the case were Viscount Simonds and Lords Reid, Devlin, Radcliffe and Denning.

[24] Under *Holgate-Mohammed* v. *Duke*, [1984] A.C. 437 (above, pp. 69–70), it would now seem that Glinski would have lost his action for false imprisonment as well, in view of the defendant's belief in his guilt. This conclusion is one of the most worrying implications of that decision.

[25] *e.g.* [1962] A.C. 726, 741 (Viscount Simonds) and 765 (Lord Denning).

affirmed, tort law would not have recognised that an "objectively" guilty person had any valid interest in protection from selective prosecution.

(b) False Imprisonment. The gravamen of this cause of action is simply deprivation of liberty: wrongful confinement—formal arrest is not required—without lawful justification.[26] Because the action is derived from trespass, the plaintiff need show no actual damage. The defendant must show that he has satisfied the preconditions of the statute under which he has effected the arrest; as we have seen, the House of Lords in *Holgate-Mohammed* v. *Duke*[27] has held that under the major statutory arrest power, which requires reasonable suspicion, the test is whether the constable has exercised his discretion within the bounds of the *Wednesbury* principle.[28] An arrest on charges based on false or non-existent evidence is therefore tortious.

It follows that that great English institution, "helping the police with their inquiries" is frequently the result of an act of false imprisonment. That is, to take someone under compulsion to a police station without arresting him is unlawful.[29] Since it is also false imprisonment to arrest someone without making known to him the basis of the arrest,[30] *a fortiori* it is tortious to claim to be exercising a power which does not exist. However, the plaintiff's genuinely voluntary consent to accompanying an officer or remaining at the station would be a defence, and consent is a very slippery concept. Research into the practice of warrantless searches has shown how easily the consent of people ignorant of the law can be manipulated,[31] and it is very doubtful whether most people are aware that they need not, unless arrested, accompany the police to the station. It is by no means clear whether "I went along only because I thought I had to, but I wasn't forced" constitutes consent, legally or philosophically.

(c) Assault. Probably the most common basis of suits against the police is physical violence, which legally is relatively unproblematic. Because the defendant must show that he used a degree of

---

[26] Salmond and Heuston (1981) section 44.

[27] [1984] A.C. 437; above pp. 69–70.

[28] Presumably a very similar test will apply if the constable has made an arrest under one of the few remaining common law powers.

[29] Street (1983), p. 84, citing *R.* v. *Lemsatef,* [1977] 2 All E.R. 835.

[30] *Christie* v. *Leachinsky,* [1947] A.C. 573, although there can be exceptions to this principle, *e.g.* where the reason is obvious to the defendant, as in *Gelberg* v. *Miller,* [1961] 1 W.L.R. 138.

[31] Lidstone (1984), p. 454.

force that was "reasonable in all the circumstances" the issue becomes a virtually unreviewable question of fact for the judge.[32] This may explain the absence of reported decisions on section 3 in the context of tort law. Although an unlawful search is technically an assault—because it involves physical contact—and the number of searches lacking the requisite reasonable suspicion probably runs to the hundreds of thousands,[33] it is unknown for anyone to bring an action solely based on such conduct. Presumably this is because most people are unaware of the illegality involved; but the injury would be regarded by the courts as slight and the damages negligible. However, when to this is added the policy of the English courts of refusing to exclude evidence gained by virtue of illegal searches,[34] the result is the complete absence of any judicial effort to protect the right of citizens to be free of unlawful invasion of their persons, and to prevent police abuse of their powers of search.

(d) **Trespass to Land and to Goods.** The final category consists of actions based on violations of the rights flowing from ownership or occupation of property. The great landmark constitutional case *Entick* v. *Carrington*,[35] declaring general search warrants unlawful, was in fact an action in trespass. Seizure of goods not covered by a valid warrant, or destruction of property in excess of what was necessary to gain entry and carry out a lawful search, would also constitute trespass. Here again the important legal question turns on the scope of the defendant constable's powers. In recent years, under the leadership of Lord Denning M. R., the Court of Appeal significantly expanded common law powers of search and seizure in response to claims of trespass, in *Chic Fashions (West Wales) Ltd.* v. *Jones*[36] and *Ghani* v. *Jones*.[37] However, those decisions did not expand the constable's right to enter premises after arrest; they related solely to the right to seize goods pursuant to a lawful entry or arrest.[38] These important matters are now regulated by sections 18 and 19 of the P.C.E.A. 1984, whose broad effect is to

---

[32] Criminal Law Act 1967, s.3, which is a defence in civil and criminal proceedings.
[33] The P.S.I. Report on the Metropolitan Police (Smith and Gray, 1983) estimated that about $1\frac{1}{2}$ million stops (not all resulting in searches) occurred annually, and that about one-third of those the researchers observed lacked adequate suspicion. It also found that less than one in ten stops produced an arrest or summons. On these figures the estimate in the text is conservative.
[34] Below, pp. 143–146.
[35] (1765) 19 St. Tr. 1029.
[36] [1968] 2 Q.B. 299.
[37] [1970] 1 Q.B. 693.
[38] *McLorie* v. *Oxford*, [1982] Q.B. 1290 (D.C.).

approve Lord Denning's initiatives and to widen powers of entry, contrary to the view of the common law taken by the Divisional Court.[39] Hence much conduct that two decades ago would have constituted trespass is now unquestionably lawful.

Tort actions for police misconduct show certain legal peculiarities. The first is that the Police Act 1964 makes the chief constable liable for the torts of his constables on the basis of master-servant liability, and treats him as a joint tortfeasor.[40] Hence it is not necessary to identify the particular constables who have committed the wrong before the plaintiff's case can be established. This is quite important, because it means that a person may recover damages for police wrongdoing whereas a complaint or a criminal charge arising out of the identical incident would fail if the plaintiff could not identify the particular officers beyond a reasonable doubt. This happens more often than might be imagined, particularly on picket lines or crowd melees, or where a large group of officers raid a house.

Secondly, whilst jury trials in civil cases have largely disappeared, there remain residual categories of cases in which the right to a jury trial may be claimed by either party. These apply identically to actions in the High Court or the county court, and include false imprisonment and malicious prosecution.[41] Some American commentators have suggested that jury trials in civil rights actions against the police work to the disadvantage of plaintiffs because of jurors' prejudices in favour of the police and against blacks and persons with criminal records.[42] However, in England the number of cases that reach the courts, with or without a jury, are so few— and in any case no records are kept about the number of such actions, let alone their mode of adjudication or even their outcome—that it is impossible to tell whether this factor is at work.

Thirdly, actions of this type may attract additional damages under two special heads. Aggravated damages may be given as additional compensation to the plaintiff for particularly outrageous or deliberate misconduct which has injured or humiliated him especially severely. Moreover, and quite distinctly, exemplary damages, designed to punish the defendant for his obnoxious conduct, have survived twentieth century judicial hostility and may be

---

[39] For discussion, see Zander (1985), pp. 27–29 who notes that these sections reverse *McLorie* [1982] Q.B. 1290. Note also s.17 of the P.C.E.A. on powers of entry for purposes of arrest.

[40] s.48(1). Subs.(2) provides that the police fund shall pay out all monies required by a court award or settlement.

[41] Supreme Court Act 1981, s.69(1); County Courts Act 1984, s.66(3).

[42] Newman (1978), pp. 454–455.

awarded in three narrowly-delineated circumstances.[43] One of these is "oppressive, arbitrary or unconstitutional action by servants of the government."[44] This is peculiarly applicable to abuse of police power. Notwithstanding the view of *Fisher* v. *Oldham Corpn.*[45] that the constable is no one's "servant," exemplary damages have repeatedly been awarded against the police under this head. In perhaps the best-known incident, Mr. Justice Mars-Jones awarded £51,000 including £20,000 exemplary damages, to a middle-aged West Indian couple, Mr. and Mrs. White, who were imprisoned without cause for five hours and prosecuted on charges the officers knew were false; Mr. White was assaulted so savagely that he was off work for nine weeks because of injuries.[46] Several other such cases, disproportionately involving black victims, have been reported in the press, and the damages awards have been substantial.[47]

It is impossible to evaluate the impact of tort law as an influence on curbing police misconduct or redressing violations of individual rights. No systematic figures are kept on the number of actions initiated, settled or tried. The Home Office has disclosed some figures in response to MPs' questions. In 1983 when 135 actions were initiated, the Metropolitan Police paid out £57,455 in settlement of claims, and a further £5,855 under court awards, but the accuracy of these figures has been disputed and there is only fragmentary information available relating to provincial forces.[48] Although the number of cases brought is small, it is steadily rising, and there seem to be very few court judgements adverse to plaintiffs. The officers involved do not pay the damages out of their own pockets, though their career prospects may suffer, and the sums involved are not large enough to make a serious dent in the organisation's resources. However, the publicity surrounding such

---

[43] *Rookes* v. *Barnard* [1964] A.C. 1129, reaffirmed in *Cassell & Co. Ltd.* v. *Broome* [1972] A.C. 1027. Lord Devlin in his leading judgment in *Rookes,* [1964] A.C. at 1221, made it clear that had he not felt bound by longstanding authority, he would have abolished exemplary damages entirely.

[44] *Rookes* v. *Barnard* [1964] A.C. 1129, 1226–1227.

[45] [1930] 2 K.B. 364; above, pp. 56–60.

[46] *White* v. *Metropolitan Police Commissioner, The Times*, May 24, 1982.

[47] For a collection of several such cases, see Bailey, Harris and Jones, (1985), p. 25.

[48] These figures are reproduced from *Hansard* in [1985] P.L. 323 (Current Survey). The Police Support Unit of Camden Council produced a useful report, "Damage Claims Against the Metropolitan Police" in 1983, which includes statistics from earlier years. The GLC publication, *Policing London* No. 19 August/September 1985, p. 76, reports figures from several police authorities outside London. It appears that the number of actions brought against the police has been increasing generally; in London it rose to 184 in 1984.

cases, which seem to have received greater press coverage in recent years, is most unwelcome, as is the ammunition they provide to critics, and this can only spur senior officers to greater exertion to prevent repetition of such conduct.

From the standpoint of the victims, tort actions provide a public and independent adjudication of the merits of their allegations, denied them by the present system of complaints. Where police misconduct has been particularly brutal or outrageous, compensation may be obtained. This is facilitated by the practice of settlement, which avoids trials and judicial findings of wrongdoing and allows the force concerned to escape public admission of liability. However, in respect of unlawful searches, which may result in the evidence thereby obtained being used to convict the defendant, it is difficult to disagree with the view of Lord Fraser of Tullybelton, refuting the argument that a civil action is an adequate remedy in such cases: "one has only to mention that to see how ridiculous it is in real life in most cases."[49]

Criminal Sanctions

The individual constable has theoretically always been subject to a number of criminal sanctions designed to prevent and punish neglect of duty in curious ways: *Crouther's Case*[50] held that a constable who failed to make hue and cry when informed by the victim of a burglary was indictable for contempt of the statute against burglary. More broadly, it was held that constables, as subordinate officers to the justices, were indictable for neglect of duty under statute or common law.[51] This principle, or something very similar, was recently reaffirmed in *R. v. Dytham*.[52] The defendant was a constable who had ignored cries for help and failed to pursue the perpetrators of a vicious assault. The Court of Appeal upheld a conviction for the common law offence of misconduct in office, which can be established by wilful and inexcusable failure to perform any duty required by law, in circumstances calculated to injure the public interest and calling for condemnation. This seems at least as broad as the offence upheld in the far more celebrated case of *Shaw* v. *D.P.P.*,[53] though less likely to result in prosecutions.

---

[49] H.L. *Hansard*, vol. 454, col. 940 (July 11, 1984).
[50] 78 E.R. 893, 92 Cro. Eliz. 654.
[51] *Domina Regna* v. *Wyat*, 1 Salk. 380, 91 E.R. 331.
[52] [1979] 3 All E.R. 641.
[53] [1962] A.C. 220, upholding the existence of offence of conspiracy to corrupt public morals.

In the nineteenth century, statutory offences superseded these somewhat unwieldy rules. A typical example is the provision of the County Police Act 1839 imposing penalties of up to a £10 fine or one month's imprisonment with or without hard labour upon constables convicted by justices of neglect or violation of duty.[54] Such provisions continue to rule from the grave: in speaking for the majority of the House in *Wills* v. *Bowley*,[55] Lord Bridge defended his expansive interpretation of an offence created by the Town Police Clauses Act 1847 with the argument that a narrow reading would have put constables charged with its enforcement in peril of prosecution for neglect of duty under another, now repealed, section of the same Act.

It would be eccentric, however, to claim that the possibility of criminal sanction presently serves as a serious constraint on police misconduct. This is partly because matters like neglect of duty are now dealt with under the Discipline Code. There is also a more serious set of legal obstacles. Where evidence that a constable may have committed a criminal offence arises out of a complaint from a member of the public, the procedure governing the processing of those complaints requires that the evidence be forwarded to the Director of Public Prosecutions for a determination whether to institute criminal proceedings.[56] This in effect places police suspects in a more favourable position than the ordinary citizen, who does not enjoy the safeguard of a D.P.P. veto, but is subject wholly to the decision of the police. Moreover, although by statutory instrument a chief constable[57] is required to submit to the D.P.P. information about specified offences where it appears to him that there is a *prima facie* case for proceedings, these Regulations do not mean that the D.P.P's consent is required for commencement of proceedings. That requirement is specified in particular statutes, and limited to those instances only.[58] Moreover, the offences specified include neither common assault nor any of its more serious varieties under the Offences Against the Person Act 1861,[59] the legal category under which police violence

[54] 1839 County Police Act (2 & 3 Vict. c. 93), s.12.
[55] [1982] 2 All E.R. 654, 672 and 681.
[56] P.C.E.A., ss.90 and 92.
[57] From 1986, the Crown Prosecution Service will have the power to discontinue proceedings, but the decision whether to charge a suspect will remain in the hands of the police.
[58] Prosecution of Offences Regulations 1978 (S.I. 1978/1357), reg. 6.
[59] Had the Regulations purported to add offences requiring prior D.P.P. consent before the police could initiate a prosecution, they would have been *ultra vires*. For a list of such offences, see Halsbury's Statutes, Vol. 21, under Malicious Prosecution.

would fall. Nonetheless the practice has arisen of submitting *all* potential prosecutions to the D.P.P., even if the information did not arise from a complaint, but from, for example, the report of a superior officer or colleague.[60]

The approach of the D.P.P. in these cases is highly controversial. He applies the so called "51 per cent rule," under which prosecutions are not undertaken against persons he believes to be guilty unless he also believes that there is a greater likelihood than not of securing a conviction. The present D.P.P., Sir Thomas Hetherington, has publicly stated that, in applying this rule to prospective prosecutions of policemen, he takes into account the experience of a lower conviction rate in such cases, presumably because juries are relatively reluctant to accept a citizen's word against that of a constable. In a powerful criticism of this stance, Professor Glanville Williams has pointed out that the effect of this rule of practice is that corrupt and violent policeman are not brought to book when ordinary people would be.[61] He further argues that this practice is a new departure of the present incumbent, quoting a letter from former Attorney General Sam Silkin, who stated that the rule he prescribed was "where there is a clear *prima facie* case against a police or prison officer, the greater likelihood of acquittal which he enjoys should be secondary to the public interest in ensuring and demonstrating that those who enjoy a position of authority should not abuse it."[62] The present position is a flagrant violation of the rule of law, in effect creating by executive action immunities for criminal conduct when a favoured class of official is involved. Both the rules of *locus standi* and the refusal of the courts thus far to come to grips with the problem of discretionary failure to enforce the law[63] ensure that only through the political process will this abuse be curbed.

Police Misconduct as a Shield for Defendants

A final way in which police misconduct may be brought to light is when it is raised as a defence to a criminal prosecution. Under, respectively, section 51(1) and (3) of the Police Act 1964, it is an offence to assault or obstruct a constable in the execution of his

---

[60] I was informed of this practice by a commander in the Metropolitan Police.

[61] Williams (1985), p. 116.

[62] *Ibid*. p. 117.

[63] Above, pp. 15–16. Since *Gouriet* v. *U.P.O.W.*, [1978] A.C. 435 held that no member of the public would have standing to contest the Attorney General's refusal to issue his fiat to a private citizen seeking to vindicate a public right, it would seem to follow that the same principle would apply where a private citizen sought review of the D.P.P.'s refusal to institute criminal proceedings.

duty. Where, however, the constable has exceeded his legal powers, he is no longer executing his "duty" and there cannot be a conviction. Consequently there is a strong incentive for the defendant to challenge the legality of police conduct, and these relatively minor offences have produced a substantial case law on various powers of stop, arrest and search.[64] Such litigation is valuable in clarifying and delimiting the extent of police powers, though from the defendant's point of view it is of purely negative effect. He avoids conviction and punishment, but receives no automatic compensation. Even if most actions producing acquittals in these sorts of cases are likely to be tortious, he would still have to bring a separate civil action.

Inquests

A major area of concern and dissatisfaction has been that of deaths of members of the public, either in or shortly after being in police custody, or more broadly at the hands of the police, as in the shooting of a five-year-old boy, John Shorthouse, in his Birmingham home, or in the demonstrations at which Kevin Gately and Blair Peach were killed. In the past fifteen years on average between 25 and 30 people annually have died in police custody, a figure which takes no account of non-custodial deaths.[65] In the great majority of instances, no question of police misconduct arises,[66] but the number of deaths resulting in verdicts of accident or misadventure has risen substantially, and the propriety or legality of police action in several incidents involving physical struggles with the victim has been a matter of great dispute.

For such cases the investigative procedures are inadequate. Their great weakness is that they are treated as an internal disciplinary matter, as though they originated as a complaint by a member of the public, not as an investigation into a criminal offence.[67]

---

[64] For extracts and discussion, see Bailey, Harris and Jones (1985), pp. 32–42.

[65] The figures are summarised in Reiner (1985), p. 69 and for 1982–1984, the Annual Report of the Chief Inspector of Constabulary for 1984, H.C. 469 (1985). The House of Commons Select Committee on Home Affairs published a Report on the issue: Third Report of the Home Affairs Committee 1979–1980, *Deaths in Custody*, H.C. 631.

[66] The deceased person has usually been badly drunk and death results from suffocation from his own vomit or from injuries sustained before coming into police custody. Often the police efforts are responsible for him receiving any medical attention at all. As the Commissioner points out in his Annual Report for 1984, Cmnd. 9541 (1985), p. 74 establishment of detoxification centres staffed by medical personnel to which persons in this condition could be sent as an alternative to police custody might well have prevented some of these deaths.

[67] Warwick Inquest Group (1985), pp. 41–42.

Although investigation of a complaint always involves consideration of whether the officer has committed a crime, the objections
to the police investigating themselves (albeit the investigators in
such cases will be drawn from another force) apply with particular
cogency where the possibility of a manslaughter or even murder
charge looms in the background.[68] Charges of "whitewash" cannot be proven because the investigations are themselves not subject to public review,[69] but policemen potentially subject to
criminal charges are accorded treatment that is often more favourable than civilian suspects would receive. For example, in the
investigation following the death of James Davey in a Coventry
police station after a violent struggle in which he was surrounded
by nine officers, one of those known to have been most closely
involved in the struggle was not interviewed until nearly three
weeks after the investigation began, in the presence of his solici-
tor.[70] More generally, suspects in these investigations are scrupu-
lously informed of their right to remain silent, have no difficulty in
securing access to solicitors during interrogation, and have in no
instance been arrested prior to interrogation.[71] These are all practices evincing admirable respect for the rights of suspects but since,
to put it at its lowest, the police not infrequently fail to treat
civilians in this manner, the odour of favouritism is not easily dis-
pelled.

The results of the investigation are submitted to the Director of
Public Prosecutions. Once he has decided not to initiate criminal
charges, the death is then always considered in an inquest before a
coroner's court. The criticisms of its orientation and procedures by
the Warwick Inquest Group[72] seem persuasive: the incident is presented as one in which suspicion of criminal conduct has already
been authoritatively rejected; and the 1984 amendments to the
coroners' rules have abolished the power of the jury to add a rider
to its verdict and restricted the scope of the "lack of care" verdict.
The function of the proceedings thus becomes a sort of public
absolution of responsibility for the institution involved.[73]

---

[68] The investigation of complaints is discussed below, pp. 146–149.
[69] We are brought back once again to the problem of police discretion and non-
enforcement, discussed in Chap. 1.
[70] Warwick Inquest Group (1985), p. 43.
[71] *Ibid.* pp. 42–43.
[72] *Ibid.* especially pp. 35–48. This research was undertaken, and the article written,
by colleagues and students, but I personally took no part in the project.
[73] The police are of course only one institution in whose care people die in circumstances in which misconduct or neglect may be an issue. Hospitals, mental hospitals, old peoples' homes and prisons are equally affected, and may take
advantage of the features of inquest criticised here.

Exclusion of Evidence

English law has been strongly hostile to the exclusion of evidence in criminal trials on the grounds that it has been improperly obtained. Violation of the Judges Rules—which extended only to the questioning of suspects—was held early on not to prevent admission of the evidence thereby obtained.[74] Nineteenth century judges bequeathed a jurisprudence excluding confessions obtained by oppression whose purported generosity towards defendants embarrassed their successors,[75] but otherwise the basic principle was that the judge at trial was concerned only with how the evidence was used in his court—whether it would be unfairly prejudicial to the accused—not with how it was brought there. For a long time this was thought to encompass a discretion to exclude unlawfully obtained evidence whose admission would be unfair to the accused.[76] but in *R.* v. *Sang*,[77] a unanimous House of Lords decided that no such general power existed. In practical terms, as Lord Diplock pointed out, it had hardly ever been used.[78] This was a far more restrictive view of the judge's function compared with that prevailing in Scotland, Australia and even more the United States, where the so-called Exclusionary Rule is grounded in federal and state Bills of Rights.[79]

The rationale for excluding unlawfully obtained evidence is contentious. Ashworth identified two justifications: the disciplinary principle and the protective principle. It is the latter, he argued, that properly supports the practice in appropriate cases.[80] Indeed the disciplinary principle has never found favour in English jurisprudence, on the ground that the purpose of a criminal trial is adjudication of the defendant's guilt, not punishment of the errant policeman, which is properly left to disciplinary action by his superiors. This argument would carry a great deal more weight if there was any evidence at all, however obtained, that the police themselves were prepared to take such responsibilities seriously. Indeed this seems *a priori* implausible, since if the organisational goal is "nicking villains," bending the rules—at least within under-

---

[74] *R.* v. *Voisin* [1918] 1 K.B. 531, 538–539.

[75] The most convenient introduction to English practice is the compilation of cases and commentary in Heydon (1984) chap. 9.

[76] The so-called *Kuruma* discretion, after the Privy Council decision in *Kuruma, son of Kaniu* v. *R.* [1955] A.C. 197.

[77] [1980] A.C. 402.

[78] *Ibid.* p. 435.

[79] Heydon, above n. 75 presents brief extracts from the leading cases in these jurisdictions.

[80] Ashworth (1977), pp. 723–725.

stood limits—is bound to be regarded as an excess of otherwise admirable zeal. Indeed, one of the most common, if bizarre, arguments offered in favour of the provisions of the Police and Criminal Evidence Act 1984 that increased police powers, was that police were regularly exceeding their existing powers and that the law should be brought "up to date" to accord with practice.

A more cogent objection to the disciplinary rationale is that exclusion of evidence may neither discipline nor deter the individual officer who has exceeded his authority. That is to say, loss of evidence in a particular case (which does not always ensure acquittal) does not necessarily cause him to suffer financially or in his career. Nor, for that reason or because other goals may be more important—for example, seizure of a large amount of contraband—will the prospect of exclusion necessarily restrain him from future illegality where the same influences are at work.[81] However, these are also empirical questions, and unless one accepts that the disciplinary rationale has some validity, one has to place a large question mark over the utility of the criminal law generally in controlling anti-social behaviour—a view the police themselves would surely be the last to accept.

The foregoing discussion forms the necessary backdrop to discussion of section 78 of the 1984 Act. Headed "Exclusion of unfair evidence," it restores to the courts the discretion to refuse to admit evidence if in light of all the circumstances including those in which the evidence was obtained, its admission would have such an "adverse effect on the fairness of the proceedings" that it ought not to be admitted.

This provision emerged at the culmination of a long and interesting parliamentary history. It was absent from the Government's Bill, but in the House of Lords, Lord Scarman introduced an amendment which would not merely have reinstated the discretion denied in *Sang* but would have put the onus on the prosecution to prove beyond a reasonable doubt that any evidence challenged was not obtained improperly; this concept was defined to include breach of any rule of law or Code of Practice issued under the Act.[82] The amendment was approved after extended debate.[83] It

---

[81] There are working limits. Sociological accounts of policing (*e.g.* Holdaway, 1983) demonstrate that whilst the police are prepared to tolerate unlawful violence by their colleagues, this will depend on its occasion or cause, and also its degree.

[82] The full text is found in H.L. *Hansard*, Vol. 455, col. 427, (July 26, 1984).

[83] H.L. *Hansard*, vol. 445, cols. 635–675, (July 31, 1984); see also Vol. 454, cols. 931–950, July 11, 1984.

was very revealing, however, that Lord Scarman was virtually alone in advancing the disciplinary principle in support of his amendment. He emphasised the importance of the "deterrence of misuse of police power in the collection of evidence," particularly in relation to stop and search and entry into premises, because the enforcement of safeguards of citizens' rights is otherwise left by the Act to the police themselves.[84] Whilst he also acknowledged the importance of a fair trial for the defendant and the protection of his rights, such protective principle considerations alone were mentioned by others who spoke on behalf of the amendment.

In the event, the Government added section 78 on Third Reading and the Lords acceded. Although it met Scarman's proposal partway, it differs in two significant respects. First, it abandons his "reverse onus" approach, which had put a substantial burden on the prosecution to prove the evidence had been properly obtained, and leaves that factual determination to the judge without the necessity of a formal trial within a trial.[85] Secondly, although the Court may "have regard to" the circumstances in which the evidence was obtained, the test of admission is whether it adversely affects the "fairness of the proceedings," *i.e.* the trial. Particularly in relation to searches and seizures or to leads obtained by unlawful questioning that does not produce a confession, the "proceedings" are not affected by the introduction of accurate information or material. The section as worded does little to prevent judges and magistrates from continuing the standard practice before *Sang* of paying lip service to legality but admitting the evidence on grounds of its probative value.[86] Certainly, whatever one's view of the desirability and appropriateness of the disciplinary principle, it cannot be expected that under present law the exclusion of evidence in criminal trials will have any impact on controlling illegal police behaviour.

Exclusion of evidence serves another important function that is frequently overlooked. It may be the only means by which the breadth of police powers may be defined, and its exercise challenged. To put the same point in reverse, its absence in English law means in some circumstances the police define their own powers. Thus, for example, they have interpreted the Misuse of Drugs Act 1971 as allowing them to take suspects to the station for

---

[84] *Hansard* Vol. 454, col. 932.

[85] This does not apply to the admissibility of confessions, which are subject to the more rigorous safeguards of s.76. Lord Scarman's amendment was also directed to evidence other than confessions.

[86] A very good example is the decision of the then Lord Chief Justice, Lord Widgery, in *Jeffrey* v. *Black*, [1978] 1 Q.B. 490.

a full search if they wish to, rather than limiting them to a "frisk" on the street.[87] Short of a civil action for damages—on grounds that themselves might be weak, since the person might well have been held to have consented to the search if at the time he was unaware of his ability to refuse—there is no way such conduct could be contested.[88] The fact that no such action has ever been pursued eloquently attests to the truth of Lord Fraser's comment.[89] Had the Scarman proposal been law, evidence introduced through such a search could have been challenged as being obtained through violation of statute, which the court would then have been required to interpret. The present position, which permits the reign of ambiguity, encourages the police to push their powers to the limit—and beyond.

Complaints and Discipline

No aspect of police governance has been so bombarded with criticism as the handling of complaints about treatment of citizens. Amidst much controversy, a new machinery was established under the Police Act 1976; since that time, no less than eight different schemes for partial or complete overhaul have been put forward by various official bodies.[90] One of these is now embodied in the 1984 Act. Because of the intense public interest, this subject has been studied and controverted in unusually great depth. Good critiques of the previous system have been written,[91] as have thorough explanations of the legislation establishing the new and largely untried procedures.[92] It is therefore unnecessary to examine the statute in detail here. Rather, what follows is an overview of the issues involved, with reference to specific procedural provisions only where necessary to illustrate a more general point.

General Criteria of Evaluation

The main criticisms of the procedures for handling complaints about police misconduct are that complaints are not always investigated thoroughly and impartially; that serious wrongdoing by

---

[87] Misuse of Drugs Act 1971, s.23(2) grants the constable a power to "search and detain" suspects in these circumstances.

[88] In these circumstances, the defendant could not, as in a prosecution under s.51 of the Police Act 1964 (above, p. 140) use the illegality of the search as a bar to conviction, for he would be prosecuted for possession of the material seized, and the question of the constable's "duty" would not be relevant.

[89] Above, p. 138.

[90] Cohen, (1985), p.247.

[91] Especially Hewitt (1982) and Cohen, *op. cit.*

[92] Notably Zander (1985), pp. 122–144. See also Marshall (1985).

police officers goes unpunished; that the process is shrouded in secrecy and never adequately explained to complainants; that it grinds on for an unnecessarily long time; and that it fails to satisfy people with genuine grievances.

Part of the responsibility for these defects rests with practices, procedures and attitudes peculiar to, or at least strongly associated with, the police service. However, the root cause lies much deeper. There is no successful model of complaints procedure at any level of British government. Indeed the police complaints machinery, for all its failings, is better than nothing, which is what exists in some other fields. The Barclay Report on social workers, for example, revealed that they were not really accountable to anyone and that clients lacked effective means of appeal or redress.[93] Birkinshaw's recent study[94] exposes the paucity of adequate procedures in local authorities. Most rely on ad hoc and inconsistent methods, which tend to revolve around complaints to councillors or officers and favour middle class people less likely to be intimidated by the machinery of government. Many others used committees or sub-committees from which, in the case of the latter, public attendance was often routinely barred. A substantial number use informal internal procedures which do not permit the complainant to present his grievance at any stage. The Code of Practice on complaints produced jointly by the Commissioner for Local Administration (C.L.A.) and the Local Authorities Association, is orientated towards internal efficiency and presenting an acceptable face to the public, rather than towards satisfying complainants; in any case it is advisory only and not always followed. Experience in the housing area, particularly in contentious or complex matters like homelessness or housing benefit[95] and council house allocations and evictions has shown the procedures for both the initial determination and appeal are subject to the same or analogous criticisms that have long been levelled at the police complaints process. Moreover the C.L.A., who exists to examine complaints of local authority maladministration, has substantially less power than either the new Police Complaints Authority or its predecessor, in that he cannot compel a recalcitrant authority to accept an adverse finding.[96] There is also substantial dissatisfaction with the working of the Ombudsman, who deals with a tiny caseload of complaints about central government departments.

---

[93] Barclay (1982), paras. 2.40–2.52.
[94] Birkinshaw (1985), Chap. 3, especially pp. 57–80.
[95] *e.g.* Partington and Bolderton (1984), and Birkinshaw (1982), respectively.
[96] Birkinshaw (1985), p. 144. On the C.L.A. generally see pp. 140–147.

None of these comments are meant to excuse inadequacies in the treatment of complaints against police. They are meant to indicate both that these inadequacies are symptomatic of a structural problem in local government, and that common remedies are required. Put another way, establishment of an effective procedure for complaints against the police should be part of a wider movement toward ensuring the same result throughout local government. For the public, change on this broad front is essential because local government provides services that are often the sole alternative to misery, particularly for the poor, and may also wield substantial powers of coercion (again largely against the poor), in matters such as compulsory care orders, evictions, and suspensions or expulsions from school. Although contacts between police and public are much more likely to be abrasive, and to have adverse consequences, short and long term, for the citizen, it should not be assumed that local government officers deal only in benevolence; on some occasions the effects of their misconduct can be far worse. Moreover, though there is ample evidence of racism amongst the police,[97] it should not be assumed that racist attitudes or conduct are absent among workers in other services producing equally damaging results.[98] Concern for quality of service and for fairness to the police alike require that all those employed as public servants be subject to rigorous standards of conduct backed up by effective investigation of complaints.

There are, however, a few distinctive features about complaints against the police. Because the police are, unusually among civilians,[99] a disciplined service, with a formal hierarchy of rank and a disciplinary code, a verified complaint can lead to formal disciplinary proceedings ending in a range of sanctions including formal admonishment, loss of pay, reduction in rank and, in rare cases, loss of employment. A citizen complaint is, as it were, fed

[97] Smith and Gray (1983), Chap. IV (the P.S.I. Report) document this most graphically. For a broader overview, see Reiner (1985), pp. 100–102, 129–136.

[98] This is a serious issue which requires extended comment. Although the police are not substantially different in their social origins than a representative sample of the whole population (Reiner, 1979, pp. 158–159), the ethos of the organisation is markedly working class. This means in particular a directness and lack of verbal subtlety than one would expect from occupations with a middle class style and aspirations, *e.g.* teachers. A teacher might avoid saying something, or deal in euphemisms, where a policeman would speak crudely. No one has ever done an observation study on teachers similar to the P.S.I. Report, but many black people have been complaining bitterly for years of racism—occasionally overt but generally far more subtle—which has had corrosive long terms effects on the sense of self-worth and ambitions of black pupils.

[99] So far as I am aware, the Fire Service and Prison Service are the only others.

into this internal disciplinary procedure. For example, if a person complains that "Constable Armstrong for no reason stopped me on the street, searched me and when I protested called me "a fucking troublemaker," this translates into one allegation of disobedience to orders and two of abuse of authority.[1] However, the proportion of complaints leading to disciplinary charges is miniscule: 5.8 per cent. in the Metropolitan Police, and 3.6 per cent. elsewhere.[2] Moreover, the great majority of disciplinary proceedings do not arise from complaints; in 1984 only 18 per cent. in the Met. and 24.6 per cent. nationally did so.[3] Of course an indeterminate number of complaints will be without merit, but these figures point to three problems: many complaints are inappropriate for disciplinary proceedings; the proceedings themselves are subject to undue hindrance; and the inquiry into the allegations may be inadequate. These issues are considered in turn, under somewhat broader headings.

Conciliation

In recent years, approximately one half of all complaints annually have subsequently been withdrawn or "not proceeded with" because the complainant has not pursued his initial claim. One reason, noted by the House of Commons Home Affairs Committee[4] and frequently offered by critics of the system, is that complainants may be pressured by the officer investigating the case, either because the latter believes it to be unmeritorious, or for less creditable reasons. Another fact has been the manner in which complaints are treated on receipt, *i.e.* the high figure is in part an artefact of record keeping. If it is immediately ascertained that the

---

[1] The Police Discipline Code is found in Sched. 1 of the Police (Discipline) Regulations 1985, S.I. 1985/518. Disobedience to orders (para. 3) includes failure to comply with any requirements in a code of practice—here relating to reasonable suspicion for a strip and search. Abuse of authority (para. 8) specifically includes conducting a search without good cause and being abusive or uncivil to a member of the public.

[2] These percentages are calculated from the figures for the total number of complaints received and disciplinary charges brought in 1984 found in the Commissioner's Annual Report, Cmnd. 9541 (1985), pp. 47 and 51, and the Chief HMI's Annual Report, H.C. 469 (1985), pp. 59 and 61. The fit is not exact; because of time needed for investigation, those subject to disciplinary charges in a given year will almost certainly have been the subject of a complaint in an earlier year. The source of most disciplinary charges is reports of superior officers or colleagues.

[3] *Ibid.* pp. 51 and 61 respectively.

[4] Fourth Report, 1981–1982 Session, HC 98–1, para. 21.

person expressing dissatisfaction wants either a quick explanation or an apology which is readily forthcoming rather than having the matter treated as a complaint to be formally investigated, the number of withdrawn complaints drops sharply: when the Metropolitan Police introduced an initial screening to identify such cases in 1984, the number of withdrawn complaints fell by 25 per cent. with no rise in the number of complaints dismissed as unsubstantiated.[5] More generally, probably a high proportion of the nearly 20,000 complaints received each year either do not involve incidents which the complainant would wish to see treated as a disciplinary matter, or which have been brought primarily to ensure that misconduct does not recur rather than to seek punishment of the offending constable. The 1984 Act introduces a conciliation procedure known as "informal resolution"[6] which allows the chief constable[7] to decide whether the matter is appropriate for this procedure. This requires both a determination that criminal or disciplinary proceedings would not be justified if the complaint proves valid, and approval of the person complaining.[8] Neither the Act nor Regulations specify how conciliation should proceed. Presumably it will track the 1983 White Paper, which suggested that the complainants might be given an explanation or apology, be told that the officer will receive a talking to, or be invited to discuss the matter with the officer in the presence of a lay third party.[9] Complaints involving surliness, bad language, delayed response to a 999 call and the like are the sort of matters expected to be covered. So long as the complainant is not pressured by the investigating officer into accepting conciliation in place of the possibility of sanctions against the constable, the informal resolution procedure should benefit all concerned.

The Disciplinary Process

For more serious cases, disciplinary sanctions are appropriate where misconduct is proven. Such behaviour may come to light as a result of a complaint, but far more commonly from reports by fellow officers or superiors. The Code ranges very widely, subsuming but going well beyond criminal offences. The investigating offi-

---

[5] Cmnd. 9541 (1985), pp. 47–48.

[6] P.C.E.A. 1984, s.85.

[7] The Police (Complaints) (General) Regulations 1985, S.I. 1985/520, reg. 13 allows the chief constable or commissioner to delegate its function; in most forces it is the deputy chief constable who is actively concerned.

[8] P.C.E.A., s.85(10).

[9] "Police Complaints and Discipline Procedures," Cmnd. 9072 (1983).

cer, who must be at least of the rank of chief inspector and of equivalent rank of the person being investigated,[10] is therefore seeking to assemble evidence of possible disciplinary and criminal offences simultaneously. This is only sensible use of resources, but it creates one serious obstacle to the disciplinary process. A police officer, like anyone else suspected of a criminal offence, is entitled to the benefit of the right to silence, and to be cautioned that evidence obtained from him during questioning may be used against him at trial. However, the Discipline Regulations provide, and have long provided, for a similar right in investigations related to disciplinary offences.[11] This is far more dubious, because the penalties are at most verbal or financial and no other occupation enjoys a similar protection: a worker who refused to answer an employer's questions about misconduct at work could almost certainly be fairly dismissed.[12] Moreover, there is a strong public interest in ensuring that good behaviour towards members of the public and high standards of service are unremittingly maintained.

It would seem that the only way the right of silence could be preserved in relation to criminal proceedings alone would be to establish, not two investigations, but two separate sessions of questioning. This is not as absurd as it sounds. If a constable, having duly been cautioned, makes clear his refusal to answer questions related to a prosecution for A.B.H., such questioning would cease and he could then be told that all the ensuing interrogation related to the disciplinary offence of abuse of authority. Failure to answer these questions would call down adverse inferences in the disciplinary adjudication. This seems a fair balance of the competing considerations; however, there must be an inviolate rule that if the officer responds to questions in the disciplinary interrogation, his answers may never be used in criminal proceedings against him.[13] Given the expertise an officer may be expected to possess in handling their interrogators it is hardly surprising that criminal convictions of police are, and will remain, very difficult to

---

[10] P.C.E.A., s.85(8).

[11] Discipline Regulations, *op. cit.* reg. 7. For discussion, see Hewitt, *op. cit.* pp. 35–37.

[12] This would follow by close analogy to cases like *Harris and Shepherd* v. *Courage Eastern*, [1982] I.R.L.R. 509, (C.A.), and *Harris Ipswich (Ltd)* v. *Harrison*, [1978] I.R.L.R. 382 (EAT), although the precise question in unfair dismissal law would not be whether the employee has a right to silence, but whether the employer, seeking to ascertain the truth about a particular incident, acted reasonably in all the circumstances in dismissing him.

[13] To ensure that this restriction is observed, a tape recording of all questioning for disciplinary purposes should be made, as is now becoming the norm with criminal interrogations under s.60 of the P.C.E.A.

obtain.[14] But a disciplinary system which granted them no greater rights than are enjoyed by other public servants would go a considerable distance towards securing justice for complainants.

A second feature of the disciplinary process that unduly favours the constable is the burden of proof. Apparently as a matter of custom and practice—the point was not covered by any rule of law—disciplinary charges have always had to be proven beyond a reasonable doubt. No convincing reason has ever been offered as to why a criminal standard of proof should govern these civil proceedings. The anomaly is especially glaring because under unfair dismissal law, even before the Employment Act 1980 muddied the waters, the employer has only to discharge the civil standard of proof—balance of probabilities—for a dismissal to be adjudged fair. Dismissal is a far graver sanction than most policemen ever face, yet their misconduct can involve far more serious malefactions than ordinary workers could possibly commit.[15]

At one point the practice did receive judicial approval in a curious way. In 1983, in the course of a judgement holding invalid the so-called double jeopardy rule that had sheltered policemen from disciplinary proceedings when the D.P.P. had refused to approve criminal proceedings, McNeill J., more or less in passing and certainly *in dictum*, accepted that the criminal standard of proof applied.[16] However, in a case challenging the application of the civil standard of proof to disciplinary charges under the Fire Service Code, which is very similar, the Court of Appeal took a different view.[17] It rejected the challenge, and O'Connor L. J., whilst unwilling to make a formal ruling because the Police Federation was not represented in the litigation, expressed his doubts that McNeill J. had been correct[18]; his colleagues, though less explicit, took the same position. The judges accepted the principle that the graver the offence charged, the higher degree of probability required. However, this does not mean that a sort of sliding percentage scale operates, but that the adjudicator must think longer

---

[14] We return to the point made in the Prologue, influenced by McConville and Baldwin (1982), that the primary goal of criminal investigation is to obtain a confession, and that the police station rather than the courtroom is the main locus of criminal process. To put the point another way, in the absence of a confession, it is difficult to secure the conviction of an ordinary person, let alone a policeman.

[15] In 1984, only 44 policemen in the entire country, 26 of them from the Met., were dismissed after disciplinary proceedings. All persons in such circumstances may appeal to the Home Secretary. Unfair dismissal claims, which obviously reflect only a minority of all dismissals, average approximately 30,000 annually.

[16] *R.* v. *Police Complaints Board, ex p. Madden,* [1983] 1 W.L.R. 447, 467.

[17] *R.* v. *Hampshire C.C. ex p. Ellerton* [1985] 1 All E.R. 599.

[18] *Ibid.* p. 603.

and harder before accepting that the civil standard of proof has been satisfied.[19] The *Ellerton* case was decided on January 3, 1985, and was presumably soon made known to the Home Office. None the less the Discipline Regulations, laid before Parliament three months later, state explicitly for the first time that a criminal standard of proof is required.[20] The change went through on the nod when the Regulations received Parliamentary approval. Thus there now exists the absurdity that substantive offences governing firemen and policemen, some of which are the same word for word, can be more easily proven against the former than the latter. In effect, as with the D.P.P.'s prosecution criteria,[21] the police are a uniquely favoured class of wrongdoer.

The likelihood that complainants would achieve a measure of redress would be significantly increased if the norm of equality before the law were to be reinstated and the investigatory and evidentiary privileges abolished in the disciplinary process. However, such a reform would still leave untouched an even more fundamental objection: that complaints are not adequately investigated because the police investigate themselves and cannot be trusted to bring their own colleagues to book.

Internal v. Independent Investigation

After years of debate, a broad consensus—including Lord Scarman and embracing groups normally as chasmatically apart as the Police Federation and the N.C.C.L. but not, unfortunately, the Government—was finally reached on the necessity for an investigatory body wholly independent of the police service. In the late 1970s and early 1980s, there were a series of incidents of police violence which led only to complaints being declared unsubstantiated, as well as several deaths in custody never adequately explained.[22] Coupled with the failure of Operation Countryman in circumstances suggesting sabotage within the Metropolitan Police,[23] the result was to undermine fatally public confidence in the trustworthiness of internal investigations. One consequence, as Lord Scarman reported,[24] was that people refused to complain. Among black people this feeling could be supported by evidence from the Home Office Research Unit showing that complaints by

[19] *Ibid.* p. 604 (O'Connor L.J.) and 608 (Slade L.J.)
[20] Above n. 1, reg. 23(2)(b).
[21] Above, p. 140.
[22] For a brief review, see Hewitt, *op. cit.* pp. 13–14.
[23] Doig (1984), pp. 243–252 discusses this episode in depth.
[24] Scarman (1981), para. 7.14.

whites were three times as likely to be found substantiated.[25] The
Police Federation, after years of powerful resistance, joined the
chorus, having recognised that its own members would be better
protected if people could no longer blame a rigged system when a
constable was exonerated of wrongdoing. Although an "independent element" had supposedly been introduced into the system
with the creation of the Police Complaints Board (P.C.B.) in 1976,
its performance satisfied no one.

The problem is particularly acute with respect to serious allegations, involving police criminality, harassment and racism.
Figures are only available for the Metropolitan Police. In 1984, 8
percent. of all complaints actually investigated were held to be
substantiated. *Not one* complaint involving harassment, racial discrimination,[26] false evidence or perjury was found substantiated;
the same was true in 1983. Only 20 of 1410 complaints of assault—
1.5 per cent.—were substantiated.[27] Either those who do bother to
complain are all liars, or there is something wrong with the system.

Two factors seem to be primarily responsible for this failure of
the complaints machinery. The first is an intractable problem
which will survive any procedural and administrative changes in
complaints investigations however otherwise desirable. There is an
unusually strong sense of solidarity among the police work group,
a phenomenon often noted by observational studies.[28] Its sources
are various, but perhaps the most important are the two key
elements Skolnick identified in his classic study of the policeman's
"working personality": authority and danger.[29] The need to pro-

---

[25] Stevens and Willis (1981), p. 16. Asian complainants were more than twice as
successful as blacks, but still less so than whites.

[26] Racial discrimination was not then a specific offence against discipline, but
would have been treated as a matter of discreditable conduct under the Discipline Code. As a result of a Government defeat in the House of Lords when
Lord Scarman introduced an amendment (now P.C.E.A. s.101(1)(b)) requiring
that racial discrimination be made a specific disciplinary offence, para. 9 has
been added to the Disciplinary Code. It forbids racially discriminatory behaviour, defined as abuse of authority or any other improper treatment of any person on grounds of his colour, race, *etc.* For symbolic reasons, this addition to the
Code is important. However, it would wholly unrealistic to expect that it will
materially assist complaints who have been maltreated in this way. The offence
requires proof of two elements: conduct and motive. Apart from racist verbal
abuse, this is likely to be extremely difficult to establish, for all the reasons cases
of employment discrimination often fail for want of proof. For an extended discussion of the reasons, see Lustgarten (1980), chap. 11.

[27] Above n. 2, p. 139.

[28] *e.g.* Holdaway (1983), pp. 114–119; Smith and Gray (the P.S.I. Report) (1983),
pp. 70–75.

[29] Skolnick (1966), Chap. 3.

vide instantaneous and unhesitating support to a colleague threatened with physical danger, or who is exercising his powers over a resistant citizen, creates an ethos in which total reliability is required if an individual is to be an acceptable member of the relief or specialist group, and breeds a sense of social isolation from both the public and organisational superiors. In certain situations this degree of trust is necessary, but it can also be very dangerous, supplanting obedience to fundamental moral and legal duties. One of the most important conclusions to emerge from the P.S.I. study was that "we believe that police officers will *normally* tell lies to prevent another officer from being disciplined or prosecuted, and this is the belief of senior officers who handle complaints and discipline cases"[30] (emphasis added). In a different occupational setting this is known as the code of *omerta*.

The result is a wall of secrecy that is very difficult to demolish. Many valid complaints fall at this wall, which is further shored up by the expertise in criminal process that is, uniquely, part of police occupational skills. Short of the unacceptable step of giving police suspects fewer rights than are enjoyed by members of the public, this problem can only be attacked on two fronts. Probably the most important for long-term effectiveness is change in the ethos of the police organisation. The norms of behaviour must be altered from within so that lies and conspiracies of silence come to be generally regarded as unacceptable. Here the notion of professionalism is crucial, and the 1985 statement on Principles of Policing and Guidance for Professional Behaviour, issued by the Metropolitan Police to all officers, meets this issue head on.[31] However, for those cases in which professional training and leadership are insufficient, there must exist an investigative body whose members can at least match police suspects in interrogation and detection skills, and whose separation from the group solidarity is beyond question.

The Government's response to the calls for an independent investigatory body was to transform the P.C.B. into a Police Complaints Authority (P.C.A.) with new personnel and some new powers. The existence of the P.C.A. in no way alters the basic fact that investigations of complaints continue to be undertaken by the police themselves. Its function is "supervisory," a term that is as unclear as it is broad. By statute and Regulation[32] all complaints

---

[30] *Op. cit.*, p. 329.
[31] Metropolitan Police (1985), pp. 54–56.
[32] P.C.E.A., s.87(1) and Police Complaints (Mandatory Referrals etc.) Regulations 1985, S.I. 1985/673, reg. 4.

involving death, serious injury, A.B.H., corruption, or a serious arrestable offence[33] must be referred by the force involved to the P.C.A. It may order that the investigation be conducted by someone from another force[34] and impose reasonable requirements relating to the investigation.[35] How much effective influence it will have on the conduct of the investigation cannot yet be judged. The investigating officer must submit a report to the authority, which must then issue a statement saying whether it was satisfied with the conduct of the investigation, and specifying its reasons if it was not.[36] Presumably its power to impose requirements will minimise the number of occasions of dissatisfaction. In cases where the authority has not supervised the investigations, it is entitled to receive a report from the chief constable explaining why he has decided not to send a report to the D.P.P. with a view to bringing criminal proceedings. If it disagrees with that decision, it may then direct that all relevant information be sent to the D.P.P.[37] Where the chief constable has refused to bring disciplinary charges, it may first recommend and if necessary direct him to do so.[38]

For complainants sceptical of officialdom's trustworthiness, these provisions remain unsatisfactory. One important indication that little had changed came very early on. The West Midlands Police Authority and its chief constable jointly requested that the report of the investigation, supervised by the P.C.A., into the shooting of a five-year-old boy hiding under his bed, be made public. The P.C.A. quickly rejected their request, on the grounds that witnesses might withhold information if they knew the report would be published. As a *Guardian* leader pointed out,[39] the only witnesses were the officers involved in the shooting: "by their silence and secrecy"—more accurately, that of the P.C.A.—they are "creating a no go area for public accountability over what is not only an exceptionally serious individual incident but also a more general issue of wholly legitimate public concern."

---

[33] A term of art created by the P.C.E.A. and particularly important for the extended powers its commission gives the police. It is defined in s.116 of the P.C.E.A.

[34] P.C.E.A., s.89(4).

[35] Mandatory Referrals Regulations, reg. 5(2). However, reg. 5(3) provides that any requirement relating to the obtaining or preservation of evidence of a criminal offence must be approved first by the D.P.P.

[36] P.C.E.A., s.89(6)–(11).

[37] P.C.E.A., s.92

[38] P.C.E.A., s.93(1) and (3). Here the P.C.A has simply taken over the function previously exercised, sparingly, by the P.C.B.

[39] September 3, 1985.

It is unlikely that the P.C.A. will satisfy critics of the complaints system. It is not accountable, directly or indirectly, to Parliament. It is neither fish nor fowl. It does not conduct investigations itself, and though its chairman is a lawyer and former Ombudsman, its members have little experience or knowledge of criminal investigations. These limitations ensure that the police will continue to dominate investigations of complaints against themselves. Justice may not be done, and at all events will not be seen to be done. What is required is a corps of skilled investigators independent of any police force under the direction of a politically accountable authority, which can only be located in central government. Once again we return to the imperative of rethinking which functions of police governance should be the responsibility of local and central government, and of the institutions through which these should be exercised: this is one of the main issues taken up in the following chapter.

The final point relating to complaints is the role of the police authority. It is required to keep itself "informed" about the working of the complaints system, as are the Inspectors of Constabulary.[40] It has no power in relation to investigations and, despite a suggestion to this effect in the White Paper, the Regulations[41] do not provide it with a right of access to the record that must be made of the outcome of informal resolution of complaints. The one new power it has been granted is that of referring a case to the P.C.A., on grounds of gravity or exceptional circumstances, where no complaint has been filed but it believes that an officer has committed a crime or disciplinary offence.[42] This may prove useful when a local *cause célèbre* arises but the victim distrusts the system too much to present a complaint.

Perhaps the most important role allocated to the police authority is as the disciplinary body relating to senior officers—those above the rank of chief superintendent. Its tasks, however, are limited to deciding whether to refer the case to the P.C.A., appointing the investigating officer and selecting a one-person tribunal, drawn from a list nominated by the Lord Chancellor, to conduct the hearing.[43] Should the tribunal find the charges proven, it is for the police authority to impose punishment.[44]

Though the police authority can hardly be expected to make a

[40] P.C.E.A., s.95.
[41] Police (Complaints) (Informal Resolution) Regulations 1985, S.I. 1985/671.
[42] P.C.E.A., s.88.
[43] Police (Discipline) (Senior Officers) Regulations 1985, S.I. 1985/519, (reg. 12).
[44] *Ibid.* reg. 20. The punishments can only be dismissal, requirement to resign, or reprimand.

major contribution to the complaints process, its existence provides the justification for an important restriction. No complaints concerning any action of the chief constable in directing and controlling his force may be the subject of a complaint.[45] The process is concerned with misconduct by individuals, not general policies; the latter are left either to the judgement of the chief constable alone or may be the subject of a request by the police authority for a report.[46] This limitation, which presumably would extend by implication to actions of officers acting in pursuance of instructions from the chief constable, would now justify the refusal of the Nottinghamshire police to accept complaints relating to their "turnback" policy of refusing to allow persons intending to picket to enter the county.

Summary and Conclusions

The diverse mechanisms that have been surveyed in this chapter are meant to serve one or more of three different functions: preventing, punishing or redressing police misconduct. Though each operates in a different context and serves different interests, they should be complementary; a monetary solatium for someone wrongfully arrested should be paralleled by disciplinary action against the offending constable. This however is seldom the case, for each mechanism has its own specific rules and limitations. Yet some general lessons can be identified./One is the value of independent public scrutiny of police conduct, at the moment achieved primarily through tort actions. Judge and jury may form their own evaluation of police credibility, unconstrained by organisational loyalties and with the assistance of vigorous cross-examination by the plaintiff's counsel. Moreover, the plaintiff in such cases is not hampered by having to satisfy an unduly high burden of proof; the application of the criminal standard to the civil process of disciplinary proceedings is a serious and unjustifiable obstacle to the substantiation of charges, some of which arise from complaints from the public. Indeed it has been known for someone to recover damages but have his complaint about the identical incident to be found unsubstantiated under the statutory complaints procedure.

This example recalls a second point: the favoured position enjoyed by constables suspected of wrongdoing. The D.P.P.'s criteria for prosecution and the manner in which police suspects are treated further illustrate this.

---

[45] P.C.E.A., s.84(5).
[46] Under s.12 of the Police Act 1964; above, p. 78.

A third is the potentially crucial impact of the new Codes of Practice on the range of these control mechanisms. Effective training and rigorous insistence on their observance by senior officers, backed up by their use in civil actions, disciplinary proceedings, and criminal proceedings by means of excluding evidence tainted by their violation, would go a long way towards strengthening the safeguards against police misconduct.

All these mechanisms are directed to individual cases. They cannot, and are not intended, to reach organisational policies or structures which in some instances may stimulate or sustain misconduct, or which bring the police into conflict with significant groups within the population. These can only be considered in relation to the constitutional structures of police governance.

Part V

Chapter 10

POLICING AND DEMOCRATIC CONSTITUTIONALISM

I

In recent years, apart from discussion of specifically legal powers, virtually all of the large literature on policing has been written by sociologists or historians.[1] They have deepened our understanding of policing practices and their historical roots. But the predominance of social science in this field has created an unfortunate analytic imbalance and left important gaps. Police governance has tended to be treated as a sub-problem of current political issues, notably race relations, rather than as a constitutional issue of fundamental importance in its own right. What has been lacking is a systematic attempt to place issues of police governance in their proper context, that of constitutional principle. This requires an analysis which proceeds at two levels: within the framework of public law—a term embracing formal rule and political practice—and of the constitutional and political theory appropriate to a democratic polity which values civil liberties. It is time for the distinctive contribution of the public lawyer.

What follows will therefore concentrate on first principles, and on institutions devoted to realising them. A key characteristic of this approach is its concentration on structural design and worst case prevention. That is, it seeks to create institutions to prevent or at any rate minimise abuses of power, which it assumes are inevitable. The likelihood of abuse is not peculiar to the police either as an institution or as individuals; it simply reflects the way people are made.[2] It follows that one cannot rely primarily on professionalism, training and reform from within, important though these are. Those, like the authors of the P.S.I. Report,[3] who place

---

[1] The major exceptions among lawyers have been Jefferson and Grimshaw (1984; 1984a) and Baldwin and Kinsey (1982); there is also of course the work of Marshall (1965; 1984), a political scientist.

[2] It is a commonplace that theories of political institutions are ultimately based on one's conception of human nature and possibilities. Mine is pessimistic, and regards persons given the opportunity to exercise power as likely, unless checked, to abuse it, regardless of their specific political beliefs or allegiances.

[3] Smith and Gray (1983), *passim*. For a critique of the P.S.I. Report which emphasises this aspect of their work, see Lustgarten (1984).

their faith in enlightened senior management rather than external institutions of control are in effect advocating the most venerable of political theories, the core idea of Plato's *Republic*: choose the best people, give them the power they need and let them get on with it. Unfortunately such a theory cannot be squared with the fundamental premises of a democratic polity. Enlightened despotism is arguably the best form of government, if we could be sure the despot would always be enlightened. As it is liberal democracies play safe and try to ensure that those who exercise the power of the state are subject to effective democratic control, perhaps supplemented by judicial control.

The ensuing discussion is organised around four main themes. The first is that of identifying fundamental principles upon which normative statements about police governance may be grounded. The second is that of independence *versus* democratic governance: the issue of whether, and to what extent, the police as an institution of government may claim exemption from the normal processes of democratic control. A third is the scope for legal rather than political mechanisms of control. Finally, the appropriate arena of control must be determined, which requires consideration of the conflict between the claims of localism and centralism.

One assumption underpinning the analysis is that the mandate of the police is the executive task of enforcing criminal law. It is true that the police perform many social service functions, but most of these could readily and perhaps more effectively be performed by other agencies, and many police officers regard them as a distraction from their real work.[4] And although sociologically and historically it makes eminent sense to talk about policing primarily in terms of the maintenance of order, in concrete terms this ineluctably political task is carried out by the discretionary invocation of legal powers. Hence for present purposes policing may be equated with law enforcement.

II

Lord Scarman in his Report attempted to start with first principles. He denominated "two well-known principles of policing a free society," which he identified as "consent and balance" and "independence and accountability."[5] The first refers to the diverse and at times conflicting functions of policing, the second to the ques-

---

[4] See Reiner (1985), pp. 110–116 for review of the empirical studies and a subtle discussion of their implications.

[5] Scarman (1981), para. 4.55.

tion of governance under consideration here. Independence and accountability, however, are not first principles. They derive from a conception of social order and must, like any alternative, be justified in the light of such a conception.

I would suggest that a conception appropriate to democratic constitutionalism may be derived from the work of the philosopher John Rawls.[6] Although entitled *A Theory of Justice* it is not devoted to specifying substantive outcomes. Rather it is concerned with underlying principles, and above all with the method by which those principles would be agreed. Rawls is fundamentally concerned to abolish interest, particularly self-interest, in that process of agreement. He therefore concludes that rational people would agree to those principles of justice which they would accept in total ignorance of whether they would be favoured or disfavoured when the principles came to be applied to them. They are the principles that would be chosen in "reflective equilibrium," not those designed to produce the greatest possible gratifications of an individual's desires.

Most of the discussion of Rawls' principles seems to have been in connection with economic or material inequalities. Yet they are of abundantly fruitful potential in relation to issues of power and political order. Rawls himself thinks they would produce agreement on "constitutional liberty"[7] but he restricts his discussion of such matters to a very abstract level. In an attempt to bring Rawlsian theory somewhat closer to the street, I would suggest that no structure of power be regarded as just unless rational persons would agree that, within its contours, they would willingly be subject to those whose material interests were radically different from their own. Hence no relationship of power would be justified unless the person in the superior position would agree to exchanging roles with those occupying the subordinate position. This principle also has implications for substantive criminal law. It would preclude any legislation granting wide discretionary power over the activities of any group within the population. For example, the prosperous or timid might indeed feel more comfortable if unemployed youths and their noise were driven off the streets, but they would hardly be willing to accept such harassment if they were to find themselves in the others' place.

This is emphatically not a prescription for anarchy or "license": it is a fundament of constitutionalism. A rational person will consent to such an allocation of power provided it is subject to limits

[6] Rawls (1971).
[7] He says this most explicitly in an earlier essay: Rawls (1963), pp. 98–125.

and controls restricting its use solely to the purpose for which it is granted. He will do so for all the reasons that mutual dependence and division of labour are essential features of modern society. In so far as the exercise of their specialist functions requires the police to be granted power over others, he will correspondingly insist that it be exercised subject to effective control. More concretely, this requires that the police—who possess a virtual monopoly of legitimate violence in the name of the political order—be subject to a regime of control which ensures that everyone, regardless of social or economic condition, ethnic origin or political belief, be treated equally.

III

Constitutional thinking about the police in Britain has been bedevilled by a particular conception of law, or more precisely, by the identification of policing with a vastly overblown notion of The Law. Most people regard law in an idealised way, as the apotheosis of fairness and justice. Hence law enforcement is seen, not so much as requiring higher standards than other government services but as not a service at all—as something higher than the merely social or political. The analysis in the opening chapter attempted to demonstrate that this view of law is untenable. There is in any society as heterogenous and stratified as contemporary Britain an inescapable conflict between law and order—between unremitting law enforcement and social stability. The corollary of accepting Lord Scarman's view that the latter consideration must be paramount, is to try to minimise the conflict by adopting a less inflated view of law—to see it as a valuable but subordinate mechanism serving to maintain a social order. It is a means, not an end; not abstract and rigid, but serving social purposes. The manner and occasions of its use will, therefore, be dictated by how it can best be used to achieve a social order which embodies justice in the sense defined above. We thus reach by an alternative route the argument developed from more empirical premises in Chapter 1: that law enforcement is inevitably discretionary, and that discretion involves political choices.[8]

Hence it is a fallacy to argue against democratic governance of policing on the grounds that the police to some unspecified degree partake of a judicial character. The analogy is misplaced; the valuable analytical contribution of *Holgate-Mohammed* is the clarity

---

[8] Above pp. 15–20. Note the definition of "political" as used throughout this book.

with which it treats the constable as a person exercising executive discretion.[9] Moreover, the constable is a key participant on one side in the partisan adversary contest; to see him as a disinterested or neutral interpreter of law is contrary to the reality of our system of criminal justice.

There is indeed a sense in which law enforcement decisions must be independent of popular control. The decision to investigate, arrest and charge a particular suspect must remain wholly a matter for the judgment of the officer in charge of the case and aware of all the relevant facts. It is important to identify the precise justifications of this principle, for they are quite distinct from the extravagant claims that are routinely made about the constitutional status of the police. The requirement of independence in this sphere has little to do with the nature of law or criminal process, and everything to do with the nature of the decision to be taken. Positively, the decision requires objective and honest application of a rule or standard of conduct; negatively, improper considerations such as favouritism, racial or political bias and the like must be rigorously excluded. This is no less true of teacher's grading of an examination. Unduly favourable marking of the script of an influential businessman's child, or conscious or unconscious devaluation of the work of black pupils is as objectionable as police favouritism or racism—for precisely the same reasons. It is the betrayal of the impartiality required of the person in whom a public trust has been placed. Fairness, moral scrupulousness and professionalism rightly understood—as standards of work and ethics—are expected of all services. Most of these, like education or social work, are under political control without these standards being threatened. Independence of decision is one means by which they are achieved, but it is exercised within the framework of political decisions taken democratically. Impartiality and like treatment of like cases are demanded of the police officer, not because he is the servant of the Crown, the Law or some other abstraction, but because they are the imperatives of a liberal democracy. And the police officer is entitled to demand that other public officials be subject to the same rigorous standards of justice, control and mechanisms of redress as himself.

Policing, then, is a public service. Generally in a democratic polity it is expected that public services be responsive to the public. In Britain several mechanisms have been created to achieve this. Most establish ways in which elected representatives can

---

[9] [1984] A.C. 437; above pp. 69–71. The thoughtful argument of Waddington (1984) is in my view vitiated by mistaken reliance on the judicial analogy.

supervise the conduct and exercise powers of state officials; in a
few limited areas, the citizenry is enabled to participate, or at least
be heard directly, in the making of particular kinds of decisions.
Supervision and participation are the two principal modes of
democratic control. Principal, but not twin: the predominance of
the former reveals the limited character of the democracy Western
states have managed to achieve. Supervisory powers generally
entail establishing broad lines of policy for officials to follow;
appointing, and in some instances discharging, senior administrators; questioning and making representations to officials on
behalf of constituents aggrieved by the decisions or behaviour of
their subordinates. Allied to these is the ability to command attention of the media to pursue grievances when the authorities prove
unresponsive.

In relation to the Civil Service and local government, the supervisory mechanisms currently in operation are seriously defective: a
matter largely of design failure but also of inadequate maintenance. Nonetheless the rudiments are there, and the principle that
supervision is an essential element in the working of democracy is
unquestioned. Yet in relation to policing, the mechanisms are all
but non-existent, and even the principle remains bitterly controversial.

How can one explain the fact that in the relationship between
the chief administrative authority and elected representatives,
policing claims a wholly unique degree of immunity from these
democratic processes? At one level the question may be treated
historically, and Chapter 3 offered an interpretation of the origin
and rise to dominance of the independence doctrine. Over and
above the contingent historical factors, however, the question is
one of policy, which means evaluating the philosophical justifications of this extraordinary claim. The main supporting argument
has been based on the nature of law and the police officer's relation to it, a view that the analysis offered through the present study
has sought to destroy.

There is, however, a second line of argument, which is that
democratic governance is undesirable because it cannot be trusted.
This view was put forward nearly a decade ago specifically in relation to police in an essay by Geoffrey Marshall, recanting his
earlier views in favour of greater democratic control of police discretion.[10] In view of his stature as a constitutional theorist and
writer on police governance, they require deep consideration. The
key passage in his argument was reproduced almost verbatim, but

[10] Marshall (1978), pp. 51–65.

with one important alteration, in his recent book on *Constitutional Conventions*.[11] The original version is given below; the amendment is discussed in the ensuing commentary. Marshall wrote:

> "In 1959 [the year the Royal Commission on Police was established] anyone who believed in the value of local control of administration and in democratic accountability could well believe in the need for greater political control of police discretion. Situations could even be conceived where, in the interests of more effective or uniform or equitable law enforcement, even positive instructions might in theory be justified . . . Nothing in British politics and administration is quite what it was in 1959 or ever will be. Suppose it to be the case that we cannot automatically assume that elected politicians will respect the rule of law, or reject bribes or refrain from exploiting their positions for self-interested or party-political, or even corrupt and unlawful, ends. Suppose that Watergates, Poulsons and Clay Crosses are not unique and unrepeatable phenomena . . . If therefore in the field of law enforcement we have to give a calculated and unprejudiced answer in 1977 to the question whether civil liberties and impartial justices are more to be expected from chief constables than from elected politicians (whether on police committees or in the House of Commons or in ministerial departments) many liberal democrats would feel justified in placing more trust in the former than in the latter."[12]

At one level, this argument is simply bizarre, managing to conflate Watergate with British politics and administration, and failing to distinguish corruption from ethical-political controversy about public issues involving the enforcement of controversial legislation. Almost equally strange is the implicit assumption that the deterioration of standards in government has left the police unscathed. Yet in the 1970s, more than 800 policemen were sacked or forced to resign from the Metropolitan Police alone,[13] and most commentators believe that investigations like Operation Countryman have signally failed to penetrate the labyrinth of corruption.[14] Moreover, if the argument is valid, it proves too much, or at any rate its implications are startling. As Marshall himself ambiguously recognises at one point, it cannot be limited to policing, but applies equally wherever "there may be a tension between techni-

[11] Marshall (1984).
[12] Above n.10, pp. 60–61.
[13] Dean (1982), p.162.
[14] For details, see Doig (1984), pp. 232–252.

cal judgment and political preference or necessity."[15] Indeed one example he gives is controlling the money supply; do we really wish to treat the knights of the Treasury as Imperial barons? In the end it means jettisoning democracy in favour of rule by administrators who are required periodically to explain what they are doing—a twentieth century version of enlightened despotism which is as implausible as it is unhelpful as a solution to the real difficulties of governance of any organ of public administration.

Marshall clearly recognises the constitutional significance of his revisionism, for it is linked to a fully-developed theory of what he calls "explanatory accountability." The model here is found in the relation between quangoes or the boards of nationalised industries and Parliament, in which "a Minister gives information or explanations to the House without possessing any executive authority to issue instructions to those from whom the information is obtained."[16] In relation to police, he advocates its implementation to all subjects, "police operations and prosecution matters, even sometimes to particular cases of prosecution or non-prosecution, as well as to general policies."[17] The weakness of democratic institutions is thus to be at least partly offset by the breadth of the subjects on which they may require reasoned explanation; and Marshall believes that the requirement of justifying one's actions and policies publicly exerts a significant restraint on anyone in a position of power.

The examples that seem to have inspired the idea of explanatory accountability hardly give one confidence. Quite apart from the privatisation controversy, nationalised industries have been attacked for years for their remoteness from consumers and excessively "bureaucratic" management and—from a different line of fire—of being too easily manipulated by ministers for political ends. Quangos, rightly or wrongly, are regarded by many as insufficiently responsible to Parliament. Neither provides a model that one would enthusiastically seek to spread to other areas of government.

Perhaps an even graver weakness of relying on this mode of accountability is the unsatisfactory nature of explanations. They may be defensive, dogmatic or simply unilluminating. If the decision maker is not required to furnish detailed supporting information he may, inadvertently or otherwise, present a partial and misleading account. Nor is it unknown even where full democratic

[15] Above n. 11, p. 143.
[16] *Ibid.* pp. 77–78 and 119–20. The quotation is from p. 119.
[17] *Ibid.* p. 146.

control is supposed to operate, for information to be concealed or destroyed; under the explanatory mode, conduct of that kind is even less likely to be discovered. Moreover, explanations are often simply couched in vague generalities, with heavy reliance on terms like "the public interest" which themselves embody controversial political choices. And even where general criteria may be broadly acceptable, controversies arise about their interpretation or application in particular instances. Thus, to take an example involving the generally uncontentious prosecution criteria enunciated by the Attorney General in 1983,[18] a statement that "We did not bring charges against X because although we believe he committed a housebreaking three years ago, we regarded the offence as both relatively minor and stale" is a full explanation of the standards applied; what may remain in issue is whether protection of the public and justice for the victim has been adequately served by that interpretation. Those who disagree will want to reverse the original decision, which the limits of the explanatory mode would preclude. Finally, the explanation may reveal a policy that is simply unacceptable. The Director of Public Prosecutions has revealed his prosecution criteria with respect to police officers,[19] and has apparently remained deaf to criticism; Marshall's approach requires that the public simply must live with it. That conclusion seems far worse than the evils the explanatory mode purports to avoid.

Marshall's original formulation, quoted above, expressed greater trust in chief constables than politicians. In the revised version "chief constables" has been replaced by a "body of rules or conventions that restricts their [*i.e.* politicians] scope for intervention in police operations."[20] Yet it is not really a substitution at all. The practical impact of such a convention is precisely to place one's faith in chief constables. And that is eccentric, for chief constables are not what they were in 1959 either. The last decade or so, beginning with the tenure of Sir Robert Mark as Commissioner of the Metropolitan Police, has seen the emergence of politically outspoken chief constables who do not hesitate to sermonise on society's ills and who, through A.C.P.O., have overtly entered the political arena and attempted to influence legislation and public policy. This politicisation of the police, which extends equally to the organisations representing the lower ranks,[21] is both irrever-

---

[18] See Sanders (1985) for discussion.
[19] Above, p. 140.
[20] Above n. 11, p. 144.
[21] For a full account of these trends, see Kettle (1980) and Reiner (1983).

sible and a change of constitutional magnitude. It means that the police as an institution, and chief constables particularly, can no longer be seen as merely executors of parliamentary command but as carrying a significant responsibility for the content of criminal law, particularly its procedural elements. This undermines one of the central pillars of the independence doctrine. Their attempt to influence the outcome of the legislative process implicitly recognises that their work is fundamentally political, in all but the most narrowly partisan sense. In these circumstances, "many liberal democrats would feel justified" in searching for more effective means to prevent the police from dominating the making of policy, for in a democracy those engaged in carrying out political decisions must always be subordinate to elected representatives. Indeed the movement in the 1980s for greater democratic control is in significant part a *response* to the earlier police entrance into the political arena, not the cause of it.

There is also a fundamental inconsistency in the independence doctrine, whatever reasons are urged on its behalf. Research for the Royal Commission on Criminal Procedure showed that roughly 20 per cent. of all prosecutions were brought by some public body other than the police—primarily customs and excise, Inland Revenue, D.V.L.C., DHSS, and local authorities.[22] All these bodies operate under direct political control. Their prosecution policies are openly acknowledged, are subject to public scrutiny and criticism, and altered in response to the change in priorities or values that occurs as new governments or ministers take office.[23] The offences involved are in no way less serious in terms of the penalties that may be imposed upon those convicted than are the vast majority of traffic and property offences dealt with by the police, and the officials responsible for investigating and prosecuting these offences can hardly be held to a less rigorous standard of legality than is expected of the police. Their activities are governed by detailed instructions as to the conduct of investigations, and such other critical matters as when and whether to accept restitution or other forms of settlement rather than initiate legal proceedings. These instructions are drawn up by civil servants responsible to a minister, but no one has ever suggested that this is a constitutional impropriety. Nor does anyone regard customs and excise officials as personifications of the ideal of law,

[22] Lidstone *et al.* (1980).
[23] For extended discussion of these policies and the practices that flow from them in the field of revenue law enforcement, see the Report of the Keith Committee (1983).

although historically they are more accurately associated with detection and prosecution of crime than those relative latecomers, the police.[24] A theory of law or of political responsibility that simply ignores one in five of all prosecutions has a gaping hole at its centre. Neither the idea that the police uniquely perform a function embodying the ideal of apolitical legality, nor that those who perform that function are always granted a unique degree of self-governance, will withstand serious scrutiny.

A final point may be conveniently addressed here. The police increasingly see themselves as a professionalised body of experts whose claim to freedom from "interference" rests as much on superior knowledge and skill at their craft as on the abstractions of constitutional theory.[25] They claim the same status and restriction from lay control that is asserted in the name of professionalism by teachers, doctors, planners and lawyers. One response might be to deny that professionalism is an appropriate label for police work. This, however, is to assume that there is something called professionalism which is objectively identifiable and that the only problem is whether policing satisfies its criteria. A more fruitful approach is to question the validity of the label itself. The point is most succinctly made in Bernard Shaw's comment: "all professions are conspiracies against the laity." The claim of professionalism is often a means by which an occupational group asserts power in the sense of autonomy from public or governmental scrutiny.[26] These claims to self-regulation now receive increasing scepticism from a public which has seen or had to live with the planning disasters, cases of wrongful confinement to mental institutions, maltreated children and inflated fees that have followed from treating decisions requiring human empathy or political choice as matters of technical expertise beyond the abilities of the unitiated. Indeed in recent years there has been a welcome movement towards challenging hitherto unbridled professional dominance, for example by the requirement that a majority of school governors be parents—the nearest approximation to users of the service—and that teacher performance be systematically evaluated. Much remains to be done, particularly in relation to doctors and lawyers or, as they would have it, the medi-

---

[24] Customs and excise officials have been undertaking these activities for at least three hundred years whilst, as has been seen in Chapter 3, only late in the last century did the police achieve a near monopoly on prosecutions and many forces remained without specialist detective squads until much later.

[25] Holdaway (1977).

[26] See further Johnson (1972) and Larson (1977).

cal and legal professions[27] who have been given extraordinary power over services financed from public funds, as with the Law Society's control over legal aid. There is indeed a valid sense in which "professionalism" can be used to describe policing, but as has been seen,[28] this sense is fully shared with other public services. Those who try to urge professionalism as a basis of immunity from democratic governance, however, are cloaking themselves in a mantle that is coming apart at the seams.

IV

The police, then, perform the public service of law enforcement. They should be subject to democratic control to the same extent as other services. That extent is a limited one. One limit—the commands of impartiality and like treatment of like situations—has already been mentioned.[29] The others reflect the nature of the particular service provided: execution of law as laid down by Parliament. The fundamental constitutional norm of the sovereignty of Parliament means that the substantive laws cannot be nullified by local, or even unenacted national, majority sentiment. The inevitability of discretion does not mean negation, and although the difference is one of degree, no one would mistake the angle of the Tower of Pisa for one of 90 degrees. A closely related limit is that there can be no infringement by intermediary democratic bodies on the exercise of the discretion Parliament has conferred on the constable directly. We have already seen that chief constables are similarly restricted; the remarks of Lawton L.J. in the C.E.G.B. case are important for their emphasis on the personal and non-transferrable nature of the discretion.[30] Only the constable personally aware of the facts can form the reasonable suspicion necessary in law for an arrest or search. For any political body, however popularly representative, to order the arrest of X or non-arrest of Y is—quite apart from the question of motive—to usurp a power Parliament has allocated elsewhere.

These limitations apart, democratic governance may encompass policies of the greatest breadth to matters of the most specific detail. One can identify certain guidelines for the effective and

---

[27] It is absurd and arrogant for doctors to equate themselves with the profession of medicine, since so much of the work of treatment is actually done by nurses, physiotherapists and similar people. Ditto the work of managing clerks in relation to conveyancing, the bread and butter of solicitors.

[28] Above, p. 164.

[29] *Ibid.*

[30] Above, pp. 13–15.

efficient exercise of this power. First, political decisions and those shaping organisational capability—listed and analysed at length in Chapter 1—should always be taken by elected representatives. So too should those concerned with the immediate priorities of policing—which offences should receive particular attention and resources. It is quite legitimate for the police authority to say, in response to a neighbourhood petition, "Put an extra patrol car in North sub-division where there has been a spate of burglaries." It is equally legitimate, indeed imperative, for the chief constable to say, "Yes, but to do so I must take the car from South sub-division, where the people have expressed concern about street robberies." The elected representatives must then make the hard choice, without the luxury of pointing the finger at the police when the people in South sub-division complain. If they refuse the petition after considering the chief constable's observation, they must take the responsibility of explanation, and face the criticism.

Second, whilst investigation or surveillance of specific persons or specific crimes should remain entirely under the direction of the police, generalised activities like patrolling or search operations in particular areas, roadchecks and the like—which inevitably result in large numbers of innocent persons being subjected to stops, searches and questioning—should be subject to disapproval by elected representatives of those areas. Having been informed why the police regard the particular measures as necessary, they are the appropriate persons to decide whether the gain is worth the intrusions and conflict that may result.[31] Conversely, it is equally legitimate for elected representatives to insist upon particularly rigorous action, for example against unlawful conduct by pickets. If they were to decide to deploy a massive number of police on extended picket duty, their constituents would have to live with the consequences—long-term absence of local police, less effective detection of crime, higher expenditure due to overtime. It is perfectly legitimate for politicians to decide that these are acceptable costs; and it is up to those they represent to disagree and press for a reordering of priorities. The essential point is that, precisely because of these multiple consequences, these are political decisions, and should be clearly presented as such, not disguised as technical or "operational" ones. The role of elected representatives here is part of what should be a fundamental aim of the prac-

---

[31] Police work can on occasion require an emergency response which has few analogues in other services. In situations where approval of the authority should be sought, it should not be impossible to devise a procedure for short-term authorisation by a designated group consisting of the chairman and selected members.

tice of policing: to contribute to popular participation in law enforcement and to create a climate in which the police are seen as a service, not a force. This may be optimistic in a society as stratified as Britain today, but it is not utopian.

Thirdly, where the police themselves have adopted generalised policies to deal with particular classes of offender or offence—*e.g.* to caution juveniles or first offenders, or not to prosecute teenagers engaging in sex below the age of consent if consent in fact existed—these should be put to the elected representatives for approval. Usually such decisions are not controversial (although one could think of others that would be, like non-prosecution of those possessing small quantities of cannibis), but it is the constitutional principle, not the substantive policy, that is of greatest importance. Such decisions are presumably based upon judgements about public feeling or the dangers of excessively rigid law enforcement, yet they involve deviations from the strict duty of equal and evenhanded enforcement. It is only democracy, not administration, that can supply the legitimacy for deviation from that duty.

Finally, all managerial and technical decisions not coming under the foregoing heads should be left to police management, which would periodically inform its political superiors of its work. This is simply good administrative practice; as has been said in an analogous context, it is unnecessary and unwise to bark alongside one's own dog.[32] The vast bulk of day to day management and operational decisions fall into this category, and it is to be expected that those who specialise in these matters will make better decisions than part-time generalist politicians who are outside the organisation. This conclusion applies uniformly to all government services; heads and teachers are best left to decide the organisation of the timetable and technique of instruction, as is the engineering department to assess the condition of streets and sewers. This is rational allocation of decision-making, not incantation of a myth about law.

V

What would be the dangers in such a regime of democratic governance? One might be an attempt by a police authority to do indirectly what it could not do directly. Barred from ordering that a particular law not be enforced, it could direct deployment of an

---

[32] Barker (1982), p. 18.

inadequate number of police so as to make enforcement impossible—for example that no more than 20 officers be sent to any one
picket line, even though hundreds of pickets had assembled and
there was reasonable apprehension of unlawful conduct. Equally
serious, and perhaps more likely, it could actively seek to suppress
the activities of political dissenters or cultural deviants. Directing
that forceful treatment be meted out to peaceful demonstrators, or
that black youths be dispersed when gathering on street corners,
or that travelling people be moved on, are some examples. These
possibilities raise the questions of what checks on police authorities should exist for protection of civil liberties and, more
broadly, where the locus of democratic governance should lie.

Democratic Control and Legal Control

The primary legal check on police authorities is provided by the
general principles of administrative law. The police authority
would be made statutorily responsible for law enforcement in its
area, and would thus be subject to the various principles that have
come to govern discharge of local authority functions. Much the
most important of these is the *Wednesbury* principle.[33] Its requirements of good faith and inclusion of proper considerations only
would adequately deal with the possibility of indirect nullification.

These primary *Wednesbury* criteria allow the authority sufficient
margin of appreciation or latitude to take a decision which many
might regard as wrongheaded without falling foul of the courts,
but do require an adequate factual justification of the true basis of
the decision. An attempt to make the laws on picketing ineffective
in the manner suggested above could not survive scrutiny under
this standard of review. Conversely, and precisely because its
application enmeshes the judiciary in political decision making, it
is vital that the residual *Wednesbury* test[34] be returned to the
bottle from which it has escaped and firmly recorked in place.

A second and related long-stop principle has emerged from all
the Blackburn litigation.[35] It is now tolerably clear that the courts
would intervene if a deliberate policy of non-enforcement were
adopted, but will otherwise leave discretionary decisions about
deployment and resources to those in charge of the police organisation. Hence any attempt by the police authority to adopt such a
policy could be challenged by a member of the public. Taken

[33] Above, pp. 70–71.
[34] Above, pp. 123–124.
[35] Above, pp. 62–67.

together, these principles embody the practical corollary of the *grundnorm* of Parliamentary sovereignty.

The other limitation on democratic governance stipulated earlier—that a police authority could not interfere with the discretion vested directly in the constable—also finds support in general legal authority. Closely connected to the principle that delegation of discretionary authority is impermissible absent unambiguous authorisation [36] is the rule that someone to whom a discretion is entrusted cannot act under direction but must exercise the discretion personally.[37] Hence the constable's necessary independence in this sphere is shored up by administrative law.

Recourse to the courts may, as has been seen, be of value to an individual who seeks redress when he has been treated in a manner unauthorised by law, such as use of excessive force or an arrest for which reasonable suspicion was lacking. It cannot, however, be of assistance to victims of repressive policies or harsh but lawful treatment motivated by political or ideological animus. The norm of equal treatment, identified earlier as the fundamental requirement of a just system of policing, cannot be achieved through the courts. This is not primarily due to the ideological orientation of most judges, although that is one factor. More important is that the common law does not recognise equality as the norm to be protected, nor indeed does it understand any conception of human rights unless translated into an established category of legal interest. These categories are almost invariably confined to the incidents of property ownership or notions of fair procedure; they do not encompass political or civil rights like freedom of speech or assembly. This critical point can be illustrated by numerous examples. To take two which do so with unusual clarity, consider the fate of Lord Denning's attempt to establish a right to demonstrate in English law, as distinct from political rhetoric.[38] Secondly, there is Dicey's trenchant analysis of the right to freedom of discussion, which has lost none of its force or accuracy over the years:

[36] *Delegatus non potest delegare*; though as both Wade (1982), pp. 319–20 and Craig (1983), p. 372 point out, using slightly different vocabularies, this is a presumption or general principle, not a rigid rule; everything turns on the construction of the specific statute creating the power.

[37] Wade, *op. cit.* p. 329, citing *Simms Motor Units Ltd.* v. *Minister of Labour* [1946] 2 All E.R. 201.

[38] *Hubbard* v. *Pitt* [1975] 3 W.L.R. 201. His eloquence did not prevail with his brethren; Stamp L.J. was more concerned about the profits that the plaintiff estate agent might lose than about the rights of freedom of expression and assembly. See [1975] 3 W.L.R. at 220. For valuable commentary, see Wallington (1976).

> "At no time has there in England been any proclamation of
> the right to liberty of thought or to freedom of speech . . .
> Any man may, therefore, say or write whatever he likes, sub-
> ject to the risk of, it may be, severe punishment if he pub-
> lishes any statement (either by word of mouth, in writing or in
> print) which he is not legally entitled to make."[39]

The peremptory dismissal of Miss Arrowsmith's objection to
selective prosecution,[40] and the narrowness accorded the tort of
malicious prosecution,[41] are further examples of a deep structural
flaw in the common law: its failure to protect freedoms necessary
for democratic participation in political life. This is hardly surprising in view of the antiquity of common law and the latecoming of
democracy, but it does mean that one could not look to the courts
if civil liberties were threatened by a police authority, any more
than one could do now when the responsibility would lie with the
chief constable. People in Britain, whose relation to their government—subjects rather than citizens—well expresses their legal
subordination, simply do not have legal rights in the sense possessed by persons living in Federal Germany or the United States.
It would be misconceived, however, to advocate the introduction of entrenched rights such as are found in the constitutions of
those countries to remedy this deficiency.[42] One would then
unavoidably become ensnared in the much wider debate about
whether it is appropriate to grant non-accountable judges the
power to invalidate acts of the legislature. In relation to the specific point under consideration here, the benefits of such an enactment would only be realised in the very long run: and as Keynes
said, in the long run we are all dead. It would take generations
before the habits of thought and moral outlook necessary to nur-
ture and sustain a judiciary committed to civil libertarian values
became firmly established within the legal profession.[43] Most
important perhaps, protection of minority rights cannot be effective if it is hived off and left to the courts. It must become part of
the political process, a core element of the political culture. It is

---

[39] Dicey (1908), pp. 239–240.
[40] Above, p. 15.
[41] Above, pp. 132–134.
[42] I pass over the thorny constitutional problem of whether it is possible within the
legal context of Parliamentary omnipotence to entrench rights against future
legislation.
[43] Such a change could only occur as part of a radical change in the legal profession—its structure, sources of recruitment, education and occupational socia-
lisation of its members. "Long run" is probably an optimistic time scale.

necessary to create political institutions that place civil liberties and minority rights at the heart of their concerns.

The Local-Central Balance

The one point that commands near-universal agreement is that a national police force is undesirable. Beyond that, however, there is a sharp disagreement about where the primary power should lie. Most policemen and Conservative politicians, and the Home Office, would oppose any attempt to roll back the tide of central government dominance that has flowed strongly over the past two decades, let alone restore the degree of local autonomy that existed before 1919. Since what is proposed here is a radical shift in the balance towards local democracy, it is necessary to examine the claims made on behalf of localism and centralism.[44]

The arguments on both sides are a mixture of the philosophical and the practical. In favour of localism it may be said that areas vary in their needs and the wishes of their inhabitants, to which only a locally based administration will be attuned and indeed be capable of responding. Small units are quicker to respond to changes in feeling or life circumstances of the people affected; the greater size of national administration makes it more remote from the public. Centralism may also result in an excessively long chain of command, with unnecessary administrative costs and delays. Localism also effectuates the important value of participation in political life: that people should have control over matters that affect them directly, and both be able personally to have a say in them and accept responsibility for the consequences.[45] This is easier when units of government are small, both in the sense that an individual has an arithmetically greater chance of making his own voice heard, and of the greater feasibility of joining with others to create an influential movement able to secure access to and influence elected representatives. Moreover, if mistaken decisions are taken, localism limits their impact to the particular area; a national mistake may harm millions.

Central control is necessary where there is a need for co-ordination and uniformity, as with electricity grids or motorways. It may

---

[44] There is a large body of literature on this subject. See especially Sharpe (1970), Hill (1974) and the debate between Page (1982, 1983) and Jones and Stewart (1982).

[45] This is not solely an argument about quality of decision; it is also a theory about human good, of the realisation of human potential that comes of being more than nominally responsible for one's own fate. For a powerful statement of this position, see Barber (1974), Chap. 1.

also achieve economies of scale—an argument that has tended to be exaggerated—and may be indispensable where massive investment beyond the capabilities of one or even a few localities is required. Centralism may also serve quite different values. It may compensate for local inequalities of resources which lead to unacceptable inequalities in the service or opportunities available to individuals in different areas. It may be necessary to achieve uniform standards—although the need for these has also been exaggerated—and, much more validly, *minimum* standards of service. Granting power to a central government body may also be the only means to prevent the rights and needs of minorities being trampled upon by politically secure local majorities. However, to achieve these ends and avoid these dangers it is not necessary to have administrative control vested in central government; it is sufficient to grant it powers of inspection and subsidy with default or withdrawal powers to be used as back-up in serious cases.

Thus important values are safeguarded by both localism and centralism. Each has its virtues, but the main responsibility for policy and administration should remain close to the persons using the service; the national function consists of standard-setting, equalisation and protection of minorities. Moreover, it is dangerous to concentrate all power over a particular service at any one level of government. Permanent, institutionalised tension between different levels of the political process is as firm a guarantee against abuse of power as democracy can devise.

Applied to police governance, this means that the wholly-elected police authority, an organ of local government, should exercise the full scope of legitimate control. Central government should continue to insist upon maintenance of minimum standards of technical competence, and should also incorporate human rights concerns within its brief. To assign this task to the Home Office is to will its failure. The Home Office is the Ministry of Repression. Its entire orientation, reflecting its historical succession to the prerogative power of maintaining the Sovereign Peace, is towards order and restriction. Prisons, subversion, official secrets, Sunday trading, drugs, civil defence and the admission of aliens all comprise a disparate catalogue whose sole common feature is that they involve prohibitions or strict controls. The grip of what Griffith calls "the cold dead hand of the Home Office"[46] needs to be removed from policing. Yet some national and politically accountable body is required.

---

[46] Griffith (1984), p. 91.

Perhaps the most promising approach would be to create a Ministry of Justice. Although the idea has been intermittently suggested in response to various defects of law and government for well over a century,[47] it is particularly needed in the era of the Welfare State in which a high standard of administrative justice, access to the courts and other mechanisms of redress, and full information about the workings of government are an imperative for millions of people. Many functions now scattered between the Home Office, the Lord Chancellor's Office, various semi-independent bodies or left by default to the judiciary, but which are conceptually and practically best treated together, could be joined in a Ministry of Justice. Equally important, it would be a real gain if civil liberties questions like contempt of court, the right to demonstrate, or freedom of information could be made the responsibility of a new department which started afresh with a libertarian brief. In relation to policing, a Ministry of Justice could use the Inspectorate of Constabulary to obtain information and provide guidance to the police authority and its chief constable about a wide range of matters of public concern, ranging from ensuring suspects' access to solicitors to greater sensitivity to rape victims. It would also take over responsibility for the national functions now performed by the Metropolitan Police which it would be inappropriate to leave to whatever elective arrangements emerged from London. It would also be the home for a specialist corps of investigators—to whom it could offer a reasonable career prospect so as to attract high calibre people—to handle complaints that are not handled by informal resolution. It would educate police authorities about the limits of their powers, and encourage them to use those powers to their limits.

VI

There is a final point which should be addressed. Some commentators, particularly sociologists in the phenomenological tradition, have argued that the issues of governance considered in this book are of relatively minor importance in altering police behaviour. Some stress the dominant influence of the occupational subculture and work practices of the police[48]; others the difficulty of subjecting street-level decision to regulation by superiors[49]; yet

---

[47] For a brief survey, see Beynon (1982), pp. 260–264.

[48] *e.g.* Manning (1979) and Holdaway (1982).

[49] *e.g.* Waddington (1984).

others the greater impact of organisational structures compared with externally-imposed rules.[50] It is right to sound a note of caution that structures and regulations drawn up in the legislature or the office of the chief constable are mediated through an organisation which is likely to resist change, particularly if its spirit is contrary to current values and practices. There are the serious weaknesses with any strong version of the argument, however. Empirically it is dubious. Lawrence Sherman, in his analysis of the improvement in relations between blacks and police in American cities, argues persuasively that this came about largely due to changes in police conduct.[51] After examining several possible explanations—including expensive reforms such as more and better training, increased exposure of policemen to higher education and, in some cities, additional recruitment of blacks into the force—he concludes that the key factor was the growth of black political power, sometimes galvanised by anger at police malpractices, which under American political practice could be translated into hiring and firing the chief of police. The people selected made sure their subordinates began acting in less objectionable ways.[52] At least one other study came to a similar conclusion about the importance of the attitudes of the political and police leadership in changing practices on the ground.[53] It is likely that some forms of conduct are less susceptible to this sort of pressure than others[54] but it is simply dogmatic to assert that internal resistance will always nullify policy changes sought by external institutions of governance.

The second objection strikes even deeper. It is that what sociological investigation has observed is not the deepest level of determinant. The custom and practice of police work has evolved within *contexts*: it did not just "happen." One of these contexts is substantive law. Treatment of suspects is not simply the result of what the police think appropriate; it has flourished within a structure of rules and judicial attitudes that puts few restraints upon them. It is not primarily that the sub-culture or organisational norms encour-

[50] *e.g.* Baldwin and Kinsey (1982).
[51] Sherman (1983), *passim.*
[52] *Ibid.* pp. 218–228.
[53] Rossi *et al.* (1975), cited in Sherman, *op. cit.* Note also Sherman's study (1983a) of the impact of policy change on one salient aspect of police behaviour, the use of firearms.
[54] Activities that are highly visible, of serious consequence and which raise emotive responses, such as gun use or overt racist abuse, are probably more likely to be amenable to change than matters such as permitting access to solicitors, or behaviour on picket lines where there is great confusion, difficulty of identification, and violence from the other side.

age rule violation, but that the rules are sufficiently permissive and support practices many object to but are wrong to describe as unlawful.[55] Of course it is impossible to prove a counterfactual, but it does seem highly likely that more restrictive rules, effectively enforced, would seriously modify police behaviour. Hence what is visible to the ethnographer, and therefore seems inherently determinative, is in reality contingent upon the taken-for-granted legal structure.

The same point applies to the constitutional context. Police policies and behavioural norms have grown up in the soil of non-intervention by local democratic institutions. They have simply not had to take account of the possibility of policy direction, performance monitoring and disciplinary sanctions imposed by the local authority. One certainly should not expect complete and automatic compliance with the wishes of the political authorities; the relative autonomy of bureaucracies from their ostensible masters is one of the intractable realities of modern government. But there is no reason at all to assume *a priori* that the police organisation is less amenable to political direction than any other "street level bureaucracy."[56]

It is unlikely that democratic governance of policing will be markedly effective if existing local machinery is left unimproved. Councillors will need support staff, a right of access to information[57] and a dedication to their work which are rarely found at the moment. This strengthening of the machinery of control should have beneficial spill-over effects in every local authority service, where officials often enjoy undue latitude. Young and Lea argue with eloquence that the establishment of democratic control of policing would be a central part of the movement to reconstitute decaying local communities as political entities to which their inhabitants are genuinely attached.[58] I have argued that the constitutional principles of liberal democracy require no less. The alternative—a continuation of the present system of encroaching national influence joined to the formally irresponsible authority of

---

[55] This has been one of the central insights in the work of Doreen McBarnet (1981), which has been important in restoring the content and influence of legal rules to their proper place in sociological investigation.

[56] A useful term invented by Lipsky (1980) to describe organised services such as social work, teaching, emergency medical treatment and policing which deal with members of the public on a highly individualised basis.

[57] This has two aspects: ensuring that officials generally do not withhold information councillors need to formulate and monitor policies, and the specifically police-related problem of ensuring that the *sub judice* rule is not misused to conceal relevant material.

[58] Young and Lea (1984), pp. 231–240.

the chief constable at local levels—is a blueprint for an increasingly distant and militarised police force. Constitutional principles are intimately connected to the quality of policing and thereby to the quality of democratic life.

BIBLIOGRAPHY

Allen, C., *The Queen's Peace* (1953) (London: Stevens)

Ashworth, A., "Excluding Evidence as Protecting Rights" [1977] Crim. L. Rev. 723

Bailey, S., Harris, D. and Jones, B., *Civil Liberties: Cases and Materials* (1985) (London: Butterworths)

Bailey, V., "Introduction," in *Policing and Punishment in the Nineteenth Century* (Bailey, V. ed. 1981) (London): Croom Helm)

Baldwin, R. and Kinsey, R., *Police Powers and Politics* (1982) (London: Quartet Books)

Barber, B., *The Death of Communal Liberty* (1974) (Princeton: Princeton U.P.)

Barclay, P. (Chairman), *Report of a Working Party on Social Workers: their Roles and Tasks* (1982) (London: Bedford Square Press)

Barker, A., *Quangos in Britain* (1982), (London: Macmillan)

Beynon, H., *Independent Advice on Legislation* (1982), (unpublished) D.Phil. Thesis, Oxford University.

Birkinshaw, P., "Freedom of Information, the Elected Member, and Local Government" [1981] P.L. 545

Birkinshaw, P., "Homelessness and the Law—the Effects and Response to Legislation" (1982) 5 Urban L. and Pol. 255

Birkinshaw, P., *Grievances, Remedies and the State* (1985) (London: Sweet and Maxwell)

Bittner, E., "A Theory of the Police," in *The Potential for Reform of Criminal Justice* (Jacob, H. ed. 1974) (Beverley Hills: Sage)

Blewitt, N., "The Franchise in the U.K., 1885–1918," *Past and Present*, December 31, 1965.

Bottoms, A. and McClean, J., *Defendants in the Criminal Process* (1976) (London: Routledge and Kegan Paul)

Branson, N., *Poplarism 1919–25* (1979) (London: Lawrence and Wishart)

Branson, N. and Heinemann, M., *Britain in the 1930s* (1971) (London: Weidenfeld and Nicolson)

Brogden, M., "A Police Authority—The Denial of Conflict" (1977) 25 Soc. Rev. 325

Brogden, M., *The Police: Autonomy and Consent* (1982) (London: Academic Press)

Brown, A. (ed.), *Models of Police/Public Consultation in Europe* (1985) (Cranfield: Cranfield Institute of Technology)

Burney, E., *J.P.* (1979) (London: Hutchinson)

Clarke, R. and Hough, M., *The Effectiveness of Policing* (1980) (Farnborough: Gower Press)

Clarke, R. and Hough, M., *Crime and Police Effectiveness* (1984) (London: Home Office Research and Policy Unit)

Cohen, B., "Police Complaints Procedure: Why and For Whom," in *Police: The Constitution and the Community*, (Baxter, J. and Koffman, L. eds. 1985) (London: Professional books)

Cohen, P., "Policing the Working Class City," in *Capitalism and the Rule of Law* (NDC/CSE ed. 1979) (London: Hutchinson)

Craig, P., *Administrative Law* (1983) (London: Sweet and Maxwell)

Critchley, T., *A History of the Police in England and Wales,* (2nd ed., 1978) (London: Constable)

Damaska, M., "Evidentiary Barriers to Conviction and Two Models of the Criminal Process" (1973) 121 U.Pa.L.Rev. 506

Damaska, M., "Structures of Authority and Comparative Criminal Procedure" (1975) 84 Yale L.J. 480

Davis, J., "Criminal Prosecutions and their Context in Late Victorian London," in *Labour, Law and Crime in Historical Perspective* (Snyder, F. and Hay, D. eds. 1986 forthcoming) (London: Tavistock)

Davis, K., *Discretionary Justice* (1969) (Baton Rouge: Louisiana State U.P.)

Davis, K., *Police Discretion* (1975), (St. Paul, Minn.: West Pub. Co.)

Dean, M., "The Finger on the Policeman's Collar" (1982) 53 Pol.Q. 153

Desmaris, R., *The Supply and Transport Committee, 1919–26* (unpublished 1970) Ph.D. Thesis, Univ. of Wisconsin

de Smith, S., *Judicial Review of Administrative Action,* (4th ed., 1980 by Evans, J.) (London: Stevens)

Dicey, A., *Law of the Constitution* (7th ed., 1908) (London Macmillan)

Doig, A., *Corruption and Misconduct in Contemporary British Politics* (1984), (Harmondsworth: Penguin Books)

Dyson, K., *The State Tradition in Western Europe* (1980) (Oxford: Martin Robertson)

East, R., "Jury Packing: A Thing of the Past?" (1985) 48 M.L.R. 518

Ebsworth, R., *Restoring Democracy in Germany: The British Contribution* (1960) (London: Stevens)

Edwards, J., *The Law Officers of the Crown* (1964), (London: Sweet and Maxwell)

Evans, H., "The London County Council and the Police" (March 1889) *Contemporary Review* 60

Fisher, C. and Mawby, R., "Juvenile Delinquency and Police Discretion in an Inner-City Area" (1982) 22 B.J.Crim. 63

Flynn, S. and Leach, M., *Joint Boards and Joint Committees: An Evaluation* (1984) (Birmingham: INLOGOV, Univ of Birmingham)

Fine, B. and Miller, R., *Policing the Miners' Strike* (1985) (London: Lawrence and Wishart)

Garner, J. and Jones, B., *Administrative Law* (6th ed., 1985) (London: Butterworths)

Gatrell, V., "The Decline of Theft and Violence in Victorian and Edwardian England," in *Crime and the Law* (Gatrell, V. *et al.* eds. 1980) (London: Europa)

Gilbert, K. and Khan, A., "The Constitutional Independence of a Police Constable in the Exercise of the Powers of his Office" (1975) 48 Police J. 55

GLC (Greater London Council), *A New Police Authority for London* (1983) (London: GLC)

Goldstein, A. and Marcus, M., "The Myth of Judicial Supervision in the French System of Criminal Procedure" (1978) 87 Yale L.J. 240

Goldstein, J., "Police Discretion Not to Invoke the Criminal Process" (1960) 69 Yale L.J. 543

Grant, A., *The Police—A Policy Paper* (1980) (Ottawa: Law Reform Commission of Canada)

Griffith, J., "The Democratic Process" in *Civil Liberties 1984* (Wellington, P. ed. 1984) (Oxford: Martin Robertson)

Grosman, B., *The Prosecutor* (1969) (Toronto: Univ. of Toronto Press)

Hewitt, P., *A Fair Cop* (1982) (London: NCCL)

Heydon, J., *Cases and Materials on Evidence* (2nd ed., 1984) (London: Butterworths)

Hill, D., *Democratic Theory and Local Government* (1974) (London: Allen and Unwin)

Holdaway, S., "Changes in Urban Policing" (1977) 28 B.J.Soc. 119

Holdaway, S., "Police Accountability: A Current Issue" (1982) 60 Pub. Admin. 84

Holdaway, S., *Inside the British Police* (1983) (Oxford: Basil Blackwell)

Jefferson, T. and Grimshaw, R., *Controlling the Constable* (1984) (London: Frederic Muller)

Jefferson, T. and Grimshaw, R., "The Problem of Law Enforce-

ment Policy in England and Wales: The Case of Racial Attacks"
(1984a) 12 Intl.J.Soc.Law 117
Johnson, T., *Professions and Power* (1972) (London: Macmillan)
Jones, G. and Stewart, M., "The Value of Local Autonomy: A
Rejoinder" (Sept./Oct. 1982) Local Govt. Studs. 8
Jowell, J. Judicial Control of Administrative Discretion" [1973]
P.L. 178
Kamisar, Y. *et al.*, *Modern Criminal Procedure* (5th ed., 1980) (St.
Paul, Minn.: West Pub. Co.)
Keith, Lord (Chairman), *Report of the Committee on Enforcement
Powers of the Revenue Departments,* Cmnd. 8822 (1983) (Lon-
don: HMSO)
Keith-Lucas, B., "Poplarism" [1962] P.L. 52
Kettle, M., "The Policing of Politics and the Politics of Policing"
in *Policing the Police* (Hain, P. ed. 1980), Vol. 2 (London:
Calder)
Kettle, M., "Quis custodiet ipsos custodes," (July 17, 1980a) *New
Society*, 53
Kettle, M., "The National Reporting Centre and the 1984 Miners'
Strike" in Fine, B. and Millar, R. (1985), *op. cit.*
Landau, S., "Juveniles and the Police" (1981) 21 B.J.Crim. 27
Langbein, J., *Comparative Criminal Procedure: Germany* (1977)
(St. Paul, Minn.: West Pub. Co.)
Langbein, J. and Weinreb, L. "Continental Criminal Procedure:
'Myth' and Reality" (1978) 87 Yale L.J. 1549
Larson, M., *The Rise of Professionalism* (1977) (Berkeley: Univ.
Cal. Press)
Leigh, L., *Police Powers in England and Wales* (1975) (London:
Butterworths)
Lidstone, K. *et al.*, *Prosecutions by Private Individuals and Non-
Police Agencies* (1980) Royal Commission on Criminal Pro-
cedure, Research Study No. 10 (London: HMSO)
Lidstone, K., "Magistrates, the Police and Search Warrants"
[1984] Crim.L.Rev 449
Lipsky, M., *Street Level Bureaucracy* (1980) (New York: Russell
Sage Fdn.)
Lustgarten, L., *Legal Control of Racial Discrimination* (1980)
(London: Macmillan)
Lustgarten, L., "McKinsey at the Met" (1984) 12 Policy and Pol.
297
McBarnet, D., *Conviction* (1981) (London: Macmillan)
McConville, M. and Baldwin, J., "The Role of Interrogation in
Crime Discovery and Conviction" (1982) 22 B.J.Crim. 165
Maitland, F., *Justice and Police* (1885) (London: Macmillan)

Maitland, F., *Constitutional History of England* (1908) (Cambridge: CUP)

Manning, P., "Social Control of Police Work," in *The British Police* (Holdaway, S. ed. 1979) (London: Edward Arnold)

Marshall, G., *Police and Government* (1965) (London: Methuen)

Marshall, G., "Police Accountability Revisited," in *Policy and Politics* (Butler, D. and Halsey, A. eds. 1979) (London: Macmillan)

Marshall, G., *Constitutional Conventions* (1984) (Oxford: OUP)

Marshall, G., "The Police Complaints Authority" [1985] P.L. 448

Matthew, C. *et al.* "The Franchise Factor in the Rise of the Labour Party" (1976) 91 Eng. Hist. Rev. 723

Merseyside Police Authority, *Role and Responsibility of the Police Authority* (1980) (Liverpool: M.P.A.)

Metropolitan Police, *The Principles of Policing and Guidance for Professional Behaviour* (1985) (London: Met. Police)

Moody, S. and Tombs, J., *Prosecution in the Public Interest* (1982) (Edinburgh: Scottish Academic Press)

Morgan, R. and Maggs, C., *Following Scarman?* (1984) (Bath: Univ. of Bath Social Policy Paper)

Morris, G., "The Emergency Powers Act 1920" [1979] *P.L.* 317

Morris, G., "The Regulation of Industrial Action in Essential Services" (1983) 12 I.L.J. 69

Newton, K., *Second City Politics* (1976) (Oxford: Clarendon Press)

Newman, J., "Suing the Lawbreakers" (1978) 87 Yale L.J. 447

Nott-Bower, W., *Fifty-two Years a Policeman* (1926) (London: Edward Arnold)

Page, E., "The Value of Local Autonomy" (July/Aug 1982) Local Govt. Studs., 8 July/Aug

Page, E., "Reply to a Rejoinder" (Jan./Feb. 1983) Local Govt. Studs. 9.

Partington, M. and Bolderton, H., *Housing Benefit Review Procedures: A Preliminary Analysis* (1984) (London: Brunel Univ.)

Pellew, J., *The Home Office, 1848–1914* (1982) (London: Heinemann)

Phillips, D., *Crime and Authority in Victorian England* (1977) (London: Croom Helm)

Phillips, D., "Good Men to Associate and Bad Men to Conspire," in *Labour, Law and Crime in Historical Perspective* (Snyder, F. and Hay, D. eds. 1986 forthcoming) (London: Tavistock)

Plehwe, R., "Police and Government: The Commissioner of Police for the Metropolis" [1974] P.L. 316

Project, "Suing the Police in Federal Court" (1979) 88 Yale L.J. 781

Rawls, J., "Constitutional Liberty and the Concept of Justice," in *Nomos VI—Justice* (Friedrich, C. and Chapman, J. eds. 1963) (Cambridge, Mass: Harvard UP)

Rawls, J., *A Theory of Justice* (1971) (Cambridge, Mass.: Harvard UP)

Redlich, J. and Hirst, F., *Local Government in England* (1903) 2 vols. (London: Macmillan)

Regan, D., *Are the Police Under Control?* (1983) (London: Social Affairs Unit)

Regan, D., "Police Status and Accountability: A Comparison of the British, French and West German Models" (1984) (Paper delivered to ECPR Workshop, Salzburg, Austria)

Reiner, R., "The Politicisation of the Police in Britain," in *Control in the Police Organisation* (Punch, M. ed. 1983) (Cambridge, Mass: MIT Press)

Reiner, R., *The Politics of the Police* (1985) (Brighton: Wheatsheaf Books)

Reiner, R., "Policing Strikes" (1985a) 1 *Policing* 138

Reiner, R., "A Watershed in Policing" (1985b) 56 Pol.Q. 122

Salmond, J. and Heuston, R., *Law of Torts* (18th ed., 1981) (London: Sweet and Maxwell)

Sanders, A., "Prosecution Decisions and the Attorney General's Guidelines" [1985] Crim.L.Rev. 4

Scarman, Lord, *The Brixton Disorders*, Cmnd. 8427 (1981) (London: HMSO)

Seabrook, J., *The Idea of Neighbourhood* (1984) (London: Pluto Press)

Sharpe, L., "Theories and Values of Local Government" (1970) 18 Pol.Studies 153

Shearing, C., *Organizational Police Deviance* (1981) (Toronto: Univ. of Toronto Press)

Sheehan, A., *Criminal Procedure in Scotland and France* (1975) (Edinburgh: HMSO)

Sherman, L., "After the Riots: Police and Minorities in the United States, 1970–80", in *Ethnic Pluralism and Public Policy* (Glazer, N. and Young, K. eds. 1983) (London: Heinemann)

Sherman, L., "Reducing Police Gun Use," in *Control in the Police Organization* (Punch, M. ed. 1983a) (Cambridge, Mass: MIT Press)

Simey, M., "Police Authorities and Accountability: The Merseyside Experience," in *Policing the Riots* (Cowell, D. *et al.* eds. 1982) (London: Junction Books)

Simpson, H., "The Office of Constable" (1895) 10 Eng. Hist.Rev. 625

Skolnick, J., *Justice Without Trial* (1966) (New York: Wiley & Sons)

Smith, D. and Gray, J., *Police and People in London—IV The Police in Action* (1983)

Snyder, F. and Hay, D. (eds.), *Labour, Law and Crime in Historical Perspective* (1986 forthcoming) (London: Tavistock)

Spencer, S., "The Eclipse of the Police Authority," in Fine and Millar (1985) *op.cit.*

Steedman, C., *Policing the Victorian Community* (1984) (London: Routledge)

Stevens, P. and Willis, C., *Ethnic Minorities and Complaints Against the Police* (1981) (London: Home Office Research and Planning Unit)

Storch, R., "The Plague of Blue Locusts: Police Reform and Popular Resistance in Northern England 1840–57" (1975) Int. Rev.Soc.Hist., Vol. 20

Storch, R., "The Policeman as Domestic Missionary" (1976) J.Soc.Hist., Vol. 9

Street, H., *Governmental Liability* (1953) (Cambridge: CUP)

Street, H., *The Law of Torts* (7th ed., 1983) (London: Butterworths)

Stuart, J., "The Metropolitan Police" (1889) Contemporary Rev., Vol. 60

Thomas, D., "Police Discretion" (1982) 53 Pol.Q. 144

Thompson, F., *English Landed Society in the Nineteenth Century* (1963) (London: Routledge and Kegan Paul)

Troup, E., "Police Administration, Local and National" (1928) 1 Police J. 5

Verba, S. *et al.*, *Participation and Political Equality* (1978) (Cambridge: CUP)

Waddington, P., "The Role of the Police Committee: Constitutional Arrangements and Social Realities" (Sept./Oct. 1984) Local Govt. Studies, 10.

Wade, H., *Administrative Law* (5th ed., 1982) (Oxford: OUP)

Wallington, P., "Injunctions and the Right to Demonstrate" [1976] Camb.L.J. 82

Warwick Inquest Group, "The Inquest" (1985) 12 J.L.&Soc. 35

Weinberger, B., "Police Perceptions of Labour in the Inter-War Period: The Case of the Unemployed and of Miners on Strike," in Snyder and Hay (1986) *op.cit.*

Williams, G., "Letting Off the Guilty and Prosecuting the Innocent" [1985] Crim.L.Rev. 115

190   *Bibliography*

Young, J. and Lea, J., *What is to be Done About Law and Order?* (1984) (Harmondsworth: Penguin Books)

Zander, M., *The Police and Criminal Evidence Act 1984* (1985) (London: Sweet & Maxwell)

INDEX

191

CIVIL ACTIONS—*cont.*
  trespass, 135–136
CODES OF PRACTICE, 128–132
  civil actions and, 131, 132
  complaints procedure and, 130 *et seq.*
  enforcement of, 128–130
  trials, effect of violations on, 130–132
COMBINED POLICE AUTHORITY, 81–82.
    See also POLICE AUTHORITY.
  access to confidential information, 89
  financial powers of, 116
COMMISSIONER FOR LOCAL
    ADMINISTRATION,
  Code of Practice on complaints, 147
COMPLAINTS, 126–130, 146 *et seq.*
  conciliation and, 149–150
  criticisms of procedure, 146–148
  disciplinary process and, 150 *et seq.*
    See also DISCIPLINARY
    OFFENCES.
  effects of, 148–149
  failure of process, factors responsible,
    154–155
  false, 126
  independent element, need for, 154 *et
    seq.*
  informal resolution procedure, 150
  police authority, role of, 157–158
  Police Complaints Authority,
    155–158
  Police Complaints Board, 154, 155
  policy matters and, 158
COMPOUNDING, 28
CONCILIATION, 149–150
CONFIDENTIAL INFORMATION,
  Police Authority members and, 87–89
CONFESSIONS,
  adversarial system and, 2
CONSTABLE,
  complaints against, effect on, 148–149
  control by superiors of, 11–13
  development of office, 25–31
  discretion of, 10 *et seq.*
  eighteenth century, in, 27–28
  head constable, 37
  independence of, 175. *See further*
    INDEPENDENCE.
  neglect of duty, 138–139. *See also*
    CRIMINAL OFFENCES.
  status of, 25–31
  statutory powers of, 28–29
  twentieth century, in, 29–30
  vicarious liability for, 56–61
CONSTITUTIONAL TORT (U.S.), 7–8

CONSULTATION, 89–94
  aims of, 89–91
  exclusions from, 93–94
  financial matters and, 98
  Home Secretary, role of, 94
  joint boards and, 93
  Police Authority, relationship with,
    91–94
  reconciliation as aim of, 90
COUNCILLORS,
  confidential information, access to,
    88–89
COUNTY POLICE FORCES, 41–48
  Home Office, relationship with,
    42–48
  standing Joint Committees, 42
  police committee, 80–81
CRIMINAL OFFENCES, 138 *et seq.*
  Director of Public Prosecutions, role
    of, 139–140
  double jeopardy and, 152–153
  independent investigation of, 153–158
  investigation of, 150–153
  silence, right of, 151–152
CROWN ATTORNEY (TORONTO), 6
CROWN PROCEEDINGS,
  police, exclusion from, 59
CROWN PROSECUTION SERVICE. *See*
    PROSECUTION SERVICES.
CROWN SERVANTS,
  police, exclusion from, 59

DAMAGES,
  aggravated, 136
  exemplary, 136–137
DEATHS IN CUSTODY, 141–143
DEMOCRATIC CONSTITUTIONALISM,
  policing and, 160 *et seq.*
  Rawls and, 162–163
DEPLOYMENT, 19. *See also* MUTUAL
    AID; OPERATIONAL.
  Drug Squad, "operational" or
    "policy" decision, 21
DIRECTOR OF PUBLIC PROSECUTIONS,
  criminal offences by policemen and,
    139–140
  deaths in custody and, 142
  "51 per cent rule," 140
DISABILITIES, 39
DISCIPLINARY OFFENCES, 129–130, 139,
    146–158
  burden of proof in, 152–153
  double jeopardy and, 152–153
  independent investigation of, 153–158